AF208592

International Perspectives of Crime Prevention 7

Contributions from the 8th Annual International Forum 2014
within the German Congress on Crime Prevention

Eds.

Marc Coester and Erich Marks

with contributions from:
Klaus Beier, Frank Buchheit, Marc Coester, Petra Guder, Rita Haverkamp,
Claudia Heinzelmann, Harrie Jonkman, Wolfgang Kahl, Ruža Karlović, Daniela
Köntopp, Patricia Martin, Richard Ross, Wiebke Steffen, David Stucki, Jörg Ziercke

Forum Verlag Godesberg GmbH 2015

Bibliographic information published by the Deutsche Nationalbibliothek

The Deutsche Nationalbibliothek lists this publication in the Deutsche Nationalbibliografie; detailed bibliographic data are available in the Internet at http://dnb.d-nb.de .

© Forum Verlag Godesberg GmbH, Mönchengladbach.
All rights reserved.
Mönchengladbach 2015

Produced by: BoD - Books on Demand, Norderstedt
Printed in Germany

Print layout: Kathrin Geiß and Isabell Becker

Cover design: Konstantin Megas, Mönchengladbach

978-3-942865-38-8 (print)
978-3-942865-39-5 (ebook)

Content

Introduction

The German Congress on Crime Prevention is an annual event that takes place since 1995 in different German cities and targets all areas of crime prevention: Administration, the health system, youth welfare, the judiciary, churches, local authorities, the media, politics, the police, crime prevention committees, projects, schools, organizations, associations and science. The desired effect is to present and strengthen crime prevention within a broad societal framework. Thus it contributes to crime reduction as well as to the prevention and the reduced risk of becoming a victim as well as fear of crime. The main objectives of the congress are:

1. Presenting and exchanging current and basic questions of crime prevention and its effectiveness.
2. Bringing together partners within the field of crime prevention.
3. Functioning as a forum for the practice, and fostering the exchange of experiences.
4. Helping to get contacts at an international level and to exchange information.
5. Discussing implementation strategies.
6. Developing and disseminating recommendations for practice, politics, administration and research.

Since its foundation the German Congress on Crime Prevention has been opened to an international audience with a growing number of non-German speaking participants joining. Because prevention is more than a national concern and should be focused internationally this step seemed crucial. Bringing together not only German scientists and practitioners but also international experts in crime prevention and therefore developing a transnational forum to foster the exchange of knowledge and experience constitutes the main focus of this approach. To give the international guests a discussion forum, the Annual International Forum within the German Congress on Crime Prevention was established in 2007. For non-German guests this event offers lectures in English language as well as other activities within the German Congress on Crime Prevention that are translated simultaneously. International guests are able to play an active role by presenting poster or displaying information within the exhibition.

This seventh edition of "International Perspectives of Crime Prevention" includes the outcomes of the 8th Annual International Forum which took place within the 19th German Congress on Crime Prevention on the 12th and 13th of May 2014 in Karlsruhe and gathered together more than 4.000 people from the field of crime prevention in Germany and worldwide. All articles in this book reflect worldwide views on crime prevention as well as the current status, discussion and research in crime prevention from different countries.

We hope to find a broad audience, interested in the upcoming events of the Annual International Forum as well as the German Congress on Crime Prevention. For more information please visit our website at http://www.gcocp.org.

Marc Coester and Erich Marks

Lectures and Documents from the 8th Annual International Forum

Wiebke Steffen

Report for the 19th German Congress of Crime Prevention
May 12-13, 2014 in Karlsruhe

Prevention requires practice, policy, and science

Crime prevention requires prevention practice, prevention policy, and prevention science

Wiebke Steffen

Heiligenberg (Baden) / Munich

Content

Preamble

In the last quarter of a century, crime prevention has been developed and established in Germany in many ways: in the meantime, a new field of action and policy has been created.

As a consequence of this development, the familiar original prevention protagonists (police and justice system) are now supported by additional protagonists such as schools, children's and youth organizations, and civil society organizations. Cooperation commissions have been instituted at all levels – local, regional, national, international – in order to live up to the understanding of crime prevention as a social responsibility which requires cooperation between protagonists and institutions.

The drivers of this development are the numerous programs and projects of the respective specialized practices, i.e. the organized practice of governmental and non-governmental instances and institutions. However, crime prevention not only requires practice if it is to establish and develop.

Crime prevention also requires prevention policy, especially a wide socio-political consensus that crime should be primarily counteracted with preventive strategies and concepts. A consensus that creates the necessary (legal) framework and provides the needed personnel and financial resources.

Crime prevention also urgently needs prevention science as a supplier of the theoretical and empirical foundations, as consultant in the planning, implementation, and spread of preventive programs, and for the verification of projects for their practical suitability and effectiveness.

In crime prevention, practice, policy, and science are the central work areas. For this reason, the 19th German Congress of Crime Prevention has moved its tasks in and for crime prevention into focus with the demand "prevention requires practice, policy, and science". The Report on the emphasis topic "crime prevention requires prevention practice, prevention policy, and prevention science" poses the following questions for the three areas of work:

- whether and how they have implemented their tasks in and for crime prevention, i.e. how crime prevention has developed in practice, what support it receives from the policy side, and what contributions science has made,
- what challenges had to and have to be overcome considering the individual not always (easily) reconcilable action objectives and action logic in the three areas of work, whether there are indications that they are cooperating in the implementation of their responsibilities for crime prevention and possibly even have profited from each other,

- what conclusions can be drawn and what requirements made in order to further develop, establish, and systematize crime prevention with the three areas of work.

0

Summary and conclusions

In the last quarter century, crime prevention has been established and developed in many ways in Germany.[1] In the meantime, this task has created a new field of action and policy at the level of municipalities, states, and the federation. Crime prevention as the active cooperation of many social forces and disciplines with the goal of preventing crimes requires practice, policy, and science. These are its central areas of work which each must contribute its own performance for crime prevention and should act in relation to each other and in cooperation as much as possible.

Definition and goals of crime prevention

Crime prevention is an alternative, non-punitive response to the challenge of preventing crime as a social phenomenon or as an individual event, reducing it, or minimizing its consequences.

Compared to repression, prevention takes precedence in terms of content and timing: the negative impact of the crime and the victim's suffering are avoided, it is more effective, material and immaterial costs are lower.

Crime prevention also has risky aspects, e.g. due to the tendency to blur the boundaries of crime and prevention terms and forward shift preventive actions.

For this reason, crime prevention should be understood in its narrow sense:

Only those strategies, measures, and projects should be considered crime prevention which have as goal the direct or indirect prevention / reduction of crime and from which one can reasonably expect that they are targeted towards preventing / reducing crime with a reasonable and plausible connection – either on the basis of convincing empirical evidence or based on plausible assumptions.

Generally supportive measures of social or universal prevention are indispensable and the responsibility of many policy areas but must be understood and used as what they are, namely social policy and not crime policy / crime prevention.

Crime prevention specified in this way is a general social responsibility which must be fulfilled and implemented in a networked and interdisciplinary cooperation spanning departments and institutions at several levels: at the local / communal level, state

---

[1] A decisive date with signal function for the development and implementation of crime prevention even outside of police and justice in the states and municipalities was the year 1990: the foundation of the first crime prevention State Council, the „Council for crime prevention in Schleswig-Holstein" based on Scandinavian role models.

level, federal level, and the international / global level. It requires specialized knowledge and should be evidence-based.

Central areas of work in the field of action and policy "crime prevention" are thus
prevention practice, prevention policy, and prevention science. Areas of work which
must each make its own contribution to crime prevention and should act in relation to
each other and in cooperation as much as possible.

Prevention practice

With its numerous programs and projects, the organized crime preventing specialized
practice of governmental and non-governmental institutions was and is without a
doubt the driver of development in the area of crime prevention. The focus of crime
prevention programs and projects was and is on the communal / local level. It makes
sense to influence and prevent crime and fear of crime in those places where they arise
and are enabled.

The most important protagonists of prevention practice are the police, children's and
youth organizations, schools, and – with reservations - penal law and/or the justice
system. In the meantime, the police as first responder and probably still most important protagonist of crime prevention sees itself as one protagonist in local problem
resolution processes. Children's and youth organizations hesitated for a long time to
deal with delinquency but in the meantime pedagogical crime prevention has established itself. Schools also fulfill their role in the area of crime prevention as part of their
information and education responsibilities through a variety of prevention and intervention programs. Crime prevention is also the subject of penal law and the justice
system, but their preventive effects are limited to what is possible within the framework of crime repression – and it has been shown that these effects are very small.

The concept of communal crime prevention has had an extremely positive effect
on the development of crime prevention. Since the start of the 1990s, cooperation
and communication networks have arisen in many German cities and municipalities
between communal administration and policy, police, justice, schools, associations,
churches, economy, social institutions, children's and youth organizations, and other
protagonists.

Summary and conclusions

Communal crime prevention provides some of the most pressing indicators and evidence to what extent crime prevention requires practice, policy, and science:

It requires practice for "on-site work". However, practitioners should be specially
selected for this task and receive training and education which meets today's requirements for professionalism and competence. For this, science must develop and provide corresponding training and educational programs.

It requires policy, both on the communal and the state level. Nothing can be achieved without policy support, at least not anything effective and sustainable.

It needs science to provide the theoretical and empirical basis of prevention work, consulting and supervision for the implementation and evaluation of projects, for the development of training and education programs, for the development and maintenance of databases and information systems.

Even though it has been around for a long time and developing continuously, the practice of communal crime prevention still has a lot of potential for optimization. However, since this concept still is "a just plain common sense idea", everything should be tried to realize this idea for the long term.

Prevention policy

While crime prevention is considered an important goal of criminal policy, the increased orientation of policy towards crime prevention and its sustained development which is demanded by science and practice has not taken place to a sufficient degree. This is at least true for criminal policy at the federal level, i.e. for policy which is responsible for penal law, i.e. repression – and thus really also for prevention, which precedes repression in both time and content. However, at the federal level, crime policy not only sticks with its criminal-law reaction patterns, it has even enhanced them. The trend towards a control-oriented preventive penal law supports the prevention state, into which Germany has been turning for a few years now.

This criminal policy is deaf to theoretical and empirical knowledge which criminology and other scientific disciplines have developed a long time ago and provided to policy makers because this knowledge goes against the trends of criminal policy as it is practiced today. Empirical criminology and other scientific disciplines have never produced as much knowledge as today – and have never had as little influence on criminal policy as today. Even the two *Periodical Security Reports* commissioned by and submitted to the federal government had and have practically no impact on criminal policy in Germany – its political convictions are apparently impervious even to the best knowledge available. We can certainly not speak of evidence-based criminal policy at the federal level.

This is underlined by the fact that, until now, the federal level has not exhibited any will to support crime prevention by installing a "National Center for Crime Prevention" with sufficient organizational, personnel, and financial equipment. The foundation Deutsches Forum für Kriminalprävention [German Forum for Crime Prevention] (DFK) is unable to even begin to meet its goals and core responsibilities and has remained alive only thanks to the commitment of its participants.

While the local / communal levels and the state levels are bound to federal criminal policy in terms of penal law and penal law practice[2], it still looks better here in terms of policy support for crime prevention. For communal crime prevention this can be seen in the – often applied – demand "prevention is the responsibility of the mayor". At the state level, this can be seen by the initiation and implementation of prevention-oriented programs and in particular the installation of state prevention councils and comparable commissions which not only have the responsibility consulting for crime prevention policy but also strengthen and support communal crime prevention.

Summary and conclusions

In view of an overall favorable development of crime, the municipalities and states should not ease up on their crime prevention efforts but at least keep them at the same level if not increase them. In this sense, all levels should (again and again) create a wide social consensus in terms of facing crime primarily with preventive strategies and concepts.

At the local level, the concept of communal crime prevention definitely has a future and should be implemented and developed (in an area-covering manner), for instance in the direction of a communal security policy, institutionalized for instance in an "Office for crime prevention".

Due to the tight budget restrictions in many communities, financial support is urgently needed, also so that the other actors at the communal level can continue their outstanding and indispensable work in crime prevention and possibly even expand it further.

State prevention councils should be installed in all states and suitably equipped with organization, personnel, and finances. The integration of councils into the government and not a ministry should also be studied, as should the creation of an "Office for crime prevention" at the state level. One should strive for the development of crime prevention into a systematic prevention strategy and/or prevention policy.

At the federal level it is urgently necessary to create a "National Center for Crime Prevention" with sufficient organizational, personnel, and financial resources, possibly by expanding the foundation Deutsches Forum für Kriminalprävention (DFK) into such a center and integrating the Kriminologische Zentralstelle [Central Criminological Office] (KrimZ). This center should also not be connected to a ministry but to the Federal Chancellery.

Even if the crime policy impact of the two previous Periodical Security Reports (PSR) were hardly noticeable, the creation of – actually – Periodical Security Reports based on a legal regulation or decision of the German Bundestag is urgently necessary. These reports should be compiled by an interdisciplinary scientific commission on a regular basis, for instance once in every legislative period.

---

[2]   In the meantime, only the penal system has become the responsibility of the states.

It should be checked at all levels whether 5% of the current expenses for crime response – by police, justice, and penal system – should better be invested into effective crime prevention.

Prevention science

Crime prevention should be based on evidence, i.e. on the basis of theoretical and empirical scientific insights. Prevention practice and prevention policy thus require science and research.

The fact that prevention policy looks different in reality, at least on the federal level, has already been discussed. At the communal and state levels, policy makers appear to be more open to evidence. In the meantime, this is also the case for prevention practice.

This is not lastly due to science having performed numerous "services" for practice and having increasingly and systematically supported prevention practice.

This not only provides prevention practice with the necessary theoretical and empirical scientific insights, but the planning, implementation, and effect of prevention measures and programs (implementation and evaluation) is scientifically monitored and verified. In particular the evaluation of projects has become much more frequent and standard in the meantime and implementation research is gaining in significance.

Evaluation should be a core goal of prevention policy, in particular in form of lasting regulatory impact assessment, evaluation of the usefulness of a law, and monitoring of the parameters originally targeted by the law. Not just in terms of legislative activities but especially also for practical prevention policy up to the level of cities and municipalities.

The time that research takes in general can become a problem. Practice and policy want to – must – act as quickly as possible in order to remedy recognized problems. But science needs time to be able to make well-founded statements about effects or lack thereof. It is likely as difficult in prevention practice as in prevention policy to perform empirical studies and collect data before a prevention measure has started and/or a law passed.

Problems could arise from the current position of criminology as relevant reference science: while Germany has a highly developed theoretical and empirical science of criminology, it is apparently seriously endangered due "structural depletion". A lot of criminological research takes place outside of the criminology of law schools and is significantly dispersed over various scientific disciplines. However, this also means that criminological questions enjoy widespread scientific interest.

Summary and conclusions

Many scientific disciplines are and have been involved in developing the knowledge about what works and what doesn't, what makes sense for of crime prevention and what doesn't; however, at the center there was always criminology whose existence is at risk at German Universities. Something similar applies to neighboring disciplines.

Since this could have effects on crime prevention, Universities should intensify the instruction in particular in sociological and juristic faculties and bundle, coordinate, and thus promote the diverse criminological activities by developing interdisciplinary Central Criminological Offices.

We welcome the 2012 foundation of the endowment chair "Crime prevention and risk management". In order to give crime prevention the necessary weight in the research spectrum of criminology and other disciplines, it is necessary that this Chair should be financed past 2017 and be made permanent.

But in particular, the close association between criminology and penal law should be dissolved and criminology established as an independent social science. A well-positioned criminology department is a necessary (if not sufficient) prerequisite for the implementation of the requirement for interdisciplinary prevention science.

Crime prevention requires prevention practice, prevention policy, and prevention science

The German Congress of Crime Prevention (DPT) is probably the best example for how far the demand that crime prevention requires prevention practice, prevention policy, and prevention science has already become a reality. This can be seen not only in its development from very humble beginnings – 1995 in Lübeck with 168 registered congress participants and a very manageable program of this "work conference" to the last 18th DPT 2013 in Bielefeld with almost 2,000 congress participants from 17 specified work areas, a comprehensive program (169 speakers for presentations and project spots), informational booths, special exhibits, etc.

The evaluation results (of DPT evaluated since the 13th DPT) find: "Overall, the evaluation results show that the 18th German Congress of Crime Prevention can be considered a successful event. Almost 92% of the surveyed visitors thought that the 18th German Congress of Crime Prevention was very good or good." The German Congress of Crime Prevention has without a question developed into an important forum for the discourse between practice, science, and policy in the field of crime prevention.

In 2013 another field of work started with the "DPT institute for applied prevention research" (dpt-i) in order to strengthen this development and develop it systematically. An important task of this institute could be to develop a systematic strategy for crime prevention to handle their tasks for crime prevention and the demands and challenges for these areas of work based on the findings on performance and deficits of the areas of prevention practice, prevention policy, and prevention science.

1

Crime prevention

In the last quarter of a century, crime prevention has been developed and established in Germany in many ways: in the meantime, a new field of action and policy has been created at the municipal, state, and federal level. As the active cooperation of many social forces and disciplines with the goal of preventing crime, crime prevention requires practice, policy, and science: these are its central areas of work which must make their own contributions for crime prevention and should act in relation to each other and in cooperation as much as possible.

Prevention practice with its numerous protagonists, the governmental and non-governmental instances and institutions with its many programs and projects, was and is the driving force of the development of crime prevention. However, without the support of the prevention policy, this "engine" may easily run out of steam. Crime prevention needs "fuel", especially a wide socio-political consensus that crime should be primarily counteracted with preventive strategies and concepts. Such a consensus is the prerequisite for creating the required (legal) framework conditions for prevention practice and providing the necessary personnel and financial resources. Prevention policy will only achieve this (at least in the long term) if prevention practice is evidence-based and has an effect ("success"). That means that crime prevention urgently needs the prevention science as a supplier of the theoretical and empirical foundations, as consultant in the planning, implementation, and spread of preventive programs, and for the verification of projects for their practical suitability and effectiveness.

It would be optimal for crime prevention if its three areas of work would not only provide these contributions but also work together in this process. However, this cooperation is still "in its infancy" (Marks 2014) – and this not lastly because crime prevention has not been systematically planned and implemented at either the communal, state, or federal level in the sense of a prevention strategy or even a prevention policy but has instead more or less "grown organically".

In addition, the three areas of work each have their own action objectives and action logic which generally makes cooperation difficult. Even within the respective areas of work, the network that overarches cooperation, protagonists, department, and disciplines is not easy to create.

In the following, we will discuss the three areas of work in crime prevention, based on available knowledge

- whether and how they have implemented their tasks in and for crime prevention, i.e. how crime prevention has developed in practice, what support it receives from the politics side, and what contributions science has made,

- what challenges had to and have to be overcome to balance the individual and not always (easily) reconcilable action objectives and action logic, what indications there are of whether and how they have cooperated and profited from each other in the implementation of their responsibilities for crime prevention,

- which conclusions should be drawn and what requirements made in order to further develop and establish crime prevention with and through these three areas of work.

First, however, we specify what understanding of crime prevention this discussion is based on.

1.1

Definition, goals, positive and risky aspects[3]

Crime prevention includes all governmental and private efforts, programs and measures which use to prevent, reduce, or alleviate the consequences of crime as a social phenomenon or as an individual event.[4]

In general, crime prevention deals with the development / strengthening of protective factors and the elimination / reduction of risk factors.

Crime prevention is an alternative, non-punitive response to the challenge of preventing or at least reducing crime and the fear of crime. Crime prevention is thus not part of the criminal justice system but basically another "pillar" in the area of crime control, next to the pillars police, justice, and penal system. Crime preventive action does not assume already perpetrated crimes but attempts to prevent crimes from happening in the first place (Welsh/Farrington 2012, 128; Waller 2011, 2013).

In terms of perpetrators, situations, and victims, it is still usual to distinguish between primary, secondary, and tertiary crime prevention (PSR 2006, 667 et seq.; Schwind 2013, Section 1 marginal note 42, each with further evidence).

This distinction should be forgone since it leads to misunderstandings which do not help the idea of crime prevention (Steffen 2013 b, pp. 492 et seq.):

---

[3]   The following explanations are based on the meaning of crime prevention used in the previous expert opinions for the German Congress of Crime Prevention.

[4]   According to the definition in the „Guidelines for Police Crime Prevention" 1998 (see Steffen 2013 b, footnote 12).

- This structural model imposes a hierarchy, a valuation of the prevention areas: primary is better than secondary and for tertiary it is already (almost) too late anyway. But in fact, all three areas have their own meaning and content.

- On the other hand, this differentiation leads to the incorrect conclusion that "primary prevention" has something to do with the age of the subjects, that it is crime prevention directed at children and maybe adolescents.[5] However, this is not at all the case.

More meaningful and clearer is the distinction between universal or social prevention, between selective or situative crime prevention and indicated crime prevention.[6]

Universal or social ("primary") prevention

targets the general public and/or overall groups with general supportive, non-occasion-related programs and measures without the need for specific risk factors in these groups.

Without the need for "specific suspicions", consistent social, work, youth, family, economic, education, and cultural policies are supposed to create optimal conditions to prevent deviant behavior and crime in the first place. Universal prevention is the responsibility of many protagonists and institutions, from family and schools all the way to youth support, community, and politics, but less frequently police and justice system.

Due to its very unspecific "universal" orientation, it is debated whether social prevention should even be labeled and understood as *crime prevention* – even if there is no doubt that socialization and education, individual and social life conditions etc. have a significant impact on the development of crime. But it is not possible to find direct connections between such "global framework conditions" and crime.[7] In order to counteract the risk of blurring crime and prevention terminology and focusing more on preventive action, crime is not the suitable frame of reference for strategies of universal prevention.[8]

---

[5]   Feltes addresses this (mis)understanding when he describes the withdrawal of the police in North Rhine-Westphalia from primary prevention which occurred because children generally are not the target group of police measures for the prevention of juvenile crime (2012, 36).

[6]   See also Steffen 2011, 102 et seq.; 2013 b, 492 et seq.; Work place 2007; Eisner/Ribeaud/Bittel 2006.

[7]   This „universal orientation" of primary prevention is also the decisive reason why primary prevention measures are almost inaccessible to targeted impact research despite the fact that they unquestionably have an effect (Bannenberg/Rössner 2002, 5).

[8]   Michael Walter summarized this in 2004 in a presentation given at the 26th German Youth Court Day in Leipzig: „The idea of crime prevention may be connected with almost everything and is unbounded in this respect. If one were to look at all of our living conditions, installations, and relationships from a crime prevention perspective this would signify a terrible degree of human impoverishment. Education even in the Kindergarten stage no doubt has preventive components. When viewed like this, almost everything is part of crime prevention."
The label „crime prevention" almost always imposes a connotation which suggests that the target group is

Measures of universal prevention, such as the restoration of social justice through the reduction of income, education, and integration disparity with the goal of equal economic, political, social and cultural participation of all population segments are indispensable but must be understood and used as what they are, namely as *social policy* and not as criminal policy and/or crime prevention,[9] even if they can without a doubt have a crime preventive effect. But this is not their objective, and certainly not their primary objective, and for this reason they should not be instrumentalized for the purpose of crime prevention – especially since this does not live up to the significance of these measures.

Especially since the protection of social state from the different social risks can help counteract (the increase of) crime and fear of crime, especially because crime prevention work can only be successful if it is embedded in a fair social policy – life circumstance policy[10] - one must clearly distinguish between social preventive and crime prevention strategies, programs, and measures, at least as far as this is possible: because there are always overlaps and mix-ups, at least the terminology should be clear.[11]

Selective or situational ("secondary") crime prevention,

like universal prevention, it wants to prevent crimes before they happen but has a more specific approach by focusing on risk situations and attempting to influence potentially delinquent persons and criminogenic situations. Selective prevention targets specific sub-groups, individuals, or situations which are characterized by greater exposure to risk factors and thus are subject to increased perpetrator and victimization risk ("persons at risk as perpetrators and victims") and/or, in situations, are at risk because crime can occur ("opportunities for crime").

Selective crime prevention directly or indirectly aims at preventing and reducing crime and fear of crime and/or improving the safety situation and feeling of safety.

It tries to remove personal and social deficits as possible causes of crime, reducing opportunities for crime, and increasing the risk of discovery (Steffen 2013 b, 494).

---

at least potentially prone to criminal behavior. This unavoidably creates a risk of stigmatization (Holthusen/Hoops 2012, 27; Steffen 2006 a, 1151)

[9]   Problematic socio-political developments – key words: preventive government, safety society - which may be associated with blurring the term of prevention, with mixing criminal policy and social policy, were discussed in detail in the Report for the 17th German Congress of Crime Prevention (Steffen 2013 a); see also Chapter 3.1.2 below.

[10] For this reason, too, „an orientation on empirical and/or expert descriptions, analyses, and assessments on the life situations of their target groups has become increasingly important for policy in the last decades" (Pluto et al. 2014, 7).

[11] Kahl (2012, 26) sees things differently, asking that the field of action of crime prevention should not be further narrowed but in fact expanded / liberated and this also in terms of terminology.

The important aspects here are

- help and support for persons in special problematic situations (through help in family and education etc.),

- increasing the effort required to commit a crime and the risk of being caught as well as reducing the benefit of the crime by changing the structure of crime opportunities correspondingly[12], and 3.1.2 below.

- the reduction of crime-promoting situations, also by providing corresponding information and training to potential victims.

Indicated ("tertiary") prevention

begins after crimes have already been committed. Suitable measures, if necessary special therapy, is supposed to prevent recidivism as effectively as possible; this includes support in finding employment and reintegration of the offenders (PSR 2006, 668).

Indicated prevention also includes programs and measures for situations in which crimes have occurred with greater frequency ("crime hot spots").

(Governmental) control and intervention measures are supposed to counteract crimes and re-socialize persons with criminal tendencies with the goal of preventing and/or reducing further delinquency and crimes, reducing the crime rate, and reducing the victimization risk of the population (Steffen 2013 b, 495).

Indicated crime prevention also includes help for victims of crimes with the goal of preventing repeated victimization and especially secondary victimization due to reactions of the instances and the social environment.

Positive aspects of crime prevention

Especially the following considerations speak for crime prevention:[13]

- avoiding effects of crime and suffering of victim:
  crime prevention is more humane than crime repression. This not only applies to the perpetrator side in terms of punishment but in particular also to the victim side. It makes more sense to prevent crimes from every happening than to have to pursue them subsequently at great expense. In addition to material and physical damage, crimes often lead to severe psychological consequences for the victims. No matter how successful criminal prosecution is, it cannot repair or even reverse damage already done.

---

[12] Heinz 1998, 31 et seq.: „Secondary prevention through changes to the structures of crime opportunities ... is the method of choice under the consideration of proportionality."

[13] DVJJ 2007, 5; see also Waller 2011, 2013 and Heinz 1998, 18 et seq., 2005, 9.

- Greater effectiveness:

  Crime prevention-oriented action can reduce potential conflicts and opportunities for crime, reduce fears, improve communication, defuse disintergrating situations. Criminal prosecution always comes too late: individual and social problems which are expressed by crimes have already occurred. In addition, the criminal justice repertoire has only very limited crime-reducing effects.

- Lower cost:

  Where crime prevention is effective, it usually also pays in terms of the personnel and financial resources that are used. Investment in effective prevention means fewer victims, fewer damage, lower costs for tax payers, and the reduction of the work load for police, justice, and penal system.

Risky aspects of crime prevention

However, crime prevention also has risky aspects. Crime prevention has an effect[14] – and thus may also have risks and side-effects. It is not automatically good for the mere reason that it wants to prevent bad things from happening (see Steffen 2012 a, 108 et seq.):

- Prevention is based on the assumption that it is able to recognize risks and pre-empt them through action in the present. However, the future depends on many things, knowledge is still somewhat uncertain, and prevention in this sense *action based on suspicion*. This carries the risk the present is restricted for fear that things may develop in the worst possible manner (Ohder 2010, 16).

- Crime prevention tends to *blur the terms of crime and prevention and to shift the preventive action forward:* in case of failure prevention was simply too late, one should have acted earlier and possibly more intensely (Holthusen et. al. 2011, 23).

- There is the danger that the idea of prevention could be used as *blank check to legitimize* just about any measure as long as it is labeled "prevention" (11th Children's and Youth Report 2002, 243).

- Just like repressive measures, preventive measures are always *interventions*, can have a stigmatizing effect, and must therefore meet certain requirements and a verification for negative side-effects and consequences (Ohder 2010, 17).

- When completely normal projects, like youth work, are performed with the goal of "crime prevention" – even if only to get financing for them - then not only

---

[14]   In the words of the State Councilman for Crime Prevention Mecklenburg-Western Pomerania (LfK): „Prevention works – provided that certain conditions are met. This includes e.g. its overall social approach, its factuality, and its sustainability. Both long-term practical experience and scientific studies show that ... prevention work has a decisive impact on the actual and the subjectively perceived development of crime ... In the last 17 years, Mecklenburg-Western Pomerania has become noticeably safer and prevention work has made a significant contribution to this." (impulse. Business report of LfK 2010/2011, 5).

can civilian situations be reinterpreted into criminal situations and a whole generation, namely the young adults, be stigmatized as (potentially) "criminal" or "violent",[15] but the *social policy itself* may also become *"criminalized"*, i.e. social policy issues be processed like crime policy issues (Steffen 2012 a, 100 et seq.).

- Crime prevention may promote a *"safety hysteria"*: crime prevention provides a further perspective on crime in addition to repression and this may overemphasize the problem and lead to "safety hysteria" (Ostendorf 2005; see also Sessar 2011).

- Crime prevention is based on the *logic of suspicion* – this contradicts the presumption of innocence and is deficit- and not resource-oriented from a pedagogical perspective. In addition, this logic of suspicion again presents the significant risk of stigmatizing persons (Holthusen et.al. 2011, 24).

- Crime prevention has its place where something is supposed to be prevented which would have a certain likelihood of occurring without corresponding measures and which would be connected with significant damage. Crime prevention should be viewed with skepticism in terms of *processes and developments to be created where not the failure to prevent but a lack of suitable support could lead to a negative outcome* (Ohder 2010). The use of the term prevention in itself imbues the affected persons with the connotation of a possible negative development. It would be better to use the terms "support" or "aid", in particular if these concepts – corresponding to the tendency for shifting actions ahead – are used very early on (Holthusen et. al. 2011, 23).

Prevention is an operation fraught with assumptions and ambivalence (Holthusen et. al. 2011, 25). For this reason, one should definitely take precautions against the trend for blurring and shifting of preventive action and understand crime prevention in a narrow sense:

Only those strategies, measures, and projects should be considered as crime preventive that directly or indirectly prevent / reduce crime and from which one can reasonably expect that they are targeted towards preventing / reducing crime with a reasonable and plausible connection – either on the basis of convincing empirical evidence or based on plausible assumptions.[16]

This requirement for "tightening" the prevention idea is rarely met by universal crime prevention, but is generally met by selective and indicated crime prevention.

---

[15] A good example for this are the numerous projects and programs established in the meantime for supporting life and behavior skills which are forced on entire school classes under the label „preventing violence" - thus being placed under the suspicion of having criminal or violent tendencies, completely independently of their actual conduct.

[16] This definition corresponds to the definition used in the work place 2007, 17 et seq. and in the previous Reports for the German Congress of Crime Prevention.

Apart from that, one should avoid taking over standardized programs without verifying their necessity and suitability first. Rather, crime prevention programs, projects, and measures should take into account the local, social, and cultural conditions and contexts of crime, be based on a thorough analysis of problems and causes on site, be implemented carefully, and of course be evaluated for their effectiveness. All this should happen in close cooperation of the areas of work of practice and science, supported by politics.

1.2

Development of crime prevention: the origin of a new field of action and policy

"Crime prevention as the sum of precautions and measures used to prevent the occurrence of crime and to prevent recidivism in case a crime does occur has a long tradition as idea and commitment, but only a short history as practical reality ... Until recently, the significance of crime prevention has always been emphasized for criminal policy and practice, but the specific implementation has been somewhat neglected" (PSR 2001, 470 and 455).

"When looking ... at the development of the current 'landscape' of prevention of delinquency and crime, including the prevention and/or at least effective reduction of all kinds of risks which may contribute to deviant behavior, then one can fix the targeted discussions and plans for the 'start' of current crime prevention movement that slowly spread all over Germany to the period between 1970 and 1980." (Kerner 2012, 38).[17]

However, a clear "prevention pioneering spirit" only arose in the 1990s:[18] the first state prevention councils in Germany are founded – Schleswig- Holstein (1990), Hesse (1992), Lower Saxony (1995); already in 1988 the first permanent work group for interdisciplinary prevention efforts had convened in the City of Neumünster, named "Council for crime prevention" since 1992 – the beginning of communal crime prevention as a (new) general social responsibility; in 1995, the Federal Ministry for Justice created the first expert department "Prevention" in a Ministry in Germany and the

---

[17] Kerner mainly lists the different activities of the police, such as police programs for drug prevention, the special volume of the BKA research series from 1986 „Systematic crime prevention – with practical examples" or the BKA Annual Conference 1987 on the general topic „Crime prevention as a general social responsibility." Already in 1975, the BKA held its annual conference on the topic of „Police and prevention".

Since 1970, all federal states have participated in the „Criminal police prevention program (KPVP)"; in 1972, a decision of the permanent Konferenz der Innenminister und –senatoren der Länder (IMK) [Conference of Interior Ministers and Senators of the States] installed a project management for the KPVP, also in order to place it on a firm financial basis. The PSR 2001, 458 et seq. explains in this connection: „The newer German discussion about crime prevention was started in a work meeting of the Federal Office of Criminal Investigation in November 1975. Event though not much happened in practice afterwards in terms of institutions and organization, a statement was made to turn the motto ‚crime prevention is the noblest task of the police' (which until then was really not more than a platitude) into a factually changed reality of police work for the long term".

[18] See Marks 2013, 129.

Bundeskriminalamt (BKA) [Federal Office of Criminal Investigation] starts with the "Infopool Prevention", a collection of recommended projects from the area of crime prevention; in 1997, the Deutsches Jugendinstitut [German Youth Institute] installs the still existing Office for Children's and Juvenile Crime Prevention and the police restructures its prevention-related commission work: the Kriminalpolizeilichen Vorbeugungsprogramm (KPVP) [Criminal Police Prevention Program] becomes today's Programm Polizeiliche Kriminalprävention (ProPK) [Program for Police Crime Prevention]; in 1995, the first German Congress of Crime Prevention is convened, in 1999, the legally independent "Association of Shareholders of the German Congress of Crime Prevention" is founded; in 2001, the foundation Deutsches Forum für Kriminalprävention (DFK) [German Forum for Crime Prevention] is founded.

In the meantime, crime prevention as a new field of action and policy (Kahl 2013, 39) has formed as the active cooperation of many social forces from practice, policy, and science with the goal of preventing crime.[19] "Crime prevention develops strategies to keep the crime load as low as possible. Its significance and value for criminal policy and practice are undisputed in the meantime" (PSR 2006, 665).

Today it is not disputed that "crime prevention attacks long before penal legislation, penal law, (police-based) criminal prosecution, criminal justice, sentencing, and implementation (enforcement and execution with alternatives) and/or goes far beyond them" (PSR 2001, 456). "In terms of criminal policy, the guiding principle 'precedence of prevention over repression' is therefore not disputed" (Heinz 1998, 18).

Also undisputed, if by no means completely implemented everywhere, is the following understanding of crime prevention:

- crime prevention is considered as a **general social responsibility** which involves not only police and justice but (see above) many social forces from practice, policy, and science.[20]

This is because the causes of crime cannot be remedied merely by means of police and penal law. This can already be seen in the variety of these causes but also from the experiences made with the limited effect of penal law measures on behavior and behavioral changes,[21] as well as the theoretical considerations and practical insights into the causes of fear of crime: A majority of the factors recognized and shown to be causes of the occurrence of crime and fear of crime, cannot be influenced at all by the means of penal law or at best to a very (too) limited degree. Here, – and not only

---

[19] According to the State Prevention Council Lower Saxony.

[20] „Preventive behavior modification is not particular to penal law, but a common characteristic of all social norm systems and institutions that aim at socialization" (Kunz 2011 Section 24 marginal note 3). See also the brochure of the DVJJ 2007 „Together with distributed roles".

[21] Since criminal prosecution always comes too late, see above.

here – prevention is clearly superior to repression, comes first, and has precedence in terms of content (Heinz 1998, 19 et seq.; Steffen 2013 b, 487).[22]

- Crime prevention is a task that must be performed and implemented at **several levels**: at the local / communal level, state level, federal level, and the international / global level.

According to the principle of subsidiarity,[23] crime prevention should primarily be the responsibility of citizens, then of public collectives such as municipalities, cities, and districts, and only then of states and federation (Marks 2014).

- The understanding of crime prevention as a general social responsibility leads to the conclusion that it should be performed in a **networked cooperation involving institutions and protagonists**. This is not only true for communication and cooperation networks at the communal level but for instance also for state prevention councils.[24]
- Crime prevention requires **specialized knowledge**: the demands on those who (are supposed to) implement crime prevention programs and measures to practice have increased. This also in view of the fact that crime prevention meanwhile has become a "market" which is also subject to economic interests. This is not only true for the manufacturers and retailers of preventive safety technology but also for providers of behavior-oriented prevention programs and concepts:

Many of these programs cost money, e.g. for training operators ("trainer") and/or for materials. The local prevention protagonists must be capable of assessing the "value" of these programs for the goals and intended targets of their prevention enterprises.[25]

In the meantime, the training is not only "protagonist-internally" but trans-regional training possibilities are also offered – and used! - for instance the "Beccaria qualification program crime prevention" of the State Prevention Council Lower Saxony since 2008 or the Master's program "Preventive social work with emphasis on criminology & crime prevention" at the Ostfalia University for Applied Sciences in Wolfenbüttel since the winter semester 2011 (see Chap. 4.3).

---

[22] See also Heinz 1998, 17 et seq.

[23] According to the principle of subsidiarity, tasks, actions, and solutions should be performed as far as possible by small units in a self-directed and responsible manner. Only when this is not possible, should successively larger groups, public collectives, or higher levels of an organization support and take over the responsibilities and actions in a subsidiary fashion (Marks 2014)

[24] For instance, the State Prevention Council (SPC) Lower Saxony comprises of the following members: communal prevention commissions; statewide active NGOs; ministries, state representatives, and subordinate agencies; scientific institutions.

[25] Supported not only by a corresponding qualification but also by databases such as the „Green List for Prevention".

- Crime prevention should be **evidence-based**: i.e. based on theoretical and empirical scientific insights, as well as in terms of the assessment of its planning, implementation, and effectiveness (implementation and evaluation).[26] This not only makes demands on the "acquisition readiness" of the practical side but also the "provision performance" of science.

1.3

Summary and conclusions

Crime prevention has been developed and established in many ways in Germany in the last 25 years: in the meantime, a new field of action and policy has arisen which needs practice, politics and science and creates (new) challenges for them.

Large parts of this development occurred somewhat unplanned and accidental. One essential reason for this is that the cooperation between the three areas of work in crime prevention – practice, politics and science – occurred (if at all) also somewhat unplanned and accidental and was by no means developed systematically.

However, crime prevention requires a structured and intensive cooperation in its three areas of work. Which challenges arise and what demands must be imposed will be discussed in the following using the findings concerning the actual status in practice, politics and science.

2

Prevention practice

2.1

Development and status

With its numerous programs and projects, the organized crime preventing specialized practice of governmental and non-governmental institutions was and is without a doubt the driver of development in the area of crime prevention – also towards more cooperation, networking, and professionalism.

Crime prevention was initiated and developed by the practical side before policy and science also started participating.

---

[26] Already in 2006, the 2nd PSR considers the necessity to focus more on an important basic aspect in the development of crime prevention in Germany, i.e. the evaluation of crime preventive initiatives and programs in view of their actual impact, to be mostly accepted in the meantime (2006, 670, 676).
Newer research shows that prevention programs should focus especially on systematic implementation (Foundation German forum for crime prevention 2013 b, 32). The „Beccaria quality initiative" of the State Prevention Council Lower Saxony includes not only the Beccaria qualification program but also the Beccaria standards, requirements and stipulations for the quality of planning, implementation and evaluation of crime prevention programs and projects (www.beccaria.de; Marks 2014).

2.1.1

Dominance of communal / local level

The focus of crime prevention programs and projects was and is on the communal / local level. Its dominance not only fulfills the principle of subsidiarity (see footnote 23) but also derives from the insight that crime in all its forms is basically a local phenomenon: many of the socio-cultural, scientific, and infrastructure factors relevant to the criminal act are clearly local. About 70% of the offenses registered by the police are perpetrated in the local residential community of the perpetrators and/or victims, i.e. where the perpetrators are socialized and the victims (unintentionally) co-create opportunities for crime. Social control also has clearly local relations – notwithstanding the nationalization of the communal police departments that already occurred years ago and an already trans-regionally unified (federal) justice system (Steffen 2006 a, 1145; PSR 2006, 670). Children's and youth organizations are communal responsibilities anyway; the same is true for many school systems.[27]

Apart from that, the story is not only about crime but also about the fear of crime, not just safety but also the feeling of safety – and this is affected mainly by local conditions, in particular those in the close surroundings: "In the meantime, in Germany empirical research on situations and behaviors in public that trigger fear of crime has also repeatedly confirmed the finding that citizens attach their worries to signs of disorder, decay, and neglect (partially focused on space, partly on buildings, partly on groups of persons). This finding is very important to the future design of practical crime prevention which takes the concerns and needs of citizens seriously "(PSR 2001, 461).[28]

It thus makes sense to influence and prevent crime and fear of crime in the place in which it arises and is enabled and to do so with joint responsibility of citizens of the respective community and their communal and governmental institutions, in an interdisciplinary and institutionalized form (Steffen 2013 b, 488).

2.1.2

Protagonists of crime prevention: police, children's and youth organizations, schools, penal law, and criminal justice

Many protagonists and institutions are committed to the field of crime prevention, which becomes clear in the composition of the crime prevention commissions. The most important ones, like e.g. children's and youth organizations, which themselves represent several governmental and non-governmental organizations are probably those described in the following.

---

[27] PSR 2001, 470: „The weight of local initiatives is appropriate to the problem if large portions of crime which citizens encounter in their everyday life occur in the immediate vicinity of perpetrators and victims."

[28] For fear of crime, its triggers, and its extent see also the explanations in the Report for the 17th DPT 2012, Steffen 2012 a, 97 et seq.).

2.1.2.1

The Police

The first – and probably still the most important – protagonists of crime prevention are the police:[29] Since the "defense against dangers to life, limb, health and property of the people ... which according to the current general constitutional view is the core responsibility of the government ... it is to a certain extent in the nature of the thing that the police participated in the more recent developments (crime prevention) the quickest and most visible to the outside in various ways. The police was also exposed to corresponding pressure from expectations of the population, being basically the only guarantor of internal security and thus for measures for crime prevention" (PSR 2001, 459).[30]

This "pressure of expectations" was intensified by practical and theoretical insights on the adverse effects on the feeling of safety of the population and the practical policing and criminal policy reactions to them. In Germany, the "alternative approaches in terms of formal and informal social control from the USA" (PSR 2001, 460) were being discussed since roughly the start of the 1990s, in connection with demands for a "police force that is close to its citizens and commonwealth-oriented",[31] which works "closely together with other institutions, associations, and individual citizens (or groups) in order to create effective crime prevention together and maintain it long term" (PSR 2001, 460).

In November 1997, the *Police crime prevention commission for states and federation (KPK)*[32] developed the template "Communal safety and order partnership – the adaption of community policing for Germany". The commission feels that such "commu-

---

[29]   „The high significance of crime prevention in the spectrum of police responsibilities is not only the result of the outstanding importance of protection from crime for the population, but also of the insight that it makes more sense not to let crimes arise in the first place than to have to prosecute them later at great cost. In addition to material and physical damage, crimes often lead to severe psychological consequences for the victims. Criminal prosecution, no matter how successful, cannot make up for this" (Guidelines Police Crime Prevention 1998).

[30]   However, this position of the police also results in a very specific problem: its responsibility for both prevention and repression definitely makes the cooperation with other protagonists of crime prevention more difficult, for instance with social work. See e.g. DVJJ 2007, 16 et seq.

[31]   This being the – most common - German term for the concept of „community policing". This concept is by no means just an „import" of foreign ideas and procedures but also the „revival" of a traditional principle of German police work that has often fallen into disrepute: ensuring safety and order. Its core elements include the consequent inclusion of citizen interests in short, medium, and long-term police plans and current policing actions; the expectation of citizens and in particular their feeling of safety become the focus of police work (Steffen 2006 b, 120 et seq.).
More details on „police work in Germany that is close to its citizens and commonwealth-oriented" Steffen 1995; Steffen 2002 and Steffen 2006 b.

[32]   This commission is made up of one representative each of the respective centers for crime prevention in the 16 state police agencies, the Federal Office of Criminal Investigation, the German University for Police, and the Federal Police. It is responsible for all police-relevant topics and responsibilities in the area of crime prevention which requires coordination between the police departments of the states and in the federation.

nal safety and order partnerships" could integrate the many individual developments towards police work that is close to citizens into a targeted overall concept (Steffen 2006 b, 119 et seq.).

In February 1998, the Permanent conference of interior ministers and senators (IMK) passed the concept "Partnership for more safety in our cities and communities". Among other things, the security work is supposed to orient itself more on the specific needs of citizens and support the installation of communal prevention councils and security partnerships.

In October 1998, the AK II (Work group interior security of the IMK) approved the *"Guidelines for police crime prevention"* which have applied since then in unchanged form and have also entered into the Polizeidienstvorschrift [Police Service Regulations] (PDV) 100 which is the basis for the police's perception of responsibilities. The text states among other things: "A sustainable strategy of crime prevention must take into account the variety of causes. This requires an overarching, integrated overall concept. Crime prevention is thus a general social responsibility for which not only the police but also in particular policy, other governmental and non-governmental agencies, the economy, the media, and the population themselves bear responsibility and to which they must make their own specific contributions ... At the communal level, crime prevention can be performed especially effectively with targeted project work since crime occurs and is experienced mainly locally. For this, all locally relevant prevention carriers ... should be included. One goal is to network the respective projects and measures and increasingly institutionalize citizen participation. The institution of communal prevention councils and/or security and order partnerships can contribute to this."

This development shows especially one thing: The police no longer sees itself as "basically the only guarantor of internal security and thus for measures for crime prevention" because police (and penal law) measures alone do not suffice to reduce or even prevent crime and fear of crime effectively. The understanding of crime prevention as social, especially local, responsibility also changes the self-understanding of the police: the police as protagonist in local problem solution processes gives up its professional security monopoly (Steffen 2006 b, 122).

Ziercke 1997 comments: In the development process of communal crime prevention, the police will continue to play an important role. But it must redefine the limits of police-based prevention. "It must say goodbye to a self-understanding that overloads the police. It is not the police who stand at the center of crime prevention but the institutions and involved citizens at the communal level. Police crime prevention must consciously network, coordinate, and partner with other departments at the communal level ..." (1998, 283).

While this appears to have somewhat succeeded at the communal level[33], there is obviously still clear need for action at the state and especially at the federal level. In 2011 the Commission for Police Crime Prevention (see footnote 32) comments in a statement on the "Conditions for successful police crime prevention": "The Police Crime Prevention of the States and the Federation will ... tackle general social fields of action and prevention topics ... The police is unable to perform such comprehensive prevention work alone, both legally or in actuality... Prevention themes that are inter-disciplinary or even lie outside of the scope of police responsibility must preferen-tially strive for cooperation with the originally responsible prevention protagonists. They should take on their role in the general social prevention work independently and if necessary only with the participation (of the police)."[34]

The development of police crime prevention towards more cooperation becomes clear, but also towards the integration of crime prevention knowledge that was ge-nerated through interdisciplinary work to that of the Police Crime Prevention of the States and the Federation (ProPK), the "pivot" of federation-wide prevention work.[35] For more than 40 years, this program has been pursuing the goal of educating popu-lation, multipliers, media, and other prevention carriers concerning manifestations of crime and possibilities to prevent it. Among other things, this happens through crime prevention-related press releases and PR work and the development and publication of media, measures, and concepts which support local police departments in their prevention work (www.polizei-beratung.de).

It was a long road until police crime prevention could be anchored as systematically as in the 1997 program Police Crime Prevention,[36] but also until the police no longer saw

---

[33] In this vein, the state prevention councils of Mecklenburg-Western Pomerania, Lower Saxony, and Schles-wig Holstein commented in their joint „advertising brochure" for the installation of communal prevention councils on the topic of how a communal prevention council should be structured to be functional: „You can't do it without the police – the police is able to bring so much technical competence and personnel support (prevention consultants) to the local prevention work. It is best able to assess actual local crime levels and suggest effective prevention proposals. Police officers should be part of any prevention council. However, the police can only be **one** driver in communal crime prevention."

[34] For this reason, the Police Crime Prevention of the States and the Federation has always promoted the installation of a National Commission for Crime Prevention and consequently also always supported the Foundation German Forum for Crime Prevention (DFK) (see Chap. 3.2.3).

[35] See the program Police Crime Prevention (publ.)(2013): Commission for Police Crime Prevention of the States and the Federation. Annual Report 2012. Stuttgart.
The ProPK also clarifies the high level of networking of the police in federation and the states. The De-partment of the Interior is the only department that has an identified „prevention thread" with the Police Crime Prevention of the States and the Federation.

[36] The first consulting offices for protection against break-ins and theft were already established in 1921 in Berlin in addition to a whole series of other communal and regional prevention activities. The idea of education in prevention only became really methodical in 1964 with the work of the Bavarian Criminal Agency. Other federal states then also picked up this idea and the Criminal Police Prevention Program (KPVP) was instituted, the predecessor of today's ProPK. After 1970 all federal states were represented in it. The slogan „Advice from the criminal police" became a program for decades.
Over time the responsibilities increased; a financing agreement between the states and the federation

and understood itself as "lone fighter" in matters of prevention and instead viewed and took advantage of cooperation as a success factor in police crime prevention:

Since many crime prevention services can only be understood and approached on an interdisciplinary basis, experts and cooperation partners from other disciplines and areas have become an indispensable and integral part of the prevention work of the program.[37] The successfully tested cooperation forms include: subject-related cooperation, technical exchanges, cooperation in the area of PR, technical assessment and expertise of police prevention enterprises, cooperation at the local level (Jerke 2013)

2.1.2.2
Children's and youth organizations[38]

Another central protagonist in the field of action of crime prevention are the children's and youth organizations whose contributions have become significantly more important over the last few years and decades: On the one hand, the prevention of crime in childhood and youth form a central area of crime prevention and the public debate concerning children's and youth delinquency was "sometimes quite fierce" in the 1990s (PSR 2001, 466).39 On the other hand, the insight has established itself in the institutions that strategies should be mainly pedagogical for the prevention of children's and juvenile crime.

"Children and juveniles at risk of being picked up for illegal activities or who have already been picked up should be prevented from possible future crimes using educational means" (Holthusen/Hoops 2012, 23).

---

placed the KPVP – and today the ProPK - on a secure financial basis. In 1997, the KPVP was changed from the ground up and anchored as ProPK in its current organizational structure. Since then, the Central Office coordinates all federation-wide activities of police crime prevention within the police and in cooperation with non-police prevention carriers (Source: see footnote 35).

[37]   The cooperation partners listed in the „Annual Report 2012" (see above footnote 36) over five pages are not only impressive in terms of numbers but also in terms of the expertise represented in its institutions.

[38]   The children's and youth organizations has communal responsibility and is responsible for all children and juveniles, in particular also those who are impeded in their development or grow up in conditions that are not very supportive. The design and selection of services are negotiated by local public and free carriers of youth support in consideration of the subsidiarity principle. This leads to a large, sometimes very large variety of offered services, also for the area of crime prevention (Holthusen/Hoops 2012, 25).

[39]   The 11th Children's and Youth Report (2002), Chapter B. X is dedicated to the topic „Public attention: delinquency – violence – right-wing extremism" and makes the following introductory observation: „The public discussion, especially in media and politics, concerning children and juveniles in the last few years was strongly defined by the focus on the topics of delinquency, violence, and right-wing extremism and the question how to react to this ... the focus of the public attention on the problematic behaviors and attitudes of children and juveniles has not infrequently led to the living situations and problems of the noticed children and juveniles being lost out of sight... On the other hand there is the risk that an undifferentiated image of violent and/or right-wing youth is assumed, which does not correspond to the reality of life for the majority of young people" (2002, 231 et seq.).

This educational orientation applies to all protagonists of the children's and juvenile crime prevention up to penal law for minors (Section 2 para 1 JGG), but especially to children's and youth aid organizations which are in charge of supporting children and juveniles in their development to an independent and socialized personality, protecting them from dangers to their wellbeing, and contributing to positive living conditions (Section 1 SGB VIII).

Prevention is considered one of the structural principles of children's and youth organizations since children's and youth aid groups don't merely react to impairments and damage that have already occurred but are intent on deflecting risks and dangers early on (Holthusen/Schäfer 2007, 134 et seq.; Holthusen/Hoops 2012, 25).[40]

In accordance with the task and the resulting perspective of children's and youth organizations, delinquency is understood in dependence on the living situations and problems of the children and juveniles and the embedded age-typical challenges (11th Children's and Youth Report 2002, 231). Delinquency is a risk to the wellbeing of children and juveniles and thus a challenge for children's and youth organizations, for "growing up in public responsibility".

However, the 11th Children's and Youth Report in 2002 still refers to a "blind spot in the expert discussion of children's and youth organizations": within the children's and youth organizations, "the discussion concerning the treatment of delinquency is not very well developed". Delinquency of children and juveniles is not only a problem for police, justice, and interior policy; it is also a "pedagogical problem that cannot be solved by turning the perpetrators into victims of their circumstances. One has to remember that delinquency of children and juveniles provokes pedagogical responses that have more to do with education, social control, intervention, boundaries, and norm clarification ... Not to refuse crime prevention is the response of children's and youth organizations, but to search for factually solid descriptions of the problems and proportional responses at all levels ... in the debate with all involved parties in the interest of children and juveniles" (2002, 238 et seq.).

However, at the same time, the report also warns of the "absolutely problematic far-reaching expectations of children's and youth organizations in terms of their crime prevention function and responsibility." Even the "careless talk of primary crime prevention as responsibility of children's and youth organizations all too easily leads to children and juveniles being viewed as possible perpetrators ... However, such a general suspicion cannot be justified empirically and contradicts all principles of pedagogical practice which is not based on a deficit diagnosis – no matter how uncertain and extended into the future – but begins with the resources, interest, and living conditions

---

[40] See generally the contribution by Holthusen/Schäfer 2007 for strategies in the prevention of violence in children's and youth organizations.

... for the sake of supposedly effective prevention children's and youth organizations cannot give up the one tenet which is of central significance even in penal law until proven otherwise: the presumption of innocence. Whosoever exposes their target group to the general suspicion that they could commit crimes at some point and lays out his actions accordingly suspends the general presumption of innocence." When assuming a public responsibility for raising children and juveniles, "young people may not be subjected to a generalized suspicion of deficit. Rather, the focus should lie on supporting and promoting them in the form of structural measures."

In the area of primary crime prevention, children's and youth organizations could ideally make contributions. Children's and youth organizations faced challenges more in the area of secondary and tertiary prevention, but here, too, it should not rely solely on "public problem definitions but is asked to recognize risk potential based on their own factually justified criteria and to become active accordingly."

Children's and youth organizations have provided these responses in the meantime:[41] "Pedagogical crime prevention has established itself in the last two decades – especially in project-like organizational forms but also in regular practices."[42] Many approaches and concepts have arisen during this process. "Challenges lie in ensuring the structure of the services on a permanent basis and also expanding it to full coverage so that depending on local need, the necessary approaches are available as regular services ... Central challenges can be found especially in the expansion of target-group-specific approaches ... We also detect a significant need in terms of (potential) victims."

There are also structural challenges in terms of cooperation. In particular for regular services, the continued development of the cooperation is a central wish. "The cooperation of children's and youth organizations, schools, police, justice, and possibly further protagonists is ... required not only on a case-related basis but also structurally – in consideration and acknowledgment of the respective different action logics and social duties."

From a specialized policy perspective, the in some respect unconsidered, almost inflationary use of the term prevention is worrisome. Another specialized policy challenge lies in the validation of the effectiveness of pedagogical prevention strategies. On particular, the hardly formalized pedagogical practice settings of youth aid pose as yet unsolved problems for the evaluation practice.

In the interest of the affected children and juveniles, children's and youth organizations in crime prevention are challenged always to reinject the pedagogical perspec-

---

[41] See Holthusen/Hoops 2012, 26 et seq.

[42] The regular services of children's and youth organizations include for instance the general social services, juvenile aid in criminal proceedings / juvenile legal support agency, the juvenile penal system, and probation service (Holthusen/Hoops 2012, 24).

tive into the expert discourse so that it does not lose weight compared to security policy considerations. In their everyday cooperation and communication with the other institutions, children's and youth organizations must follow "their professional, pedagogical standards which go far beyond the defense against danger and prevention / reduction of delinquency. This is exactly what makes children's and youth organizations a special protagonist with emphasized importance compared to the other institutions of crime prevention."

The Office for Children's and Juvenile Crime Prevention at the Deutsches Jugendinstitut [German Youth Institute] (DJI) has a significant share in establishing children's and youth organizations as protagonists in crime prevention. Since 1997, the Office which is supported by the Federal Ministry for Family, Seniors, Women, and Youth (BMFSFJ) has been accompanying the developments in the area of crime prevention and informs practice, policy, media, and research about concepts and action strategies of the Office for Children's and Juvenile Crime Prevention.

With their own evaluation studies and empirical research projects, the Office establishes itself as a new project type of the DJI, in which continuous counseling of policy and specialized practice are joined with science (Holthusen/Glaser 2013).[43]

2.1.2.3

Schools

The demand of the institution school to participate in the fight against violence and violent tendencies among children and juveniles is nothing new.[44] In particular in the first half of the 1990s there was a virtual "boom" in research and prevention on the topic of "violence at school" which, however, already clearly lost steam in the second half. In the meantime the discussion has become more factual, but flames up again once in a while, especially when there are incidents of spectacular violence (e.g. "running amok") at schools (Steffen 2012 b, 83 et seq.; Hanke 2007, 104).

This factualization has also been aided by the fact that the responsibility and significance of schools for crime prevention is not primarily due to there being lots of crime at schools, in particular violent crime. On the contrary: in contrast to the public perception caused by corresponding media reports of an "increase in violence at schools", all empirical evidence shows that there was no general increase in (physical)

---

[43]   When at the end of the 1990s „juvenile right-wing extremism" came into the sights of politics, at first the Office for Children's and Juvenile Crime Prevention was supposed to deal with this topic, as well. However, since the phenomena „delinquency in childhood and adolescence" and „right-wing extremism and xenophobia" apart from small overlaps are very different in terms of how they arise, spread, and their social treatment (see also 11th Children's and Youth Report), a second Office for „right-wing extremism and xenophobia – juvenile policy and pedagogical challenges" also supported by the BMFSFJ will be created in 2000 in the DJI branch Halle (Saale) (Holthusen/Glaser 2013, 71 et seq.).

[44]   See also Schubarth 2010, 9 et seq., 57 et seq., on extent, manifestations, and causes of „violence and mobbing at schools" and the possibilities for prevention and intervention.

violence and/or increasing brutalization in the last few years. In fact, the incident numbers appear to be decreasing instead – and this despite an increased awareness of school violence and an increased readiness to report such incidents (Steffen 2012 a, 85): "Criminal behavior occurs relatively rarely in this area of life" (Melzer 2013).[45]

Crime prevention at schools is thus mainly directed towards (violent) crime on and by young people in general and by no means only at offenses that actually occur in the "crime scene school":

Students should be reached via schools, teachers, and legal guardians with measures and concepts of crime prevention.[46]

The responsibility and significance of the schools very fundamentally arise from their educational mission and also from the fact that the majority of strategies of crime prevention developed over the last few years can be identified as pedagogical strategies. This orientation not only considers the fact that crime prevention for children and juveniles deals with adolescents, but also that the widely held conviction that deviance in childhood and adolescence can be treated preferentially with education, learning, and acquisition of competence. This means that especially persons with pedagogical training are needed to take on their responsibilities in crime prevention (as well) (Steffen 2008, 259; Office 2007, 281). And you can find these people not only in children's and youth aid but also in schools.

On the other hand, the significance of schools for crime prevention also comes from the fact that schools are the place at which the main target group of crime prevention, i.e. children and juveniles, can be found reliably and where they can also be generally reached for preventive measures and programs (Steffen 2012 b, 86).

For this reason other protagonists of crime prevention were - and are - preventively active at schools.[47]

---

[45]   For instance, the data of the HBSC studies „Health Behavior in School-aged Children" 2002, 2006, and 2010 – one of the few longitudinal studies – indicate a clearly positive trend for mobbing and violence at schools in Germany. From 2002 to 2010 the share of perpetrators and perpetrator-victims decreases substantially and the share of persons not involved increases. There is a time delay for children with lower family wealth (Melzer et al. 2012, 76). Fuchs et al. had already found in chronological analyses from 1994 over 1999 to 2004 that the incidence of violence at schools was generally decreasing. According to Schubarth (2010, 59) the share for „perpetrators" and for „victims" is ca. 5%; the great majority of students appear neither as „perpetrators" nor as „victims".

[46]   See also the decision of Ministry of Culture conference (KMK) at their 298. plenary session on May 23/24, 2002 in Eisenach „Support schools – strengthen education – expand violence prevention" (www.kmk.org; press release 2002).

[47]   We would like to mention in particular the police which was committed in schools beyond traffic education, initially especially with programs for drug prevention. However, here they were often the only protagonists who were given the responsibility according to the slogan: the policeman was here and gave a presentation, so we don't need to do anything else. This has thoroughly changed in the meantime: the police participates in crime prevention classes or corresponding actions only upon request of the schools and in close cooperation with the teachers. In addition, the promotion of positive social behavior cannot be

Schools should also – according to *Schubarth* (2010, 14) – "not feel shy in accepting the cooperation services of other institutions which also carry responsibility for the development of children and juveniles and to do so in time and not only when the child 'has already turned the wrong way'. There are good beginnings of cooperation e.g. with youth aid, police, or in the communal context."[48]

In the meantime a large number of school programs for prevention and intervention were developed and used: violence-specific and non-specific programs, programs for all students, and programs for students of various age groups, programs for noticed students, programs for teachers and for parents:[49] "The services include a confusing number of prevention and intervention programs. Scientists, journalists, publishers, clubs, and foundations appear as providers; not rarely, economic interests are connected with this. The respective interests and responsibilities or costs that arise with use, e.g. purchase of materials or training for protagonists, should be considered during the selection process. But the final deciding factor should be whether the available program is suitable for the specific situation at the respective schools" (Melzer et. al. 2011, 201).

Since the target group of students "have generally not (yet) been noticed for criminal activities" (see above), the "responsibilities of prevention ... are mainly at a universal level" (Melzer 2013). Thus, the warning that the 11th Children's and Youth Report issued for children's and youth organizations in terms of the effects of "careless talk of primary crime prevention as responsibility of children's and youth organizations" (see above) also applies to schools. Here, too, only measures and programs of selective and indicated prevention should be described as crime prevention and used correspondingly. "General supportive measures" such as the promotion of social or communicative competence, moral development, handling of media etc. are no doubt important and sensible, but should not be referred to as crime prevention measures (see above).

---

achieved by one-time (police) activities but only by sustained and especially by occasion-related action. The police cannot do this and is also not responsible for this (Steffen/Hepp 2007, 185).

Another protagonist is school social work which offers young people social / pedagogical help as part of youth aid which supports their school and professional training, integration into the work world, and their social integration (SGB VIII Section 13 para 1). While school social work has been practiced for more than 30 years, there are only few empirical studies on the effectiveness of this measure; the question of the impact of school social work on violence in schools has also only been treated marginally (Hermann/ Jantzer 2012, 207).

[48] After all, the core business of schools remains education, not social work or therapy, though many schools perform great social-educational work, not in addition to class but especially in class. The social learning processes of students should be appreciated as much as the results in the different subjects. Both are inseparable since education and upbringing form a dialectic unit.

[49] See overview and descriptions in Melzer et al. 2011, 201 et seq.; Schubarth 2010.
The continuing education of teachers currently forms the „central strategy of the protagonists" to strengthen violence prevention at schools on the different levels of action. The large number of education offers also indicates a lack of fundamental qualification of teachers for everyday school life. Continuing education attempts to make up for things that were not sufficiently considered in the primary education. „In addition to methodical skills for the implementation of prevention of violence projects, teachers require basic qualifications which allow them, in addition to their education mission, to meet their no less important upbringing mission" (Hanke 2007, 125).

Possibly more important than programs and measures directed at students, teachers, and parents are measures that are directed at the institution of schools itself. A specific approach for crime prevention at schools results from the determination according to which socially problematic behaviors are partly caused by the internal design of the schools and their pedagogical orientation. One can state that such behaviors do not simply 'flow into schools' from the outside but are partly caused by the internal design of the schools and their pedagogical orientation. "One can deduce from this finding that the development and improvement of various aspects of school culture can make a sensible contribution to the prevention of violence... (there) has to be a two-fold strategy .. which is directed at optimizing school and teaching culture, improving class climate, and thus also student sensitivities" (Melzer 2013).

Following and realizing this "two-fold strategy" still appears to be a (not yet mastered) challenge for schools as protagonist in crime prevention.[50]

2.1.2.4
Penal law and criminal justice

Crime prevention is always a subject of penal law. Still, according to PSR 2006, it is still not self-evident in Germany that penal prevention should be treated in connection with crime prevention. "Penal law is often equated with repression and thus differentiated from prevention. However, this polarization of prevention and repression is a thing of the past, at the latest since penal law has also committed to the goal of prevention. Juvenile penal law focuses on prevention from the start;[51] at the latest since the penal law reform in 1969, general penal law is no longer merely obligated to compensating guilt, the punishment of injustice, but also serves for the preventive protection of legal rights" (PSR 2006, 684).[52]

However, the preventive effects of penal law are limited. This can already be seen in the understanding of crime prevention on which this Report is based, namely as an alternative, non-punitive response to the challenge of preventing crime (see above). Under the aspect of this understanding of crime prevention, penal law and criminal

---

[50]   Already in 1990, the final Report of the Commission on Violence found: „Effective prevention must address the design of the institution school itself and its embedding in the social environment since schools play an important role in causing school violence." The path to a violence-free school culture goes over three intermediate goals: student and teacher responsibility for their school must be strengthened; frustration which schools generate in their students as part of its social selection function must be reduced through targeted support in case of performance deficits; schools must remember their education mission, the upbringing aspect and conveying social norms must become more prominent again compared to the transfer of knowledge, teachers must be better prepared in their training for their formative role (Schwind/ Baumann (publ.) 1990, 150 et seq.).
     See also Uhle 2012 for significance of school development for prevention of violence.

[51]   See also contributions on juvenile criminal law and juvenile penal system in Office 2007.

[52]   For justification of penal law from and according to its social utility and prevention as description of striving for socially useful effects of penal law see also Kunz 2011, Section 24 marginal note 1.

justice could not have been counted among the protagonists of crime prevention. That this is nonetheless the case is not lastly due to how limited in particular the deterrent and resocializing effects ascribed to penal law are – and how little sense a criminal policy thus makes which is especially focused on punishment for preventing or at least reducing crime (see chap. 3.1).

However, the limited effects also come from the generally repressive character of penal law. Actual crime prevention aims at removing personal and social deficits as possible causes of crime and/or creating protective factors and thus signals endangered persons (but also those who have already become perpetrators and victims) that society is taking care of them, that it has not given up on them or excluded them, but that they are part of it, are integrated and included and/or that everything is being done to achieve this. In contrast, penal law is by necessity repressive and its measures generally work to exclude (Steffen 2011, 105).

Positive preventive effects can therefore "only be achieved within the framework of what is possible with repression. In this respect, positive effects are mere side-effects of the *per se* negative threat and practice of sanctions primarily aimed at deterrence. The basically repressive orientation of penal law permits the promotion of socially constructive concerns only to the extent to which the repression purpose which is included in the medium of punishment is not undermined" (Kunz 2011, Section 24 marginal note 5).

The prevention effects intended for penal law can be distinguished by whether they are directed at the general public or the persons recorded by penal law and whether they pursue positive or negative purposes (Kunz 2011, Section 24 marginal note 3):

- In the area of *universal* (primary) crime prevention, penal law has the goal of positive general prevention and/or norm clarification: criminal prosecution and sanctions are intended to confirm (clarify) penal law norms in the population and reinforce the legal compliance of the population (PSR 2006, 685).

- *Selective* (secondary) crime prevention pursues the goal of negative general prevention: potential perpetrators are supposed to be deterred from committing crimes by the threat of punishment, criminal prosecution, punishment, enforcement, and penal system – in brief: the fear of punishment.

However, "negative and positive general prevention cannot be cleanly separated because the trust in the ability of legal order to enforce its goals partly depends on the deterrent effect of penal law" (Kunz 2011, Section 25 marginal note 1).

- Addressees of *indicated* (tertiary) crime prevention are those who have already committed offenses. Penal law uses positive special prevention ("rehabilitation") and/ or negative special prevention (deterrence of individual, securing the perpetrator) to minimize or completely preclude the recidivism probability of the perpetrator.

Whether and to what extent penal law has the postulated general and/or special preventive effects is hotly disputed and only partly verified by empirical studies.[53] The
prevention effects claimed by penal law can generally be verified empirically since
these are postulated effects which may or may not occur (Kunz 2011, Section 24
marginal note 2).[54]

In terms of the general preventive effect assumptions, empirical verification is limited
by at least two problems: "On the one hand, measurable effects are always triggered by compound effects of different moral-forming norm systems and socialization
instances, so that the general preventive effects specifically of penal law cannot be
tested in isolation.

Penal law forms a sub-section of social control whose general preventive effect can
only be studied in toto" (Kunz 2011, Section 25 marginal note 4).[55]

On the other hand, all available empirical studies on this topic refer to societies in
which there are penal law and penal law sanctions. "A comparative system verification of the general preventive superiority of a society with penal law compared to one
without penal law is thus not possible" (Kunz 2011, Section 25 marginal note 5).[56]

In terms of the expected effect "special prevention" - mostly defined as legal probation[57] - the problem for special preventive effect research under methodical aspects, as
for all evaluation research, also lies in empirically proving that the measured success,
non-recidivism, is actually an effect of the sanction.

Despite these methodical difficulties, success evaluation is urgently necessary for
both penal law practice[58] and criminal policy (see chap. 3). This includes not only
general and special preventive effect research, but for instance also population surveys concerning the wish for sanctions. However, today's "secure knowledge based

---

[53]   See for basics Schöch 1985 and the first results of the meta analysis of empirical deterrence studies by
       Dölling et al. 2006.

[54]   Anders Sessar (2011), for whom the dogma of penal law general prevention is not intended to be empirical
       but normative and thus defies factual study.

[55]   „This means that - at least at the moment - there is no empirical evidence for assuming a ‚moral forming
       force‘ of penal law" (PSR 2006, 686).

[56]   In this context, the PSR (2006, 686) points out the „variety of individual examples" which „shows that
       brief and/or temporary collapses of penal law sanctions led to an enormous increase in crime."

[57]   But legal probation, i.e. the absence of new penal law registrations within a certain period of observation,
       is a problematic criterion since it usually only refers to official figures and does not study the reasons for
       success or failure (PSR 2006, 686; Kunz 2011, Section 26 marginal note 2 et seq.).

[58]   As Kunz aptly explains: „Penal law practitioners assume the basic preventive utility of penal law... Howe-
       ver, it is a professional distortion to conclude from the need of healing an illness that the currently availa-
       ble medicine is suitable. The duty of the penal law practice to apply legally available sanctions is not a
       sufficient argument for the preventive suitability of the sanctions. It does not harm the ethos of medicine to
       test the applied medication critically for its therapeutic effects, to study harmful side effects, and develop
       new treatments" (2011, Section 25 marginal note 18).

on research" already contradicts the expectations and approaches of penal law policy and criminal justice.

For instance, the deterrent effect (negative general prevention) of threat, imposition, or enforcement of penalties is somewhat low; the idea of deterrence is not supported empirically. There is also no indication to believe that tightening penal law would have a positive effect on norm awareness.[59] Nonetheless, it is important for maintaining public trust in the government and thus preserving the government monopoly of violence that the government reacts appropriately to the violation of legal rights, i.e. to crime (PSR 2006, 665 et seq.).

Clear disapproval of the offense by society makes the greatest contribution to people acting in compliance with the law. The population expects a sign of discreditation of the committed violation of law and thus a confirmation of the validity claim of the values expressed in the penal norm.

Usually, not the formal punishment is expected, but a symbolic disapproval of the deed, accompanied by restitutive measures to restore the legal order (Kunz 2011, Section 25 marginal note 6 and 12).

In terms of possible special preventive effects of punishment one can first note that there were no comprehensive newer secondary analyses of effect research on punishment and measures of improvement and assurance of general penal law ... therefore in general a conclusion already made in 1981 remains valid: "According to today's state of international research, there is no empirical basis for the expectation that tightening threatened or performed punishments can influence crime rates (PSR 2006, 688 et seq.).[60]

However, these findings are contradicted by the activities of the legislation in the direction of punishment by enhancing the threatened sanctions (raising of maximum and minimum sentences, expansion of securing measures), the expansion of the penal scope (making more acts illegal), and reduction of the legal position of a defendant in the penal process (Kunz 2013 b, 113).[61] For this reason the implementation of the

---

[59] Any punishment which clarifies the norm violation and does not trivialize it is suitable to meet the general preventive responsibility of penal law (Schöch 1985, 1104) and Schöch 1995, 82: „There is .. such a thing as the general preventive power of our penal laws ... But it is a valuable commodity which we should use sparingly. We must beware of wasting this valuable resource through an overkill of punishment."

[60] Also Kunz (2011, Section 26 marginal note 23 et seq.): „Under a careful interpretation, the available findings overall argue that a reduction of recidivism probability cannot be expected from harsher sanctions, in particular unsuspended prison sentences. This supports the assumption of a general exchangeability of sanctions without special losses in preventive effect."

[61] According to Kunz, the German Criminal Code (without ancillary laws) was changed about one hundred times since 1990. A trend towards a control-oriented prevention penal law can be noticed which refers to any danger to society, intervenes in a precautionary manner, and uses quasi secret service evidence (2013 b, 121; see chap. 3.1.1).

call for a penal law policy and practice guided by scientifically tested information represents one of the greatest challenges for the "prevention protagonists" penal law and criminal justice.

2.2

Communal crime prevention

Communal crime prevention was largely responsible for the "prevention spirit of departure" in the 1990s: Since the beginning of the 1990s, "under the banner of 'communal crime prevention', new communication and cooperation networks arose in almost all German cities between police, communal administration and policy, justice, economy, social services, free carriers, and other protagonists in order to prevent everyday crime and ensure public order in inner city areas which wanted to assume their share of responsibility for ensuring internal security and removing the causes of crime. At the moment there are ca. 1650 federation-wide prevention commissions ... i.e. associations at the communal level which attempt to bring all decision makers to the table and bundle activities" (PSR 2001, 462).[62] Due to the "dynamics of the development", the 2nd PSR assumes that "at the moment there are probably about 2,000 prevention projects" (2006, 672).[63]

The development of communal crime prevention in Germany reads – read? – like a success story (Steffen 2004, 2005) – and indeed, communal crime prevention is, as Heinz explained at the 9th German Congress of Crime Prevention in Stuttgart[64], "from a criminological and scientific perspective ... an idea that is just plain common sense. The insight into the limited effectiveness of repressive strategies and the precedence of prevention over repression appears to have established itself in the local work."[65]

However, Heinz continues: "Of course, deficits cannot be overlooked. The available information about who does what where with what objectives and carriers is spotty ...

---

[62] The 1st PSR comments on the reasons for the installation of communal commissions: „The possibilities and competences to influence the specific creation factors (of crime) are thus mainly found at the local level. For this reason crime prevention can only be successful if it is understood as general social responsibility and in particular includes local initiatives in addition to police action" (PSR 2001, 460; see also above 2.1.1).

However, Kunz considers the culture of fear and discrediting experts to be the drivers of communal crime prevention as general social responsibility. This is „not directly about crime prevention and dealing with fears triggered by crime, but about achieving these concerns by means of (the detour of) a redesign of the living conditions in communities and regions oriented towards the goal of crime prevention" (2011, Section 31 marginal note 10).

[63] Schreiber counts 960 (2007). See also Steffen 2009, 55.

[64] This DPT had the main topic „Communal crime prevention"; see Bannenberg et al. 2005.

[65] As background of the new concept for creating security and order in cities, Frevel (2012, 215) lists: changed crime situations and order problems, changed demands and evaluations of the feeling of security of the population, modified self-understanding of the institutions involved in producing security, and new concepts of government involvement and administration as expressed in the terms ‚citizen community‘, ‚citizen-oriented police work‘, and ‚activating government‘. See also Steffen 2005 and the contributions on the cover topic „Urban security – social city" in the Forum Crime Prevention 4/2013.

The required fundamental discussion concerning goals, means, and especially limits of (not only communal) crime prevention and concerning the relationship of crime prevention to social policy is still in its infancy. Documentation of the experiences – positive and negative – are the exception, program or results evaluation mainly remain a demand" (2005, 9).

The need has been recognized to "coordinate the activities of the various public instances which are directly or indirectly involved in crime prevention in its widest sense, to utilize synergy effects, and prevent parallel work". However, the "gap between demands and reality could not be bigger."

One of the criticisms is that communal crime prevention is too police-oriented, mainly focused on agencies and institutions, and cooperation and a sense of community of citizens are not promoted enough.

At the same time there is the risk, in particular at time of tight budgets, of "criminalizing social policy": The magic word "prevention" appears to open doors and – especially – budgets, the relationship between general social policy and special criminal policy becomes questionable and uncertain; as a consequence this also affects the determination of what is a crime prevention project as opposed to a general social policy measure, e.g. youth support.

And finally: how do we know that we not only want to do the right thing but are also actually doing the right thing if systematic effect research that satisfies methodical standards is the exception? (Heinz 2005, 22 et seq.).

What results do we find ten years later - also in terms of the claim of the commissions Communal Crime Prevention of realizing a "three pillar approach": local orientation, interdisciplinary networking, citizen participation (Steffen 2005, 157)?[66]

- The "mood of departure" of the 1990s seems to have disappeared. At least in the last few years there have been hardly any new foundations and several of the "old" commissions no longer exist. However: there is no recent overview[67] of number, composition, goals, or projects of communal commissions. This is in part because there is no uniform prevention idea or a clear, binding recording criteria – commission does not equal commission – or even continuous documentation.

- But one can assume that only a few commissions do justice to the variety of criminogenic genesis conditions and the development of corresponding preventive measures also by joining the greatest possible number of relevant carriers

---

[66] Kober/Kahl (2012, 12) mention these fundamental structural principles: interdisciplinary cooperation approach, citizen participation / public, „mayoral duties".

[67] Recently Schreiber 2007 did this work.

of formal and informal control – and that the coordination and networking is successful (Kober/ Kahl 2012, 13 et seq.)

- Only very few commissions have managed to realize the claim to *citizen participation* and integrate "normal" citizens without "official office" and function – i.e. "function-less" citizens. However, citizen participation is actually considered to be the "new thing", the identifying characteristic of the commissions, also because it corresponds to the principles of citizen community and citizen society: citizens should have a direct influence (crime prevention) on matters that affect them directly (in this case crime). However, in reality there have been only a few exceptional cases in which the claim was realized turning citizens from affected persons into protagonists for crime control, to make their participation in and their responsibility for the state of security of their community possible and enforce it (Steffen 2009, 54 et seq.).

One of the few newer studies on the internal design of the commissions[68] comes up with the following results:

- The degree of institutionalization of crime prevention commissions varies greatly and the composition of protagonists is very heterogeneous. The founding protagonists determined the joint work with their specific perspectives and interpretations of the problem and looked for suitable colleagues.

- The commissions lived from the commitment of its members; in most of these cooperations this commitment level is very high. But: the more the commissions were dominated by the committed individuals, the more devastating would be the effect of that person leaving. Such an exit would endanger the commission-internal cooperation and could possible end the entire cooperation.

- The majority of the commission members can be classified as case workers. This means that the commissions have lots of technical competence but little decision-making competence.

- We can note various knowledge and qualification deficits, in particular in basic prevention training.

- There are clear deficits in PR work even though this is a stated goal of the commissions. Reaching the citizenry and wide-spread education about the topic are therefore difficult.

- The commissions generally did not perform scientifically well-founded evaluations but acted on unsystematically processed feedback and subjective impressions.

---

[68]   During the project „Cooperative security policy in cities – KoSiPol", supported from 2010 to 2012 by the Federal Ministry of Education and Research, empirical case studies on crime preventive cooperations were conducted in 16 German communities in four fields of action: domestic violence, juveniles as perpetrators and victims, drugs and addiction, and policing presence; see Frevel (publ.) 2012; Frevel/Miesner 2012; van den Brink 2012; John/Schulze 2012.

- The citizen perspective remains an outsider; the problem perception and processing of crime is done almost exclusively from the protagonist perspective.

Conclusion of study:

In connection with the concept of voluntary cooperation, the equality of partners, and the goal of consensus this leads to a cooperation which in many cases remains at the phenomenon level but does not answer basic questions about the problem, the cooperation, and the goals. On top of this, the actually existing and rather well developed systematics of crime prevention is rarely absorbed and exemplary approaches are not systematically used.

"Despite its many years of existence and continuous development the practice of cooperative security policy offers still a lot of potential for optimization" (Frevel/Miesner 2012, 219). But: this concept of cooperative local security policy has prospects. In the words of the scientists involved in KoSiPol (Frevel 2012, 39): They are convinced "that

- this form is sensible,
- it has to be qualitatively developed,
- existing weaknesses in the organization and process design of commissions can be overcome,
- the protagonists must be recruited in a targeted manner and qualified for the cooperation,
- a development of the concept is necessary,
- the information exchange between the commissions has been rudimentary up to now and should be supported, e.g. by state prevention councils or the Foundation German Forum for Crime Prevention".[69]

Communal crime prevention in Germany thus faces a few challenges if it is actually – successfully, effectively and sustainably – to be realized.

However, since it is still an "idea of just plain common sense" and the cooperation of the security and order agencies, social services of communities and free carriers, health services, and many other institutions is considered a form of complexity management which one can no longer do without (Frevel/Kober 2012, 337), every attempt should be made to realize this idea in a sustainable manner, for instance by implementing the following five (most important) structural principles:[70]

---

[69] Especially since the „Infopool prevention" of the Federal Office of Criminal Investigation and the „Information system for prevention on the net – PrävIS" developed with the guidance of the German Forum for Crime Prevention have both ended their services.

[70] See also the very instructive „Guideline for communal practice" by Kober/Kahl 2012: Impulses for communal prevention management. Insights and recommendations on organization and work of crime preven-

1st structural principle: inter-departmental networking

The interdisciplinary approach, the appearance of several institutions and groups as initiators and responsible carriers, and the networking of their activities are decisive and characteristic for the commissions of communal crime prevention. Alone the many factors influencing crime and crime prevention make communal crime prevention a cross-sectional responsibility, requiring a wide spectrum of professional experts to manage.

Members of a crime prevention commission should thus be representatives of city administration, communal offices, police and justice, and of socially active civil institutions of the community, from economy, media etc.

The specific responsibility of these representatives in the commission is to recognize the existing fields of activity in their crime prevention significance and to make the existing resources more efficient and effective through networking. This means that there are no new responsibilities that the protagonists will face but "only" new interpretations of existing responsibilities – but this is actually often a lot more difficult than it sounds or than the protagonists expected.

In addition, due to the very different logic of action and independence of the involved protagonists, networking represents a challenge that should not be underestimated.

For this reason it should always be checked whether and to what extent the networking and interdisciplinary work actually succeeds. A proven approach is the institution of a work group of the commission which is only responsible for performing and verifying the task "interdisciplinary networking".

2nd structural principle: citizen participation – creating public relations through citizen participation

Prevention at the communal level requires citizen involvement – otherwise it runs the risk of giving up what actually triggered it: the idea of creating an environment worth living in together in a community (Kober/Kahl 2012, 26).

As a role model this idea is mainly uncontroversial, however, as we have shown, in practical commission work it can be implemented only in exceptions: up to now only a few commissions have managed to integrate "normal" citizens without "official" office and function, i.e. "function-free citizens".[71]

Disregarding for a moment the question whether "function-free" citizens would have any interest in working in the commissions, i.e. whether one could even find enough citizens, it contradicts the organization and working methods of commissions to integ-

---

tion commissions at the communal level" and the results and conclusions in Frevel (Publ.) 2012.

[71]   For „ambivalences connected to the integration of citizens" see also Kober/Kahl 2012, 16 et seq.

rate function-free citizens – even if they are not very formalized as usual in communal crime prevention.

Commissions can only work in a meaningful manner if its members are responsible to another governmental or non-governmental institution, i.e. if they are members of such an institution and are sent to the commission in order to represent the insights and interests of their institution. In return, these representatives should then carry the content and results of the consulting and project work of the commission back to their institutions and implement them in order to act as multipliers of institutionalized crime prevention for the "function-free" citizens – e.g. its association members. However, this still happens too rarely, too accidental, not systematic enough.

Beyond this, cooperation is possible and sensible for "function-free" citizens who are nonetheless willing to commit to crime prevention on the local (community or neighborhood) level for projects and measures that are specific, occasion-based, and directly affect them. Based on the needs and the high competence of the citizens for matters which affect their immediate environment, they may participate in specific, short-term, action-oriented measures which go beyond crime prevention and might follow communal strategies especially in "neighborhoods with special need for renewal" – read: social hot spots – (see also Frevel et al. 2009 and Kahl/Kober 2009).

3rd structural principle: local problem analysis
A necessary, indispensable condition for a successful prevention strategy – including and especially at the communal level – is the most comprehensive possible inventory analysis of local framework conditions.

Ideal would be a criminological regional analysis which not only draws the "crime map" of a community but also its "social map".

Only based on such a – solid – basis of data and insights a "communal prevention strategy can be developed, which can be used to recognize need for action and cover it effectively by networking existing or creating needed resources" (Kober/Kahl 2012, 34).

4th structural principle: verification of success of implemented measures
Based on the results of the local problem analysis, a plan should be created which is oriented on verifiable criteria and fixed in writing and contains the measures to be used to resolve the problem.

In addition, the implementation of this plan should be monitored and checked, also in terms of efficiency, i.e. a so-called process evaluation should be performed ("are we achieving that which we had intended?")

Finally, it would be ideal to evaluate the results for effectiveness, the effectiveness of the measures and programs in terms of the degree of achieving objectives, any negative side-effects (e.g. displacement effects), and in terms of the sustainability of the achieved effects.

5th structural principle: prevention is a top management affair

The management of the crime prevention commission by the mayor of the community and the participation of high-ranking representatives of the communal offices and the community/city council underline the status of the commission and make the implementation of recommendations and decisions easier.

The principle of "top management affair" also includes that the commission has a legally defined and secured status, is clearly legitimized – e.g. by the community/city council, has clear competences, precise and goal-oriented contents, and has sufficient financial and personnel resources, e.g. in an office.

"Prevention is a top management affair" especially means that this commission would be doomed to failure without communal policy support and legitimation. According to *Frevel/Kober*, there is almost no legal doubt that commissions are entitled to act cooperatively in security policy. Police and communal administration worked on the basis of democratically founded responsibilities and are subject to political control. But such a constellation is still not uncontroversial if there is no accountability to communal commissions, i.e. city councils or district councils: "If ... the commissions act in a field of security and order that is so important to communal politics, it appears problematic to exclude the participation of politics" (2012, 344).

Communal crime prevention must become part of the community development policy and further developed in the direction of a communal security policy, designed as a communal cross-sectional responsibility, and democratically legitimized, with clear political goals and networked, interdisciplinary, and integrative procedures (Steffen 2005, 166). The proposal by *Waller* should be studied to institute an Office for Crime Prevention also at the local level and to spend 5% of "law and order" expenditures on prevention, another 2% for training and data systems which are needed to maintain this reform (2011, 235 et seq.).

2.3

Summary and conclusions

Communal crime prevention provides some of the most pressing indicators and evidence to what extent crime prevention requires practice, policy, and science:

- It requires practice for "on-site work". However, practitioners should be specially selected for this task and receive training and education which meets today's requirements for professionalism and competence – for this, science must develop and provide corresponding training and educational programs.

- It requires policy, both on the communal and the state level. Nothing can be achieved without policy support, at least nothing effective and sustainable.

- It needs science to provide the theoretical and empirical basis of prevention work, consulting and supervision for the implementation and evaluation of projects, for the development of training and continuing education programs, for the development and maintenance of databases and information systems.

3

Prevention policy

3.1

Crime prevention as goal of criminal policy

"Criminal policy means the totality of all governmental and non-governmental measures intended to protect society and individual citizens by means of prevention and fighting against crime" (Schwind 2013, Section 1 marginal note 37).[72] The corresponding activities refer not only to the purely repressive areas such as administration of justice and penal system but especially – interdisciplinary - to the use of non-penal law preventive measures which the serve crime-relevant protection of society (Schwind 2013, Section 1 marginal note 33 et seq.).

Crime prevention as prevention of and protection against crimes has "always counted - in a general sense - ... as an important goal of legal policy, in particular criminal policy." But this does not mean "that theory and practice have always tried to direct laws, measures, institutions, and organizational precautions specifically to prevention ... Instead, things generally remained with very general considerations and confessions of convictions" (PSR 2001, 455 et seq.).

Heinz therefore believes that a "course correction of criminal policy is overdue. A stronger alignment with and a sustained development of crime prevention is necessary. A criminal policy which merely uses penal law means according to the motto 'more of the same' is a 'recipe for disaster'. The question can therefore no longer be whether there will be a course correction. In view of the precedence of prevention over and its superiority to repression, there is no lack of insight, just a problem with implementation" (1998, 17).

This begs for the follow-up question whether this course correction has happened over the last few years: has the conviction also taken hold in criminal policy in the meantime that crime should be countered especially with prevention concepts – meaning concepts of a non-punitive nature? I.e. the conviction which is mostly undisputed in practice, as described above, with the exception of the protagonists of penal law and criminal justice.

---

[72] There is no uniform definition of what criminal policy is supposed to mean but in the meantime this wider sense of crime prevention has come to dominate (Kriminologie-Lexikon ONLINE [Dictionary of criminology], Article on „Criminal policy").

Has criminal policy at the different levels - local/communal, state, and federal - managed to create a wide social consensus to the effect that crime should be primarily encountered with preventive strategies and concepts, has it created the necessary legal framework conditions for this and provided the necessary resources?

And does criminal policy also understand crime prevention the same way as practice does or does it look at it mainly repressive; are we talking about prevention through repression, not just averting danger but more about taking precautions against danger; under the aspect of fighting risks, does a suspicion-free prevention as governmental means of control outrank the previous suspicion-dependent prevention (Sessar 2011) – is criminal policy on the way to a security society and prevention state?

Is criminal policy rational, can it be legitimized by social ethics and is it oriented on the results of scientific research – or is it rather emotional or even populist, can it be (increasingly) manipulated by media and opinion polls?[73]

3.1.1

Criminal policy: scientifically founded or "flying blind"?[74]

To start with the last question: a rational criminal and penal law policy is not possible without a solid empirical foundation, so Heinz (2006, 241). Schwind quotes the "old master of criminological thinking", Franz von Liszt (1841-1919) who emphasized that the "fight against crime presupposes the knowledge of crime", a sentence which refers primarily to prevention measures (2013, Section 1 marginal note 40) and again Liszt, every criminal policy-maker remains a "dilettante if he lacks a firm scientific foundation which he can only gain from the most minute and exhaustive knowledge of the facts."[75]

The federal government – i.e. the criminal policy – shares this view, at least in its statement for the 1st PSR: "There must be a sufficient level of insight into extent, structure, and development of crime on the one hand and into criminal prosecution, enforcement, and penal system on the other hand in order to be able to successfully design criminal and penal law policy measures and verify its impacts" (2001, 599).[76]

This (theoretical and empirical) knowledge "of crime, crimes, perpetrators, victims, and the different governmental and private, informal and formal reaction and preven-

---

[73]   See also Schwind 2013, Section 1 marginal note 33 et seq.

[74]   „Criminal policy flying blind" was the title of a conference at the Friedrich-Ebert Foundation on May 7, 2012 in Berlin and thus employed a „popular saying" by Wolfgang Heinz (see also Hilgendorf/ Rengier 2012, 7).

[75]   Quote from Schwind/Steinhilper 2014, 593.

[76]   With the publication of the 1st PSR, the federal government had „started down a path in official crime reporting which was equally new and promising for both the representation and assessment of internal security as well as the crime policy discussion" (Heinz 2003).

tion forms" was developed a long time ago by criminology as the relevant reference science[77] but also by other scientific disciplines and provided to criminal, social, and communal policy. The Freiburg Memorandum "On the situation of criminology in Germany" states:[78] "Empirical knowledge has become indispensable for crime prevention, criminal prosecution, enforcement, and penal system together with all associated measures of assessment, therapy, and rehabilitation, in order to continually improve the protection of citizens with rational means and their trust in the function of the penal law.

This includes identifying limits beyond which this functionality becomes questionable. The legislation of the federation and the states in their different forms may utilize the existing findings of these criminological sciences to develop modern criminal and social policy."

But do they do that? According to the Freiburg Memorandum, this knowledge "is also used when they want to ensure a sufficient scientific justification and evaluation of their respective responsibilities".[79] Kunz on the other hand laments the "deafness of official criminal policy to empirical findings", results from empirical criminological research stood "in opposition to the trends of criminal policy practiced today. The recommendations to be derived from the research for a 'rational' policy are hardly followed in reality. On the contrary, the impression is growing that official criminal policy is deaf to 'evidence-based' statements concerning great risks of error in individual prognoses, the risk of overestimating criminal danger, the doubts concerning the effect of general deterrence, the fact that harder sanctions are not preferable in terms of special prevention, and the generally somewhat de-socializing effect of prison sentences[80] and instead follows the overly dramatic crime campaigns by mass

---

[77] As social-scientific integration science, criminology combines approaches from e.g. psychiatry, neurobiology, psychology, and social pedagogics, jurisprudence, sociology, political science, economy, and historical science (Freiburg Memorandum 2012).

[78] The „Freiburg Memorandum" is the result of a conference in June 2012, with 60 participating scientists engaged in teaching or research of criminology and related disciplines.

[79] However, since the „Freiburg Memorandum" wants to draw attention to the „decreasing significance of criminology, in particular at German Universities" and „advertises" for an improvement of this situation, maybe this willingness of policy to acknowledge criminological findings and implement them into political actions is viewed in a too positive light.

[80] This is already stated in the insights of the 2nd PSR: „Contrary to a wide-spread belief, the current state of criminological research considers the deterrent effect (negative general prevention) of threat, sentence, or enforcement of penalties to be rather small. In the area of minor to moderate crime it is generally true that the amount and severity of the punishment have no measurable significance. Only the perceived risk of discovery is somewhat relevant – however only for a series of minor offenses. Until now, there is also no indication to believe that harsher penal law would have a positive effect on norm awareness ... In terms of the special preventive effect of penalties, there is no empirical evidence that – for comparable offense and perpetrator groups – the recidivism rate after a conviction is lower than after a suspension of the proceedings (diversion). If differences were observed - in comparable groups - the recidivism rates were lower after diversion. There is no evidence for negative effects of diversion compared to formal sanctions.
In the area of minor to moderate crime, different sanctions do not have a differentiating effect on legal probation; indeed, the sanctions can mostly be exchanged with no measurable impact on recidivism rates.

media and many politicians which call for harder punishments... It is simply absurd that empirical criminology has never before had as much knowledge at its disposal as today and that it has less influence on criminal policy than ever" (2011, Section 30 marginal note 23).

The question also recently posed by Heinz "What should legislators want to know?"[81] gives more cause to suspect a "criminal policy flying blind" than a "rational criminal policy".[82]

3.1.2

Criminal policy: on the way to a preventive state?

There is certainly no sign of any "overdue course correction of criminal policy" (see above) as already demanded by Heinz in 1998. Criminal policy continues to use penal law means according to the motto "more of the same". And this is meant literally: not only is criminal policy sticking to its penal law reaction patterns, it is actually making them more severe: "In the areas of non-domestic violence and sexual delinquency, 'criminal liability gaps' are being filled quickly and completely and corrections are made according to the motto "more of the same". The German Criminal Code (without ancillary laws) was changed about one hundred times since 1990... In the heat of a public influenced by the mass media, sexual delinquency has finally become the driver of criminal policy (Kunz 2013 b, 121).[83]

If there is a trend, then it is that the recidivism rate for comparable offenses and perpetrator groups is higher after harsher sanctions. In particular, until today there is no group of criminal perpetrators for which there is empirical evidence – in special preventive terms – of a superiority of juvenile detention or (unconditional) juvenile penalties compared to an ambulant reaction" (2006, 665 et seq.).

See also the recently published findings of the recidivism study „Legal probation after penal law sanctions 2007 to 2010 and 2004 to 2010" (www.bmj.de/DE/Ministerium/Strafrecht/KriminologieKriminalpraevention/_doc/Rueckfallstatistik_doc.html?nn=1470118) and Albrecht (2013 b) on recidivism statistics in international comparison. Also Spiess 2012 and Kury 2013.

[81]   Heinz posed this question in connection with the „never-ending story of the reform of German crime statistics". In particular Heinz has always pointed out the need of reform of crime statistics, especially the need of a progress statistic and emphasizes that the statistical conditions for a scientific criminal policy had deficits and that current, comprehensive, and reliable data are a necessary (though not a sufficient) condition for a rational criminal policy. However, this has achieved little to nothing with the responsible federal legislator, criminal policy (Heinz 2013).

[82]   See also Schwind (2000) concerning acceptance of scientific findings by criminal policy „Has the (anti) violence commission worked in vain?"

[83]   Which is highlighted again in the discussion concerning child pornography.
        The dictionary of criminology ONLINE states the following in the article on criminal policy: „There is no disagreement with the necessity to create legal liability conditions, threaten effective sanctions, and enforce them in a capable procedure. As much as this need exists, it is also known that penal law only deters if legal violations are uncovered and sanctioned. But it is exactly this aspect which the policy neglects... Instead of improving the quality of the criminal prosecution and making sensible investments into prevention, the legislator hectically creates penal regulations and intervention authorities. He disregards the role and the possibilities of penal law."

Kunz recognizes a "trend towards a control-oriented prevention penal law ... which refers to any social danger, intervenes preemptively, and uses quasi secret service evidence methods for this purpose... A legislation which functions for the culture of fear strives to work through the assumed punishment expectations of the population as preventively as possible" (2013 b, 121).

This is the road to a prevention state which Germany has been traveling for a few years now.[84] This is the development to which the statement refers that crime prevention has become the dominating paradigm of our time and in criminal policy:

Towards prevention through repression. In Germany, this aspect is traditionally popular, as can be seen in numerous new statutory offenses, reduced conditions for criminal liability, increased punishments, and repressive regulations in risk defense and police rights of the state (Steffen 2006, 1150).

In order to do justice to the security thinking in the prevention state,[85] it no longer appears to be sufficient if police and the other instances of criminal prosecution only ensure reliable basic protection from criminal risks. In the meantime it has become a public responsibility to recognize mere threats and alleviate them, to assuage the fear of crime, and strengthen the feeling of security – and no longer just to prevent and/or prosecute crime. This creates the risk of the rise of a prevention state: a state which, in order to minimize security risks, subjects its citizens to (massive) distrust and monitoring measures that are not based on any specific suspicion. In such a prevention state, every citizen is not only potentially dangerous – and must therefore submit to corresponding verifications which then determine that he is not dangerous after all but also endangered – and thus the target and object of risk prevention by means of in principle unlimited and undefined prevention measures. Such a development does not meet the principles of a state governed by law nor does it reduce fear of crime or strengthen the feeling of safety. On the contrary: if crime has to be prevented everywhere - even only a putative risk - this can also mean for the individual that he should expect crime everywhere and can no longer feel safe anywhere (Steffen 2013 a, 106 et seq.).

This trend to "control-oriented prevention penal law" cannot, as often claimed by the politicians responsible for this, refer to an increased desire for punishment in the population.

---

[84] See Steffen 2006a; he discusses at length the problem of a security society and prevention state in the Report for the 17th German Congress of Crime Prevention (Steffen 2013 a, 105 et seq.). See also Ostendorf (2005), for whom not only crime prevention is important. The reaction to crime by means of penal law is also still being expanded. These approaches emphasize an increasing security interest in our society. Apparently the security needs are also manufactured. Media demand security, politicians promise it. „This leads to obvious amplification effects. One can speak of publicistic-political amplification cycles that heat up things."

[85] For Heinz (1998, 19), the susceptibility to disruption of modern communities requires prevention. The risk society of the present is oriented towards taking precautions against risks in order to recognize and prevent possible risk potentials and sources of danger ahead of time.

For instance Reuband, in his inventory of federation-wide surveys on the question of increasing punitive tendencies in the population, reaches the following overall conclusion: "All in all, the empirical findings contradict a punitive trend". As before, education and resocialization are still considered to be important functions of punishment. Despite the idea that criminals are not being treated harshly enough, there is no shift towards a plea for harder punishment. On the contrary: the demand that stricter laws are needed has decreased in popularity among German citizens in the period between 1998 and 2006. In terms of the attitude towards the death penalty, the extent of the approval has significantly decreased over the years; in the meantime the opposition is in the majority (2010, 143 et seq.).

This also corresponds with the results from population surveys concerning demand for sanctions which is quoted by Kunz. In Europe there is a clear preference for community work as opposed to prison sentences; in Germany, even non-punitive reactions – at least for property offenses – are clearly preferred to punishment. Even among victims the expected punishment often only has a supplementary significance and is limited to rather mild, pedagogically sensible reactions.[86]

In general no formal punishment is expected but a symbolic disapproval of the crime, accompanied by restitutive measures to restore legal order. The population expects a sign of discreditation of the committed violation of law and thus a confirmation of the validity claim of the values expressed in the penal norm. (Kunz 2011, Section 25 marginal notes 11, 12).[87]

Penal law practice also does not show an increased punitive trend. In his careful and comprehensive analysis of data from criminal justice (until 2008), Heinz reaches the following conclusion: The "thesis of the 'new lust for punishment' (cannot be) empirically confirmed for the German sanction practice based on the aggregated data of criminal justice statistics ... According to this data, the thesis of the increasing punitive trend in the German sanction practice is a myth that corresponds to the zeitgeist but is not empirically supported. It is correct that there is an increasing punitive trend limited to certain, quantitatively very small, groups of criminal perpetrators and offenses, which now also seems to be decreasing again. This is the group of perpetrators that are classified as especially 'dangerous' and perpetrators of violent crimes. But no significant changes can be found for the overwhelming majority of informally of formally sanctioned perpetrators." That German justice has mainly not succumbed to the punitive trend is due to the law system itself: "Where judges and attorneys are elected, where the influence of lay judges is great, the influence of public opinion is greater than in a system with professional, tenured independent decision-makers..." (2011, 27).

---

[86] So also the findings on „Punitive and compensation wishes" and/or for „compensation" of victims in the Report for the 18th German Congress of Crime Prevention (Steffen 2013 d).

[87] For this reason, according to Kunz, the wide-spread practice of attorney generals to suspend investigations for opportunistic reasons without consequence or discreetly by imposing conditions, is questionably in terms of general prevention (2011, Section 25 marginal note 12).

3.1.3

Criminal policy in the media society

While there is no increasing punitive trend among the population and in criminal justice, this is not true for the treatment of the topic crime by politicians and definitely not for the presentation of crime in the mass media. They "clearly reflect an increased trend towards dramatization and thus increased punitive tendencies" (Kunz 2011, Section 30 marginal note 17).

In the reporting of the media, crime and in particular violent crime play a great role - and this reporting is (and not just since now) "in no way a correct representation of social reality".[88] The consequences of such one-sided information often focused on spectacular individual cases can be significant if one assumes (and according to empirical findings on this topic one may assume) that media use can have an effect on the perception of crime, need for punishment, and criminal policy.[89]

And the so-called political-publicistic amplification cycle[90] is one of the reasons why (violent) crime is viewed as a comprehensive problem and everyday threat:[91]

- In accordance with the attention rules of the media, reports often selectively cover attention-grabbing, brutal, and shocking individual cases, especially of "juvenile violence" and regularly note an increase in this violence and growing brutalization.

- This triggers (criminal) policy activities which appear to be forced reactions to the public discussion triggered by this dramatizing perspective: "If the media report greatly increasing numbers and if the public debate is also defined by spectacular severe crimes, then policy is under significant pressure to raise the legal penalties and make the procedural rules for the implementation of criminal proceedings stricter."[92]

- These political activities again ensure that the same topic again becomes a topic for media due to political reporting.

Security needs can thus be "manufactured": security is demanded by the media, promised by politicians (Ostendorf 2005). For Kunz, the agenda of practical crime policy in the media society is prescribed by social expectations which are formed and formulated by the mass media (2011, Section 23 marginal note 4).

---

[88] Lamnek 1990, 174. See also Schubarth 2001 and Heinz 2007.

[89] See also e.g. Pfeiffer et al. 2004.

[90] Scheerer 1978, 223.

[91] However, this political-publicistic amplification cycle is not just well positioned in terms of the perception of and reaction to violent crime, but also, for instance, in victim protection legislation. Recently, the effectiveness of this cycle became clear in the discussion of „sexual abuse of children in institutions and at home". The „wave of outrage" led to a new „Law to strengthen the rights of the victims of sexual abuse (StORMG)".

[92] Pfeiffer et al. 2004, 415.

This is because "practical criminal policy, like any other branch of politics, must justify its actions. It does not simply act but is dependent on communicating its activities, interpret it in an understandable manner, and try to gain public approval for it. This communication with the public is filtered through the mass media ... The peculiarity of the crime topic to address everyone on an emotional level and at the same time exceed their individual horizon of perception, suggests a simplifying and dramatizing presentation of problems and solutions. Practical criminal policy must come to an arrangement with this media simplification and intensification of their field of activity. The problems it tackles are defined by media processing of social problem perceptions. The crime political need for action and time pressure are defined by ideas which are the result of opinions influenced by media. The acceptance of crime policy interventions is significantly defined by how media report it" (Kunz 2011, Section 23, marginal note 4).

This significance of the media for policy is also an opportunity for criminology and other sciences: If the relevant sciences can manage to bring their findings and the resulting requirements into the media, they could also find an open ear in politics.

Not only scientists with great communication skills and the talent to "sell their products" are needed, but also good science journalism interested in criminal policy questions.[93]

3.1.4

Summary and conclusions

Criminal policy – at least in terms of its actions with Germany-wide consequences – appears to not only primarily understand crime prevention as repressive but also to turn a deaf ear to scientific-criminological findings and resulting requirements.[94] This includes the fact that criminal policy only rarely evaluates laws.[95] For instance, it

---

[93] 20 years ago the finding that „the self-representation of criminology and the representation of its approaches and results are in a poor state" resulted in the attempt to start a dialog with the media concerning criminological insights – in vain. The daily newspaper, which we thought had accepted, delayed publication of the contributions available in 1994 and then slowly pulled out. In 1996 the contributions were then published in Issue 4 of „Kriminologisches Journal" [Criminological Journal].

[94] Criminal policy at the communal level is, in contrast, much more willing to accept and implement criminological findings, as our previous explanations on prevention practice, in particular for communal crime prevention, have shown. At the state level there is also a comparatively greater willingness to implement criminological findings (p. 3.2.2).

[95] Becker disagrees. She recognizes an increasing interest in criminal policy in the evaluation of laws. Criminology could present itself as a competent contact person for this. However: „The answers would have to correspond to the practical requirements of the policy, without accepting a loosening of scientific criteria. A certain problem is posed by the time needed to conduct serious scientific evaluations." At the legislative level it is often difficult to perform empirical studies before a law is passed. „The awareness of the circumstance that law may not always have only the intended effects or perhaps not have the intended effect at all is increasingly expressed by announcements of an evaluation of the law after it becomes effective" (2012, 207, 210).

was determined for victim protection legislation that there were no evaluations of the reform measures whatsoever, nor were there insights concerning what victims need and want.[96]

The problem is not that criminal politicians do not see the need to put their concepts and legislation on a scientific basis and evaluate them. For instance in their preface to the 2nd PSR the then Federal Minister of the Interior Schäuble and former Federal Justice Minister Zypries wrote:

"In order to develop effective concepts to fight crime, policy needs a reliable, regularly updated record of the crime situation which goes beyond the mere analysis of crime statistics and criminal prosecution statistics. For this reason, for the first time in 2001, the federal government has submitted the 1st Periodical Security Report (1st PSR) as a founding work to serve for the systematic, wide-spread processing and analysis of existing data material under criminological, sociological, legal science, and statistical aspects. From the outset, this 1st PSR was planned as the start of regular reporting and was intended as verification in suitable intervals in order to adjust governmental reaction patterns to fit to changing crime situations. About five years after the publications of the initial report, the federal government now presents an updated analysis in the 2nd PSR."

These two reports are still the only ones to date – and they had practically no effect on criminal policy in Germany – at least no visible effect (Hahlen 2012, 122). In order to at least improve the opportunities for criminal policy to make its decisions on an empirically-scientific basis and thus legitimize them, regular security reports should be created. Either on a legal basis, as applicable for instance to the Children's and Youth Report to be submitted once every legislative period, or based on decisions of the Deutschen Bundestag, as in the case of the Family Report, the Report on the Elderly, or the Poverty and Prosperity Report.[97]

3.2

Levels of prevention policy

Like prevention practice, prevention policy is also a task which is performed on several levels: at the local/communal level, state level, federal level, and international/ global level.

---

[96] See the „Bielefeld Declaration" of the 18th German Congress of Crime Prevention and the Prevention News from March 22, 2014.

[97] „An orientation on empirical and/or expert descriptions, analyses, and assessments on the life situations of their target groups has become increasingly important for policy over the last decades. Such reports serve both as a factual-technical foundation of political decisions as well as for legitimation. This development can be observed supra-nationally, nationally, and at the level of the federal states and communities. This is true for many fields of policy and also for youth policy (Pluto et. al. 2014, 7).

And, just for prevention practice, the local level is the most important among the levels of political responsibility: "Preventive criminal policy (should) include all policy fields ... which can make a contribution to preventing crimes ... the design and strengthening of local relationships is absolutely essential... The possibilities and competences for influencing specific creation factors (of crime) are ... mainly to be found at the local level" (PSR 2001, 459 et seq.)

3.2.1

Prevention policy on local/communal level

The significance of the policy for crime prevention at the communal level already becomes clear in the well-known claim: "Crime prevention is the duty of the mayor".

"The communal heads in administration and policy must make prevention their own; otherwise the work has no chance! ... As part of the mandate for action of the different protagonists

... different interfaces arise with the city or community which require joint and co-ordinated action. If the head of the administration does not support the work of the prevention council, the necessary cooperation of the administration is naturally much more difficult. Add to this that volunteers or part-timers are much more likely to join if they feel that they are supported by the leadership of the communal" (Müller 2004).

The "Advertising letter" of the state prevention councils Mecklenburg-Western Pomerania, Lower Saxony, and Schleswig-Holstein "10 GOOD REASONS WHY and HOW communal prevention councils should be installed" states: "Mayor at the top – The mayor should have a firm grip on the management of communal crime prevention. He himself should take the initiative and chair the communal prevention council and ensure with all of his authority that the administration participates... The work of a prevention council around the administration or even against the administration is doomed to failure from the outset."

"Mayors at the top" stand for the significance of crime prevention in their community, give the commissions respect and legitimacy, thus motivating other communal institutions and organizations to cooperate, and facilitating the implementation of proposals of the crime prevention commissions in an interdisciplinary manner in the different departments of the administration (see also Kober/Kahl 2012, 28).

The inventory by Schreiber in the winter of 2005/2006 for local prevention commissions in Germany shows that mayors participate in more than two thirds of all commissions. This means that in many, especially smaller, communities, the requirement "mayors at the top" is fulfilled. However, this is no guarantee for successful commission work: the assessment of the effectiveness of the commission is no better when the mayor is committed to the commission, nor does their participation appear to have a positive impact on the activity of the commissions. "The often postulated assumption that the presence of the mayor generally has a positive impact on prevention work must then be considered in a more differentiated manner" (Schreiber 2007, 44).

In view of the problems mentioned above (Chap. 2.2) and/or – put more positively – the abundance of parameters for success and design which the commissions must manage, it is not really surprising if this one albeit important factor "mayors at the top" turns out not to be that decisive.[98]

However, it may be decisive what kind of support the communal commissions receive from the respective state policy.[99] An expression of such support is the institution of central commissions which primarily serve the function of providing crime prevention policy field consulting, i.e. supporting the communal level through advice and expertise in questions of institutionalization, process organization, and the design of the content (Kober/Kahl 2012, 30): The institution of state prevention councils and comparable commissions.[100]

The example of the State Prevention Council Lower Saxony (SPC) shows what support the state level can contribute to the communal level.[101]

The State Prevention Council sees itself as the "Lower Saxony competence center for crime prevention" and considers strengthening communal crime prevention to be its most important objective. Its department "communal crime prevention" coordinates all activities towards this end. This includes in particular:

---

[98] In the view of the State Prevention Council Lower Saxony, however, the association to the administration has been especially effective for the ca. 200 communal commissions of the state.

[99] In some states, legal regulations were passed to provide the communal crime prevention with the necessary legal framework. For instance, in 2000 in Hessen, Section 1 Para. 6 of the Hessen Law on Public Safety and Order was supplemented. It is stated in Clause 3: „The danger prevention agencies and police agencies are to form joint work groups as part of danger prevention (crime prevention councils); these are to accept persons and institutions from various areas and fields of responsibility which can contribute to crime prevention." (www.landespraeventionsrat.hessen.de).

[100] More details in Chap. 3.2.2
Concerning the situation in Schleswig-Holstein, Ziercke already stated in 1997: „The Initiative (for communal crime prevention) had to come mainly from central instances in the states. This was the only way to achieve the goal of establishing a state-wide network of communal crime prevention councils relatively quickly. In this respect, these state councils were an interface and control element all in one for the communities... In addition to the function of an information collection and control instance, a central state instance also provides a forum for mayors to be able to exchange information specific to crime prevention. Regional conferences on crime prevention with many interested mayors and participating institutions are such a forum!" (1998, 282)
See for instance also the „Joint framework agreement of the Ministry of the Interior Baden-Württemberg with the city, district, and community conference for the intensification of the information exchange, implementation of joint periodical analyses of the local security situation, and coordination of communal crime prevention by the lower administration agencies" from 14.9.2004 (printed in Bannenberg et. al. (Publ.)(2005), 251-255.

[101] The following information comes from the web site of the State Prevention Council Lower Saxony: www.lpr.niedersachsen.de.
At the moment there are 188 communal prevention commissions as members in the SPC.

- preparation and post-processing of content for consulting processes for communal prevention commissions (also in coordination with other department of the SPC)
- planning and organization of SPC events
- implementation of guideline for promotion of crime prevention projects
- preparation of education events on applicable topics of communal prevention work in cooperation with the department Beccaria quality initiative.

Since 2002, as part of its support program (new guideline since September 2012), the State Prevention Council has been granting contributions for crime prevention projects at the communal level.[102] Since December 2011, the support focus lies on spreading the method "CTC - Communities That Care". This method has the goal of supporting communities in making their prevention activities in the area of social development of children and juveniles more targeted, more effective, and to make its success verifiable. The State Prevention Council tested the transferability of the method that was pioneered in the US during the model trial "SPIN – Social Prevention In Networks" from 2009 to 2012 with positive results, making it available to communities in Lower Saxony since 2013.[103]

In the meantime, the State Prevention Council "has found significant qualitative changes in everyday work. Bandwidth, range, and complexity of the topics have been greater and more diverse since the creation of the first commissions in Lower Saxony at the beginning of the 90s. Add to this an increasing acceptance and perception of the work of communal prevention commissions in the public."

Another positive aspect is also the evaluation of the support services of the State Prevention Council by its "customers", the communal prevention commissions. A study with the goal to gain insights over which way the State Prevention Council Lower Saxony can optimally support communal prevention commissions came to the following conclusion: "The results of the study in terms of the assessment of the overall services and the role of the State Prevention Council allow the conclusion that its activities and services significantly contribute to the strength of communal crime prevention." However, despite the large service range of the State Prevention Council Lower Saxony, there is still room to be even better" (Müller 2010).

The concept of communal crime prevention could also receive political support from the German-European Forum for Urban Security (Deutsch-Europäische Forum für Urbane Sicherheit e.V. - DEFUS), the German forum in the European Forum for Urban Security (EFUS; see Chap. 3.3.3).

---

[102] In accordance with the support guideline, all recipients of contributions are obligated to allow verification of the measures supported by the State Prevention Council by a University or other suitable institution.

[103] More detailed information can be found at www.ctc-info.de; see also Groeger-Roth 2012.

DEFUS was founded May 10, 2010 during the 15th German Congress of Crime Prevention in Berlin; at the moment, eight cities,[104] the German Congress of Crime Prevention, and the State Prevention Council Lower Saxony are members The goal of DEFUS is cooperation in the improvement of public security in the areas of crime prevention and fight against crime, traffic safety, and the intensification of communal crime prevention. The membership in DEFUS offers an exchange of information and experiences in security questions, support of a social climate which gives crime prevention a high status, and networking of agencies, bodies, and organizations whose responsibilities include the improvement of public safety (www.defus.org).[105]

Maybe with the help of DEFUS, the commissions of communal crime prevention will succeed not only in improving and solidifying communal preventive work but also in developing an independent and long-term concept for communal criminal policy, clarifying what distinguishes their work from traditional projects and measures of social and situation-based prevention (Steffen 2005, 158).

3.2.2

Prevention policy at the state level

If crime prevention, in order to be successful, has to be embedded in an "offensive life situation policy" (see Chap. 1.1) then the states are important action levels for prevention policy. In the federal system of the Federal Republic of Germany, "state matters" (fields of action of the respective state policy) are (mainly) the areas of internal security (e.g. responsibilities, organization, and authorities of the police), penal system, media (press and broadcasting law), education and cultural support, public health and care infrastructure, and administration.

An important responsibility of the states is that for their communities (the states pass communal constitutions and help financially weaker communities as part of communal financial balancing).[106]

One way to clarify the significance of crime prevention at the state level is the institution of state prevention councils. In the meantime, state prevention councils, whose si-

---

[104] Augsburg, Düsseldorf, Göttingen, Heidelberg, Leer, Mannheim, Munich, and Stuttgart.

[105] The registered non-profit association DEFUS has its headquarters and business offices in Hanover in connection to the offices of the State Prevention Council Lower Saxony and the German Conference on Crime Prevention.
Such inter-communal networks are underdeveloped in Germany. Especially compared to the high degree of networking of the important partner of the police in the federation and the states in the area of crime prevention there is a need to catch up in the area of communal security (Marks/Schairer 2010). Since 2001, the „City network for security, tolerance, and non-violence" is an inter-communal network which now includes 17 German cities and the Foundation German Forum for Crime Prevention (DFK) as members (www.kriminalpraevention.de).

[106] See also „Information concerning political education No. 318/2013: Federalism in Germany", issued by the „Federal Center for Political Education" (bpb).

gnificance for communal crime prevention has already been discussed, exist in almost all states. Only Bavaria and Hamburg still have not yet installed such commissions; in Thüringen, the State Prevention Council no longer exists but there may soon be one in Baden-Württemberg (here, there is currently only an inter-disciplinary commission at the inter-ministry level with the "Project office communal crime prevention – KKP"). For the most part, the state prevention councils are associated with the Ministries of the Interior; in Hessen, the State Prevention Council was a part of the Ministry of Justice from the beginning, in Lower Saxony and in North Rhine-Westphalia it has been for a few years; in Berlin the "Berlin Commission against Violence" is associated with several senate departments, in Saarland with the "State institute for preventive action" established in 2009 (Steffen 2013, 489). The state prevention councils are also mainly associated with one department; the demand "prevention is a top management affair" however would require a connection to the government.

State prevention councils are consulting organs of the respective state government, mesh state action with civil-social involvement, and are "mediators" between policy, prevention, and science. Again the example of the State Prevention Council Lower Saxony (www.lpr.niedersachsen.de; Marks 2014).

The composition and activities of the State Prevention Council Lower Saxony (SPC), which sees itself as the competence center for crime prevention in Lower Saxony, clarify the understanding of crime prevention as the active cooperation of many social forces with the goal of preventing crimes.

The Lower Saxony state government founded the SPC per cabinet decision in 1995 in order to support communities in their prevention work, network experts all over Lower Saxony together, and promote the attitude of general social prevention.

The State Prevention Council is an independent consulting organ of the state government with the general objective of reducing crime and improving the subjective feeling of safety of citizens in Lower Saxony.

The offices of the State Prevention Council have been part of the Ministry of Justice since 2000. The full-time team develops concepts and coordinates measures which are necessary to achieve the objectives. In doing so, it coordinates with the chair of the State Prevention Council who represents the approximately 270 members of the State Prevention Council. In addition to the ca. 200 communal prevention commissions, the members include NGOs that are active state-wide, ministries, state representatives, and subordinate agencies and scientific institutions.

The work of the State Prevention Council includes a wide range of responsibilities, projects, cooperations, and events which are classified in seven focus areas: communal crime prevention, tailored prevention,

CTC in Lower Saxony, prevention of violence and protection of victim, prevention of right-wing extremism, Beccaria quality initiative, cooperations in Lower Saxony, national and international networks.

The State Prevention Council organizes events for the exchange of practice-relevant information and experiences for the area of crime prevention. This includes: The Lower Saxony Congress for Crime Prevention (Niedersächsische Präventionstag = NPT), the regional conferences for crime prevention, the event series "Conflict Management Congress" and "Take responsibility in the North", the annual special conference discusses domestic violence.

The services of the State Prevention Council for its members include the circular, databases, publications, schedules, prevention links, web sites of the State Prevention Council.

The current projects and focus areas of the State Prevention Council mainly grew pragmatically and were (still) not based on an overall political strategy for state-wide preventive action, an interdisciplinary prevention plan. The cooperation between the central areas of work of prevention – prevention policy, prevention practice, prevention research – is still in its infancy and has not yet been systematically developed (Marks 2014).

In addition to the state prevention councils as the "institutionalized evidence" for the significance which crime prevention has in state policy, there are of course further initiatives and actions of the states in this area. After all, crime prevention is very attractive as an action concept for policy: policy can use prevention to make clear that it no longer merely responds to problems after they have occurred,[107] but acts in a future- and action-oriented manner (Holthusen/Hoops 2012, 24, 27). In addition, these programs that are usually interdisciplinary clarify the trend to prevention policy.

For example two initiatives from North Rhine-Westphalia: In the summer of 2008, the State Parliament North Rhine-Westphalia used the enquete commission "Prevention" to "develop proposals for an effective prevention policy in North Rhine-Westphalia" – as a reaction to the murder of an inmate in the correctional facility in Siegburg. The remarkable report[108] with a focus on "recognition and removal of structural risk factors for juvenile delinquency (primary and secondary prevention)" and "optimized design of existing and conception of new measures for punishment and education of juvenile delinquents" became the foundation of many developments in state policy (State Parliament North Rhine-Westphalia 2010).

---

[107] As is typically the case in the area of repression, when legal penalties are raised after attention-grabbing crimes and/or procedural rules are made stricter (see above 3.1).

[108] Notable also in terms of the integration and consideration of practice and science by numerous hearings, expert opinions, and expert discussions.

These include the project "Turn the corner" of the Ministry of the Interior and Communal Affairs North Rhine-Westphalia, which has been installed in eight police agencies as model projects since 2011 and wants to prevent at-risk children and juveniles from becoming criminals. For this purpose, pedagogical experts of free carriers of children's and youth organizations cooperate with the police in the "Family Team".

The project is scientifically guided by the Institute for Psychology of the Christian-Albrecht-University in Kiel.[109]

3.2.3
Prevention policy at the federal level

Compared to the development of crime prevention at the communal and state level, the policy at the federal level has acted with some reservation, especially in terms of the institutionalization of crime prevention in a national commission. This corresponds to the "reservation" of criminal policy discussed above in considering (at least partially) theoretically and empirically founded scientific-criminological insights in their decisions.

While Germany is no longer "a developing nation in terms of crime prevention" as Ziercke still had to note in 1997 at the 3rd German Congress of Crime Prevention, it still has not developed very far, in particular at the national level, and not at all when compared to our European neighbors.

After all, in June 2001 the German Forum for Crime Prevention (Deutsches Forum für Kriminalprävention = DFK) was instituted as a private foundation after two years of development with the ambitious goal of promoting crime prevention in all aspects as a national service and information instance for German, European, and international cooperation.[110]

The goals and core responsibilities of the DFK are:

- Promotion of crime prevention in all aspects, utilization of prevention possibilities to the greatest possible extent, integration of all social forces by

- networking and cooperation; connection of government and non-governmental instances and carriers of responsibility; competence orientation

---

[109] See also contribution by Beckmann/Pohlmann/Unkrig at the 17th German Congress of Crime Prevention and that of Borncarriers/Pohlmann at the 18th German Congress of Crime Prevention and www.mik.nrw. de/themen-aufgaben/schutz-sicherheit/projekt-kurve-kriegen/grundkonzept.html.
Other states have also passed programs against juvenile crime and/or violence with a focus on prevention; for instance in Hamburg „Action against juvenile violence" (www.handeln-gegen-jugendviolence.hamburg.de) or Bremen „Stop juvenile violence" (www.kriminalpraevention.bremen.de).

[110] See also the motto of the foundation (www.kriminalpraevention.de).
Based on a decision of the Conference of the Ministers of the Interior (IMK) don November 21, 1997, the DFK has become a „daughter" of the interior departments with correspondingly clear personnel participation by the police in the development staff and today's offices.

- bundling; promotion of synergies and interdisciplinary approaches

- transfer of knowledge; collection and distribution of scientific and best-practice insights (national and international)

- PR work; raising awareness of the public at large and promotion of willingness of all social forces to participate.

Foundation organs are the curatorship with a total of 61 members[111] and the board. The offices are at the foundation headquarters in Bonn; the team of the offices included seven persons as of May 31, 2013;

Five of which were "borrowed" from police departments of the states. Also for personnel reasons – not to mention the completely inadequate financial basis - the DFK is not able to even begin to cover its "goals and core responsibilities"; it mainly concentrates on the prevention of violence in its work. In addition, the DFK publishes the quarterly magazine "Forum Crime Prevention".

In view of the significance of general social crime prevention at the federal level, it is more than regrettable that the even initially "tender plant" DFK just cannot manage to grow both in terms of finances and personnel – and has remained operable only thanks to the commitment of the "participants in front and behind the scenes" (Kerner 2012, 43).[112]

In the meantime there is a proposal to install a National Center for Crime Prevention in which the DFK and also the Central Criminological Office[113] "would participate in a suitable role". This proposal was made by the consortium "Crime and Security" in the "Dialog on Germany's future". In the view of the consortium it should receive

---

[111] Five federal departments, the federal states, representatives of economy and of associations, the labor unions, the major religious communities, the communal top associations.
The presidency in the curatorship changes between the Federal Ministries of the Interior and of Justice; further departments are represented in the curatorship but do not participate in the DFK with personnel or content. Another omission is the lack of connection to the Chancellor's Office, which would have made the interdisciplinary, general social mission of the DFK at least (more) visible.

[112] Details about institution, problems, and opportunities of the DFK Kerner 2012; also the interim report by Kahl 2011.
The equipment and support the DFK received did not even come close to what Ziercke 1997 demanded for the „Federal Prevention Commission" which had already been passed by the Work Group II of the Conference of the Ministers of the Interior: „I am convinced that Germany must get serious about this model of a Federal Prevention Commission. The assessment of the security situation ... makes this clear. We especially may not limit ourselves to only the area of communal crime prevention. We must also recognize that trans-regional and international crime has its roots and effects at the communal level and it is not sufficient to put all your chips on just communal prevention but also to consider the national prevention possibilities" (1998, 289).

[113] The Central Criminological Office (Kriminologische Zentralstelle e.V. = KrimZ) is the central research and documentation organization of the Federation and the states for the area of criminal justice. It has been working in Wiesbaden since 1986. The KrimZ regularly organizes specialized conferences on current topics of criminal policy, documents research results, and performs its own practice-related research projects (www.krimz.de).

"high priority". The National Center for Crime Prevention as an interdisciplinary center should develop empirically founded knowledge for an evidence-based prevention and control of crime and to prepare them in an action-oriented manner for policy makers (Dialog on Germany's future 2011/2012, 92 et seq.).

Whether this proposal will be realized is more than questionable – especially in view of the few statements which are made on crime prevention in the Coalition Agreement between CDU, CSU, and SPD "Shaping Germany's Future". The term alone hardly appears (e.g. in connection with the "prevention of extremism") and even then only provides unspecific declarations of intent, "commonplaces without detailed content, mere programmatic platitudes", which neither harm nor benefit anyone (Kreuzer 2013).[114]

For instance: "Children's and youth organizations should be developed on a well-founded empirical foundation[115] in a carefully structured process into an inclusive, efficient, and permanently capable support system ... We need strong youth agencies and a functioning partnership with free youth aid ... We will ... pursue social space-oriented and preventive approaches" (p. 99). or: "We want to better protect children and juveniles and people with disabilities from violence, in particular sexual violence" (p. 100) ... "We understand youth policy as a central policy field which is primarily designed locally by states and communities. In order to realize our youth policy goals, we need a strong coalition for youth with a new interdisciplinary youth policy which has an eye on the concerns of all young people" (p. 101) and finally under the heading "Effective criminal prosecution and effective measures for risk protection": "We want to prevent at-risk children and juveniles from slipping into criminal careers through early joint action by criminal prosecution agencies and children's and youth organizations. If a young person commits an offense, punishment should be swift" (p. 146).

It becomes more specific – and possibly more consequential - when an expert commission is to be used, e.g. in the declaration of intent: "We want to design general criminal proceedings and juvenile criminal proceedings to be more effective and practical while preserving the principles of a state ruled by law. An expert commission will develop proposals until the middle of this legislative period" (p. 146).

It would have been desirable if statements had been made in terms of children's and youth organizations as to how their programs and measures would be financed in view of the often very tight resources. Because "children's and youth support, as opposed to

---

[114] See also the analysis of the Coalition Agreement between CDU, CSU, and FDP of the 17th legislative period by Becker under the aspect of expectations of criminal policy from criminology (2013, 207 et seq.)

[115] At least, in every legislative period an expert commission presents a very comprehensive „Children's and Youth Report" which is a „report on the living situation of young people and the services of the children's and youth organizations in Germany" – it can hardly be more empirically and scientific founded. In 2013, the 14th Children's and Youth Report was created as a comprehensive report as is only usual in every third legislative period; the last comprehensive report was submitted in 2002.

police and justice, is financed by the communities which in some regions in Germany are in such bad financial shape that budgetary supervision concepts are part of every-day life, e.g. in North Rhine-Westphalia" (Holthusen/Hoops 2012, 24).

It would have also been desirable – especially in view of what was just said on the topic "national prevention commission" – if the German Forum for Crime Prevention had been mentioned which "would be a suitable partner (in addition to others) to specify a few projects and implement them cooperatively" (Kahl 2013, 2).

3.2.4

Prevention policy on the international and global level

International and global institutions are becoming increasingly significant for the design of crime prevention at the different action levels. We should mention in particular the agreements and institutions at the European level, but also the United Nations or the World Health Organization.

The European Crime Prevention Network (www.eucpn.org)[116]

Already in 1987, the Minister Committee of the European Council, in a final report of the expert commission on the organization of crime prevention for the member states, issues the recommendation for a three-level crime prevention at the local/communal, regional, and national level (Ziercke 1998, 286).

In October 1999, the European Council (in its meeting in Tampere/Finland) decides on "strategies and measures to intensify crime prevention" as part of the larger initiative with the goal of developing the EU into a "union of freedom, security, and justice".

In May 2000, the Ministers of Justice and the Interior of the EU in Lisbon welcomed the strengthening of crime prevention in a joint statement. It is emphasized that this strengthening at the European level occurs in front of the background of national prevention programs, since effective crime prevention necessarily presupposes the integration of all local social forces (PSR 2001, 472).

In implementation of the decision of Tampere, on May 28, 2001, the European Crime Prevention Network – EUCPN is founded by an EU Council decision[117] with the goal to promote measures of crime prevention in all member states. EUCPN provides a forum for the exchange of proven practices for the prevention of crime, in particular everyday crime. The network consists of one nominated "national representative"

---

[116] See for historic development of crime prevention at the European level PSR 2001, 471 et seq. and EUCPN 2013.

[117] On November 30, 2009 the foundation decision was suspended and replaced by a new Council decision. See EUCPN 2013 and Wijckmans 2013 for goals, responsibilities, and activities of EUCPN; current for structure, activities, and results also Kahl 2014.

from each of the EU member states, their respective deputies,[118] and further experts for crime prevention, including practitioners and scientists. They form the so-called contact points of the network. Germany is represented by the Federal Ministries of the Interior and of Justice and by the German Forum for Crime Prevention (DFK) as a contact point.

The EUCPN issues a newsletter and the semi-annual "European Crime Prevention Monitor", holds conferences, and presents the annual European Crime Prevention Award which is awarded during a "Best Practice Conference".

EFUS: European Forum for Urban Security (http://efus.eu)[119]

EFUS, the European Forum for Urban Security, is a city network of more than 300 European communities and regions from 17 countries which was founded in 1987. It serves for the exchange of experiences and expertise on all questions of urban security and crime prevention.

The responsibility and goal of the network is to strengthen preventive activities and policies. In addition, it is his wish to promote the role of communal administrations in this area at the national and European level. For this, a close cooperation between administrations and prevention commissions at the local, national, European, and international level is created. EFUS works on all important questions of communal crime prevention. The fundamental principles of the Forum include respect of human rights in the implementation of security and prevention policies.

EFUS is a registered association according to French law and has offices in Paris, Brussels, and Budapest. Members of the Forum are communal, regional, and national administrations. The condition for acceptance as a member is the existence of a local alliance for local security or the intent to use such a commission. Further members are NGOs and universities active in crime prevention.[120]

UNODC: United Nations Office on Drugs and Crime

The United Nations Office on Drugs and Crime (UNODC; www.unodc.org) leads the world-wide fight against illegal drug trade and international crimes and is also responsible for the implementation of the program of the United Nations for the fight against terrorism. The UNODC was founded in 1997 and has about 500 employees world-wide. The headquarters of UNODC are in Vienna and there are 20 branch offices and connection offices in New York and Brussels. The responsibilities of UNODC also include the areas "crime prevention and criminal justice reform" and "drug pre-

---

[118] These „national representatives" form the directorate which is supported by a secretariat. The chair in the directorate changes with the EU presidency.

[119] See Marks/Schairer 2010 for the following.

[120] See the EFUS Manifesto by Aubervilliers and Saint-Denis (Fontanille 2013) for the „European visions for the future of prevention".

vention and health". As part of its direct cooperation with the governments and non-governmental organizations, the field workers develop and implement drug, control, and prevention programs which are tailored to the specific needs of the respective states (www.unvienna.org/unov/de/unodc.html).

The central guideline organ of the UN in the area of crime is the Commission on Crime prevention and Criminal Justice – CCPCJ. It was founded in 1991 as the expert commission of the Economic and Social Council and also defines the political prescriptions for the practical work of UNODC in the area of the fight against crime. The Commission is also responsible for the preparation and supplementary decisions of the World Congress on Crime Prevention and Criminal Justice. The 12th UN World Congress on Crime Prevention and Criminal Justice took place in 2010 in Brazil. The 13th World Congress will take place in 2015 in Qatar (www.wie-io.diplo.de).[121]

The World Health Organization - (WHO; www.who.int) is a special organization of the United Nations located in Geneva. It was founded in 1948 and has about 200 members. Its goal is the realization of the best possible health level for all humans. The constitution of the WHO defines health as "a state of complete physical, mental, and social wellbeing which is not just characterized by the absence of illness of disability".

Since violence destroys the lives of millions in the whole world, but is preventable, prevention of violence is also a topic of the WHO. For instance, its *Violence Prevention Alliance* (www.preventviolence.info), a network of WHO member states, non-governmental and communal organizations, and private, international, and inter-governmental organizations, developed an action plan for a "Global campaign prevention of violence 2012 – 2020" as well as corresponding materials for this.[122]

The International Center for the Prevention of Crime - ICPC
The International Center for the Prevention of Crime[123] was founded in 1994 in Montreal/Canada.[124] ICPC is the only international, non-governmental organization which is solely focused on crime prevention and communal security. ICPC supports national and local governments in fulfilling these responsibilities. ICPC has international members such as states, regions, and cities, UN organizations (e.g. UNODC and UN Habitat) and NGOs. ICPC supports the exchange of knowledge and experiences in the

---

[121] See also Stolpe 2009 and the comprehensive analysis „Blue Criminology. The power of United Nation's ideas to counter crime globally" by the „European Institute for Crime prevention and Control - HEUNI" in Helsinki associated with the UN (Redo 2012).

[122] „Violence prevention. the evidence" appeared in 2010. At the 15th and 17th German Congress of Crime Prevention, Alexander Butchart of the WHO presented „Ensuring security and fundamental rights in urban settings" and/or „Preventing violence: an overview".

[123] For the following see Marks 2011 and www.crime-prevention-intl.org.

[124] At the Initiative of the French mayor Gilbert Bonnemaison, who also founded the European Forum for Internal Security (EFUS).

entire area of international crime prevention, bundles, analyzes, and processes innovative practices for crime prevention. ICPC offers technical support and training in order to support practitioners in their work; it organizes seminars, colloquia, and meetings at the national and international level and participates in a number of projects with technical expertise or support. Every two years, the ICPC publishes an international report on crime prevention and communal security, lastly in 2012.[125]

3.3

Summary and conclusions

At the communal and the state level, crime prevention is definitely an identified and supported goal of criminal policy. However, not with the same intensity and consistency in all communities and states. In some places they seem to "run out of steam" and there is probably "room for improvement" everywhere. Especially in view of the overall favorable crime development, the crime prevention efforts should not decrease but kept at least at a constant level if not increased. After everything we know about the effects of prevention and repression, prevention appears clearly superior to repression – not to mention the fact that no crime also means no victim and no damage.

At the communal level, the concept of communal crime prevention definitely has prospects and should be implemented and developed (in an area-covering manner), for instance in the direction of a communal security policy, institutionalized for instance in an "Office for Crime Prevention".

The "Fundamental discussion of goals, means, and limits of communal crime prevention" demanded by Heinz already in 1997 could help realize this. Because "only if we are aware of the limits of what prevention can achieve, will we be able – within these limits – to use the resources sensibly and effectively; only if we document the experiences – positive and negative alike - and make them available to critical inspection, will we learn and be able to use the (by no means exhausted) possibilities of prevention even better" (1998, 30).

Due to the tight budget restrictions in many communities, financial support is urgently needed, also so that the other protagonists of crime prevention at the communal level (e.g. children's and youth organizations and (most) schools can continue their outstanding and indispensable work in crime prevention and possibly even expand it further.

It is not satisfactory that the commission and project landscape is so confusing and non-transparent. After ten years it is about time to compile the local prevention commissions in Germany, their composition, their activities etc. At the moment only a few state prevention councils have this information. It would be desirable to develop a commission and project database.

---

[125] „The 2012 International Report on Crime Prevention and Community Safety"; the summary of this report is available for download in German.

At the state level, the state prevention councils have an important function, in particular as consulting organs of the state governments and the local commissions and institutions. State prevention councils (or comparable commissions) should be installed in all states and equipped with suitable organization, personnel, and finances and connected to the governments. It would make sense to supplement them with "Offices for crime prevention".

There is a significant need for action for crime prevention at the federal level, even if many crime prevention-relevant responsibilities fall into the competence areas of the states in the federal system of the Federal Republic of Germany. But only if the Federation becomes active is there a real chance that the preference of prevention over repression will establish itself in federal policy and that penal law will not be expended into a more "control-oriented prevention penal law" and that new crime definitions and harsher sanctions will be demanded.

It is urgently necessary to create a "National Center for Crime Prevention" with connection to the Federal Chancellor's Office, possibly even by expanding the Foundation German Forum for Crime Prevention (DFK) to such a Center and integrating the Central Criminological Office (KrimZ).[126] Whether and how the Police Crime Prevention of the States and the Federation can be involved should be checked.

Even if the experiences with the crime policy effect of the previous PSR were not very satisfactory, the creation of – actually – Periodical Security Reports based on a legal regulation or a decision of the Deutscher Bundestag[127] is urgently needed.

These reports should be compiled by an interdisciplinary scientific commission on a regular basis, for instance once in every legislative period.

One should discuss whether a prevention law could define the primary responsibility of crime prevention in its rule-of-law limits, clear responsibilities be defined, the multitude of governmental and non-governmental institutions recruited and obligated to cooperation for effective crime prevention.

It should be checked for all levels whether the proposal by Waller, to invest 5% of the current budget for the reaction to crime – police, justice, and penal system – into effective crime prevention (another 3% into services and rights for the victims of crimes) could be realized – because an investment into proven prevention measures will pay off in a lower number of crimes and lower costs for tax payers (Waller 2013).

---

[126] The role model for organization, responsibility, and equipment could be the Federal Center for Health Education (BZgA), an upper federal agency in the offices of the Federal Ministry for Health (www.bzga.de).

[127] As printed matter of the Deutscher Bundestag, such Periodical Security Reports at least have the chance that they could be debated in the parliament and acknowledged by the media (Hahlen 2012, 120).
How policy consulting can be successful could be seen for more than 50 years in the work of the German Youth Institute (Deutsches Jugendinstitut - DJI) one of the largest German social-scientific research institutes for children, juveniles, and families at the interface between science, policy, and practice (see also Mielenz 2013)."

4

Prevention science

Crime prevention should be based on evidence, i.e. on the basis of theoretical and empirical scientific insights (see above Chapter 1.2). Prevention practice and prevention policy thus need science and research.

The following can be noted for prevention practice in view of the information up to this point: "The significance of a scientific-empirical foundation of projects and programs for (crime) prevention has continuously gained in significance over the last two decades" (Marks 2013, 140).[128]

For prevention policy as part of criminal policy, the "deafness of the official criminal policy to empirical findings" was lamented – at least in terms of the federal level. At the communal and state level one can find "an open ear".

So the question arises whether science and research have developed the required empirical knowledge and can be provided in a way that "suits" policy and practice. The already quoted "Freiburg Memorandum" remarks that the theoretical and empirical knowledge of crime, offenses, perpetrators, and victims and the different governmental and non-governmental, formal and informal reactions and prevention forms have been developed a long time ago by criminology as the relevant interdisciplinary reference science and provided to criminal, social, and communal policy.

4.1

On the state of criminology in Germany

The conference "On the situation of criminology in Germany", held in June 2012 at the Max-Planck Institute for foreign and international penal law in Freiburg and from which the "Freiburg Memorandum" originated, comes to a sobering conclusion: Germany has a highly developed theoretical and empirical criminological science which is, however, at significant rest due to "structural depletion." Criminology is slowly dying through a gradual, almost universal reduction of its personnel and material resources which is not based on any specific political decision. Its scientific reputation is by no means in doubt. Its research results are not suspect and its international success is accepted. The reduction is creeping, as though a science is simply being drained.[129]

---

[128]   See e.g. Koop, who laments „too little specific university research" for the penal system – with the consequence that the penal system has developed its own criminological services in order to cover the demand for well-founded insights e.g. on the effectiveness or ineffectiveness of treatment measures (2013, 202 et seq.).
Holthusen/Hoops are more skeptical about crime prevention in children's and youth organizations. The topic of evaluation has been a demand for many years which up to now has hardly been met. The problem in evaluation research is especially the often weakly formalized pedagogical practice settings of youth aid (2012, 27).

[129]   From the preface of Klaus Sessar to Albrecht et. al. 2013. Out of 40 law schools, criminology was no lon-

Albrecht (2013, 73 et seq.) arrives at these conclusions: while criminology has established itself as an independent social science in North America[130] German criminology is almost exclusively connected to law schools – "The fate of German criminology is that of a still ongoing connection to penal law" (Sessar 2011) - but here, too, there have been significant losses. For instance, of the projects with criminologically relevant questions supported by the German Research Association (Deutsche Forschungsgemeinschaft = DFG), only about 8% are implemented by the criminology housed in universities. All others are implemented by other disciplines such as the general social sciences, historical sciences, forensic psychiatry/psychology, political science, ethnology, economy etc. Criminological research studies also largely take place outside of criminology in law schools and "are significantly spread over different scientific disciplines, which also indicated that criminological questions enjoy wide-spread scientific interest."

Criminology is not only being reduced at law schools but also in psychological and sociological institutes in German universities where it had "always been somewhat marginal: after their retirement, almost all criminologically active sociologists have been replaced by successors who no longer engaged specifically in criminological research and "slash sociologies" such as "social control" or "sociology of deviance" were "also no longer visible at sociological institutes with a few exceptions" (see also Reuband 2013, 140).[131] The training of police, penal system, and social work at specialized colleges and/or the German University of the Police regularly represents criminology.

Conclusion: "The withdrawal or limitation to penal law also results in a significance reduction in terms of content, in particular theoretical content, which can be seen in the fact that university criminology hardly participates in various research developments and new questions. New research fields which once took a central role in criminology are now already mainly replaced by other disciplines ... The lack of criminology becomes especially clear in questions of security and security research" (Albrecht 2013, 77 et seq.).

In view of "security as one of the central social challenges of our time" around which "new complex topics such as the research field 'security risk prevention'" formed, Sessar (2011) also demands the development and opening of criminology: "The prevailing scientific view of penal laws and crime policy is that it is the genuine responsibility of criminology which cannot be handled by other social sciences; in addition,

---

ger present at all in 11, i.e. one quarter. 6 faculty chairs are expressly reserved for criminology, 22 faculty chairs next to penal law and other related areas also for criminology.

[130] See also Schneider 2010, 475.

[131] Based on a survey conducted mid 2012 among legal, social, and behavioral science faculties and institutes, Boers/Seddig also reach the conclusion that one can „only partially speak of an institutional basis for modern criminology at German Universities" (2013, 124).

there is the observation of security policy and prevention policy to the extent they are connected with crime and the fear of crime ... Opening criminology would also mean a stronger connection with other science branches in order to tackle more complex research topics and thus participate in social theory discourses."

Since criminology is a social and behavioral scientific and thus especially empirical discipline, Boers/Seddig also demand a "clearly enhanced institutionalization of criminological research and teaching at social and behavioral scientific university institutions." This strengthening of criminology must "lead to an equal, at the core professorial cooperation in which all disciplines contribute their respective competences ... There are a few outstanding long-term examples for such interdisciplinary cooperation in Germany[132] as well as current interest from reknown sociologists and psychologists in original criminological research questions" (2013, 124 et seq.).

The endowment chair "Crime Prevention and Risk Management" which was instituted at the University Tübingen in 2012 under the sponsorship of the Foundation German Forum for Crime Prevention and with the approval of the German Bundestag was called a "kick-off for a completely new culture of crime prevention". It was taken over by Rita Haverkamp on October 1, 2013.[133] The unique in this form faculty chair in Germany is expected to develop sustainable methods for better crime fighting and creating effective strategies for the prevention of violence and crime. However, the faculty chair is only financed until 2017 and is again located at a law school.[134]

4.2

Application-oriented criminological research: opportunities and risks[135]

Criminology as a social and behavioral scientific and thus especially empirical discipline not only performs scientific autonomous basic research (we "cannot emphasize too urgently that science requires a certain independence and freedom to grow and blossom", Kerner 2013, 183) but also application-oriented research, especially in the connection of policy and practical consulting and practical research discussed here. However, this is not disputed within science due to the possible danger of a loss of autonomy for criminology and/or criminological research.

---

[132] For instance the Institute for Conflict and Violence Research of the University Bielefeld; the Max-Planck Institute for Foreign and International Penal Law in Freiburg; or the Criminological Research Institute Lower Saxony. By the way, the commemorative publication for the 70th birthday of its long-term director Christian Pfeiffer has the title „Criminology is social science"!

[133] The endowment chair was initiated by the shooting spree of Winnenden, after which politicians all over Germany and in Baden-Württemberg spoke in favor of investing more money into research on strategic crime prevention in Germany.

[134] www.uni-tuebingen.de; newsletter Uni Tübingen current No. 1/2013 and 4/2013.

[135] Thus the title of an essay by Kerner 2013.

Kunz views criminology "in its usual 'modern' version as lying in the force field between scientific autonomy and practical application: it is the science of discovering the causes for crime in the service of governmental crime control. The application fields which is opens and the insight interest which it follows are partly defined by governmental criminal policy" (2011, § 23 marginal note 1).

"The impression arises that criminology is mainly a kind of Think Tank for government-supported development of crime policy ideas and concepts.[136] As fruitful as this may be and as much as this may contribute to the social and political significance of the field, as great is the risk that this may cloud the self-view of criminology as science, which must struggle against the exploitation interest mostly dictated by current policy and in this sense demand autonomy" (Kunz 2011, Section 23 marginal note 3).[137]

Kerner (2013, 194 et seq.), in his "Plea for a diverse criminological science with foundation and application orientation" cannot completely exclude this theoretically possible risk of loss of autonomy even for the formally free university research and for basic research; however, the risk increases with increasing practice-orientation in the area of applied criminology. Risks to autonomy of independent research would have to be sought preferentially at the level of research support and might have to be questioned. "Compared to other sciences, in criminology it does not play a fundamentally different role (but possibly an amplifying role due to the specific responsibilities and structures) that the field of 'crime and crime control' is defined especially by order and security and the maintenance of the instances obligated to governmental legal order and their correspondingly socialized training...In any case, one should say goodbye to the notion of always being "heard" in a substantial sense, let alone in first position, within this tangle of forces, interests, and pressures or that being heard will translate into swift action which correspond to one's own position."[138]

Schöch summarizes the discussion of the "application of criminological research" as follows: applied criminology, in addition to basic research, which is also conducted intensively in Germany, is acknowledged as a wide and legitimate field of work in criminological research (2013, 210).

---

[136] In view of the „deafness" of criminal policy to criminological insights (see above) lamented by Kunz, this statement must be at least questioned.

[137] Maier (quoted by Schöch 2013, 211) points out the possibility that the crime policy ‚customers' may influence the methodical implementation of data collection or the interpretation of the results. This is an accusation which was often levied at so-called „state criminologists" (see also Mischkowitz 2013 and Schwind/Steinhilper 2014, 593 et seq.).
For Kunz, application-oriented criminology is still „designed to serve the instances for affirmative support of the criminal justice system. Potential topics which are critical of the instances, such as police violence, are avoided by established research" (2013 b, 106).

[138] In this connection Kerner points to the criticism „head wind" which for instance was levied by scientists against scientists – criminologists – who participated in the violence commission or the two Periodical Security Reports of the federal government. However, a wide-ranging public discussion also did not occur in this case (2013, 197 et seq.).

The "significant role" (Schöch 2013, 217) of applied criminology and its reference sciences becomes clear for instance in the documentation (conference transcripts) of the biannual meetings of the Criminological Society, the scientific association of German, Austrian, and Swiss criminologists.[139] In his analysis of five conference transcripts (appeared between 2004 and 2013), Schöch reaches the conclusion that displays "the significance of applied criminology": Of a total of 195 presentations, he estimates that 79 concern application-oriented empirical-criminological studies, e.g. about crime prevention and prognosis, about treatment and therapy research, about evaluation, or victimization and victim protection (2013, 218 et seq.).

4.3

Prevention science and prevention practice

"Application-oriented criminology" together with its reference disciplines is standing by to support practice in the implementation of the demands for evidence-based crime prevention. To provide practice thus with the necessary theoretical and empirical scientific insights and to scientifically accompany and monitor the planning, implementation, and effects of prevention measures and programs (implementation and evaluation).[140]

The willingness in practice to employ scientific insights and support when planning, implementing, and evaluating projects has clearly increased compared to the beginning years in the 1990s. This also has to do with science having provided corresponding "services", increasingly systematic forms of support for prevention practice.

---

[139] „The central responsibility of the Criminological Society (Kriminologische Gesellschaft - KrimG) is

- to support the experience-scientific research of crime, criminal perpetrators, and victims of crime and governmental and social reactions (Section 2 of the statutes)

- and to make the insights available to the practice, in particular in the areas of social work, police, and justice, but also to the public

- and thus make a contribution to crime prevention ...

The conferences serve the goal of bundling the results (which are no longer manageable for individuals, in particular practitioners) of interdisciplinary and international criminology concerning the current topics and thus stimulating wide-spread discussion among experts" (www.krimg.de).
The last, 13th, scientific conference of KrimG took place in September 2013 on the topic of „Risks of the security society. Security, risk, and criminal policy".

[140] The 1st PSR still had to find: „A special deficit in Germany is the still completely insufficient use of research capacities for process evaluation and effect evaluation of the different preventive approaches and initiatives" (PSR 2001, 470).
The 2nd PSR also complained about the same deficit: „The precise analysis of the consequences of prevention measures through accompanying research is .. indispensable for clarifying to what extent the desired effects are achieved and/or what undesirable additional effects occur.
However, such evaluation research has been hardly performed in Germany up to this point" (PSR 2006, 668).

4.3.1

Documentation and databases

The documentation of crime prevention measures and projects and the development of databases was in its infancy, e.g. the collection of information on national and international prevention protagonists, activities, projects, and models, the Infopool Prevention at the Bundeskriminalamt (PSR 2001, 467) or of PrävIS, the Prevention Information System.[141] Since its inception in 1986, the Central Criminological Office (KrimZ) has been working on the computer-aided literature documentation KrimLit which is, however, only available to a limited group of users. In contrast, freely available on the net is KrimDok, an expert bibliography for criminology at the University Tübingen; as part of the expert information service Criminology, KrimDok is to be comprehensively expanded and transferred to a comfortable search engine technology.

Other federal databases are:[142]

- "DPT-Map", the search engine of the German Congress of Crime Prevention. It can be used for targeted searches for projects, measures, institutions, and persons from the field of crime prevention.

- "Prävention im Überblick" (Prevention Overview) PRÄVÜ is provided on the internet site of the German Forums for Crime Prevention and bundles information on German prevention.

- Databases of the Deutsches Jugendinstitut (DJI), for instance "EXE project: strategies and concepts of external evaluation in children's and youth organizations";

- "PrevNet – network for addiction and health".

- "Prevention network against right-wing extremism".

---

[141] The development of this Infopool was started in 1995; it has been continuously expanded, recently also included traffic safety work, but was then – after a complete revision and expansion – taken off the net in June 2013. It received too little acceptance and resonance.
PrävIS, developed under the guidance of the German Forum for Crime Prevention together with prevention commissions and state criminal agencies in order to provide information about corresponding institutions, projects, commissions, work groups, etc. in connection with violence and crime prevention, has also been suspended.

[142] Source: www.lpr.niedersachsen.de.
English language information about the questions „What helps", „What harms", „Based on what evidence" is for instance provided by the Campbell Collaboration, which was founded in 1999 as an international network of social scientists with the goal to provide proof of the effectiveness of social intervention through systematic studies and meta-analyses and best practice projects. The focus of the content of the Campbell Collaboration lies in the areas of education, crime, justice, and public welfare. In addition, it also focuses on methodical questions (www.campbellcollaboration.org).
The Office of Justice Programs of the National Institute of Justice (USA) houses crimesolution.gov. This program offers information on „review-rated" research on the effectiveness of programs and practices (www.crimesolutions.gov).

In addition, there are databases at the level of a few states for the commissions on communal crime prevention, such as the "Prevention atlas North Rhine-Westphalia" and the "Prevention atlas Hessen" or the state-wide project database NIMAP in Lower Saxony.

4.3.2

Quality assurance, implementation, and evaluation

For the area of planning, implementation, and evaluation of crime prevention programs and projects, a "work aid for evaluation" was compiled in 2003 "for police officers ... who plan or implement prevention projects" (published by the Police Crime Prevention of the States and the Federation). In 2009 it was thoroughly revised as "Work aid for planning, implementation, and evaluation of crime prevention programs and projects", republished, and now addresses a wider audience of "persons with responsibility and planners in the area of crime fighting and traffic security. It not only addresses experts in the police but also from other institutions that are active in this area of responsibility."

The "Beccaria standards for quality assurance of crime prevention projects, issued in 2005 by the State Prevention Council Lower Saxony as part of its "Beccaria quality initiative", addressed all "developers, protagonists, and other responsibility carriers in crime prevention" from the beginning.[143] The Beccaria standards include specifications and requirements for the quality of planning, implementation, and evaluation of crime prevention programs and projects. It refers to the following seven main phases of a project:

1.   problem description

2.   analysis of genesis conditions of the problem

3.   specification of prevention goals, project goals, and target groups

4.   specification of measures to achieve goals

5.   project conception and project implementation

6.   verification of implementation and achievement of goals of the project (evaluation)

7.   final conclusions and documentation

What progress has been made in terms of the quality of prevention projects and in particular in terms of their evaluation,[144] is shown in the "Green List for Preventi-

---

[143]   Because: „quality criteria for the planning, implementation, and evaluation of crime prevention projects hardly exist. The national and Europe-wide exchange information for this group of topics is also still in its infancy" (www.beccaria-standdards.net).

[144]   Even though the „Green List" points out that, in the international comparison, Germany only produces few high-quality evaluation studies which show which programs are really effective.
And this warning by Heinz also has its justification: „Crime prevention projects should ... not enter the trap of making their justification dependent on empirical evidence of their effect; penal law does not do this either" (1998, 54).

on – CTC database of recommended prevention programs" which was developed by the State Prevention Council Lower Saxony as part of the CTC model project (see above).

This Germany-wide unique online database on evaluated prevention programs is publicly accessible. In addition to the quality of the effectiveness evaluation and the concept quality, the database also offers an overview of recommended prevention approaches in the areas of family, schools, children/juveniles, and neighborhoods based on plausible criteria (www.gruene-liste.de; Groeger-Roth/Hasenpusch 2011).[145] As the "Green List for Prevention" has seen a lot of demand from practice beyond CTC, an expansion is planned to include additional areas and an expansion of the evaluation system to include aspects of the implementation quality of programs (Marks 2014).[146]

It has almost become matter of course that crime prevention projects are planned, implemented, and evaluated with scientific support. The process evaluation alone, but even more so the effectiveness evaluation, are methodically complex enterprises which would not succeed without a scientific background (Görgen 2013).

In addition to evaluation, implementation research has become more significant in the recent past: an applied science which asks the question how evidence-based practices can be implemented with high quality over wide areas. Apparently this requires a proactive management and support; manuals or one-time training courses do not seem to be sufficient to train competent personnel. However, the effectiveness of a program can be increased two and threefold through good implementation (see the dpt-i blog dated 12.03.2014 "Implementation is key!")[147]

4.3.3

Qualification, training, and continuing education

The previous information have made one thing clear: crime prevention requires specialized knowledge; the demands on those who (are supposed to) implement crime prevention programs and measures in practice have increased.[148] Here, too, science is asked to provide practice with corresponding options – and practice is asked to use these options.

---

[145] In view of „not recommended" approaches, there are considerations whether also to offer a „Red List Prevention" (Bühler/Groeger-Roth 2013).

[146] The expert council of the Foundation German Forum for Crime Prevention developed a „quality criteria catalog for the selection and implementation of effective programs" in connection with the guideline „Development support and prevention of violence for young people" (As of: 16.04.2013 – „work in progress"). It serves to determine the quality of prevention and intervention measures or programs; it can thus be used as a basis for decisions on the selection, use, and support of measures (Foundation DFK 2013).

[147] The above quoted „Impulses" and the „Quality criteria catalog" of the DFK expert council also point to the significance of implementation.

[148] The qualification requirements have not only increased in terms of crime prevention, but also in other – all? – professional areas: Examples for this are for instance today's requirements for educators or the „Academy training wave in the police" (Schwind 2013, Section 1 marginal note 30b).

In addition to "protagonist-internal" training and continuing education[149] there is the "Beccaria qualification program" which ends with the certificate "Specialist for crime prevention", the Master's degree

"Preventive social work with afocus on criminology and crime prevention" at the Ostfalia University for Applied Sciences, and a few Master's degrees in criminology.[150]

Since 2008, the State Prevention Council Lower Saxony has offered an annual "Beccaria qualification program for crime prevention" and trains persons who are active in crime prevention. The training consists of four modules: criminology, crime prevention, project management, and project supervision. The content is scientifically founded and at the same time application-oriented. The participants are then qualified to evaluate criminological theories and empirical studies critically, develop and implement prevention projects using the latest scientific insights and data, and apply methods of project management.

The course is designed to be parallel to work, lasts one year, and every module includes two weekends. After completing all four modules, the certificate "Specialist for crime prevention" is awarded. At the moment there are more than 120 specialists.

The program was evaluated externally for the first time in 2012 and awarded the "Milestone in crime prevention" award in 2013 (www.beccaria-qualitaetsinitiative.de; see also Meyer 2008 and 2010; Marks 2014).

In the winter semester 2011, the Ostfalia University for Applied Sciences (faculty of social work) in Wolfenbüttel started the consecutive Master's degree "Preventive social work with emphasis on criminology and crime prevention". The concept for the major comes from the "Beccaria project: Training and continuing education in crime prevention" of the State Prevention Council Lower Saxony. The course is designed as full-time major (standard study period four semesters) and suitable for students who acquired their technical and professional qualifications through a major in social work and/or comparable majors and possibly have already been exposed to practical work (www.master-kriminalpraevention.de; see also Meyer 2012; Marks 2014).[151]

---

[149] Corresponding options can be found – even though there is plenty of room for growth - at technical colleges for social work or – for the police – at the technical colleges for public administration and the police education institutions. For instance the technical college for public administration NRW in its „Module manual for Bachelor's degree PVD 2012" identifies the module „crime analysis and police crime prevention". At the German College for Police, the "subject area 13: criminology and interdisciplinary crime prevention" has been installed, which not only offers events in the area of „criminology/crime prevention" as part of the annual training program but also is responsible for several modules in the curriculum of the Master's degree „Public administration – police management"; this includes the module „Crime – phenomenon and intervention" which also includes „crime prevention as general social responsibility".

[150] See the corresponding contributions from Albrecht et. al. (Publ.)(2013).

[151] The vision is an additional work-parallel education course „Crime prevention" for everyone who wants to study in parallel with their work; it combines didactically sensible live presentations and virtual learning based on new

4.4

Summary and conclusions

Crime prevention should be based on evidence, i.e. on the basis of theoretical and empirical scientific insights. Prevention practice and prevention policy thus require science and research.

The fact the prevention policy looks different in reality, at least on the federal level, has already been discussed. At the communal and state levels, policy makers appear to be more open to evidence. In the meantime, this is also the case for prevention practice.

This is not lastly due to science having performed numerous "services" for practice and has increasingly and systematically supported prevention practice. For instance through documentation and the development of databases for commissions and projects, in the meantime also by creating a database for recommended prevention projects; through the development of standards for the area of planning, implementation, and evaluation of crime prevention programs and projects; through the conception and implementation of qualification programs, training and continuing education programs, and courses for the area of crime prevention.

Prevention practice is not only provided with the necessary theoretical and empirical scientific insights, but the planning, implementation, and effect of prevention measures and programs (implementation and evaluation) is scientifically monitored and verified. In particular evaluation has become a lot more matter of course in the meantime – for supported projects it is generally an obligation - and implementation research is gaining in significance.

Evaluation should be a core goal of prevention policy, in particular in the form of lasting regulatory impact assessment, evaluation of the usefulness of a law, and monitoring of the parameters originally targeted by the law. Not just in terms of legislative activities but especially also for practical prevention policy up to the level of cities and municipalities (Becker 2012, 209 et seq.).

The time which research takes in general can become a problem. Practice and policy want to – must – act as quickly as possible in order to remedy recognized problems. But science needs time to be able to make well-founded statements about effects or lack thereof.

It is likely as difficult in prevention practice as in prevention policy to perform empirical studies and collect data before a prevention measure has started and/or a law passed. However, in the meantime prevention science has created a large stock of

---

information and communication media (Marks 2014).

knowledge about what works or does not work, what makes sense in criminal policy and what doesn't – you just have to ask.

Another problem could be that research is generally performed with open-ended results, but policy and practice would like confirmation that what they are doing is correct.

Fundamental problems could arise from the current position of criminology as relevant reference science: While Germany has a highly developed theoretical and empirical science of criminology, it is apparently seriously endangered due to "structural depletion". Criminology is not only being reduced at law schools but also at institutes of psychology and sociology. A lot of criminological research takes place outside of the criminology of law schools and is significantly dispersed over various scientific disciplines. However, this also means that criminological questions enjoy widespread scientific interest.

Still, teaching should be intensified at the Universities, in particular in sociological and law schools, and the diverse criminological activities bundled, coordinated, and thus promoted through the development of interdisciplinary Central Criminological Offices (see "Freiburg Memorandum").

However, the close association between criminology and penal law should be dissolved and criminology established as an independent social science. A well-positioned criminology department is a necessary (if not sufficient) prerequisite for the implementation of the requirement for interdisciplinary prevention science.

We welcome the 2012 foundation (for an initial 5 years) of the endowment chair "Crime prevention and risk management" at the University Tübingen, under the sponsorship of the Foundation German Forum for Crime Prevention. In order to give crime prevention the necessary weight in the research spectrum of criminology and other disciplines, it is necessary to demand that this Chair be financed past 2017 and be made permanent.

A chance for criminology and other sciences is the significance of the **media** for policy: If the relevant sciences can manage to bring their findings and the resulting demands into the media, they might then also be able to find a (more) open ear in policy. Not only scientists with great communication skills and the talent to "sell their products" are needed, but also good science journalism interested in criminal policy questions.

5

Crime prevention requires prevention practice, prevention policy, and prevention science

5.1

The German Congress of Crime Prevention (DPT)[152]

There is probably no better example to illustrate this year's main topic of the DPT, "Prevention requires practice, policy, and science", and to show whether and how far this demand has become reality than the DPT itself.

Founded in 1995 as a national annual congress especially for the field of crime prevention, its goal was from the beginning to represent and strengthen crime prevention in an interdisciplinary and inter-departmental manner and in a wide social framework. By and by, the German Congress of Crime Prevention also opened for institutions, projects, methods, questions, and insights from other areas of work in prevention.

The Congress turns in particular to responsibility carriers in prevention from agencies, communities, cities, and districts, health care system, youth aid, justice, churches, media, politics, police, prevention commissions, projects, schools, sports, associations and societies, science etc. - i.e. practice, policy, and science!

The German Congress of Crime Prevention, as an annual national congress, wants to

- convey and exchange current and fundamental questions in different areas of work of prevention and its effectiveness,
- bring partners in prevention together,
- be a forum for practice and make an exchange of experiences possible,
- make international connections, help in the exchange of information, and discuss implementation strategies,
- develop and issue recommendations to practice, policy, administration, and science.

In the meantime, the German Congress of Crime Prevention is the largest European congress especially for the field of crime prevention and related prevention areas. It thrives on the good cooperation of many people and institutions. The annual congresses take place over two days in different cities and are segmented into the central areas plenary events (opening and closing plenary), presentations and project spots, the exhibition that accompanies the congress, and the prevention workshop. The participants are mainly full-time workers in prevention and, for the most part, engaged in the practical implementation of measures and programs. They work in administration,

---

[152] www.praeventionstag.de; and Marks 2013.

management, or direction as well as in research. The largest number of members comes from the police, followed by the areas of social work, community, NGOs, state and federal agencies, science, justice, economy, schools, medicine, and sports.

The German Congress of Crime Prevention presents itself on the internet as an information and documentation platform, since 2010 also with the search-portal "dpt-map", which provides targeted searches for projects, measures, institutions, and persons from the entire field of crime prevention and related prevention areas.

The internet documentation includes all abstracts and text, film, and presentation documents of the previous German Congresses of Crime Prevention.

Since July 2011, the German Congress of Crime Prevention has been publishing the daily Prevention News, which provides information about prevention events and documents from the areas of prevention practice, research, and policy. Like the German Congress of Crime Prevention itself, the Prevention News is thus an excellent example for how far the demand "Prevention requires practice, policy, and science" has already become a reality.

5.2

The DPT institute for applied prevention research (dpt-i)[153]

In order to strengthen the development of the German Congress of Crime Prevention into a forum for the discourse between practice, policy, and science and develop it systematically, another work area of the German Congress of Crime Prevention started in 2013, the DPT Institute for Applied Prevention Research (dpt-i).

Prevention research is understood as a multi-disciplinary approach which integrates the knowledge, methods, and standards of various scientific disciplines and departments, including sociology, psychology, education science, biology, medicine, political science, legal science, economy, criminology, and victimology.

For the dpt-i, prevention research includes[154] the scientific study of

- social distributions and frequencies of events and conditions to be prevented, such as crime, violence, addiction, physical and mental illness, insecurity situations etc.
- causes and genesis conditions of these events and situations,

---

[153]   www.praeventionstag.de/nano.cms/dpt-institut and Marks 2013, 140 et seq.

[154]   In reference to the understanding of the international „Society for Prevention Research" (SPR) and the „European Society for Prevention Research" (EUSPR). The Mission Statement of the SPR states: „The Society for Prevention Research is an organization dedicated to advancing scientific investigation on the etiology and prevention of social, physical and mental health, and academic problems and on the translation of that information to promote health and wellbeing" (www.preventionresearch.org and www.euspr. org.).

- development, guidance, and evaluation of effective interventions for the prevention of these events and situations, and

- support of a wide-spread implementation of verified interventions under "real world" conditions.

In order to achieve its goals, prevention research depends on multi-disciplinary cooperation and a partnership with prevention practice and prevention policy. The dpt-i thus understands its role as an active supporter of partnerships between research, practice, and policy.

The dpt-i sees its general responsibilities especially in

- the implementation of its own research projects with the perspective of the practical application of research results,

- cooperation with other scientific institutions to implement research projects with practical relevance,

- deepening the dialog between science, policy, administration, associations, and civil society concerning the results of prevention research with the goal of a greater reliance on knowledge in the entire field of prevention,

- consultation of the German Congress of Crime Prevention and its partner organizations concerning the results and the status of prevention research.

5.3

Summary and conclusions

The German Congress of Crime Prevention (DPT) is probably the best example for how far the demand that crime prevention requires prevention practice, prevention policy, and prevention science has already become a reality. This cannot only be seen in its development from really humble beginnings – 1995 in Lübeck with 168 registered congress participants and a very reasonable program of this "work conference" - up to the last, the 18th DPT 2013 in Bielefeld with almost 2,000 congress participants from 17 identified work areas, an extensive program (169 speakers for presentations and project pots alone), information booths, special exhibits etc. The evaluation results (DPT is evaluated since the 13th DPT) find: "In total, the evaluation results show that the 18th German Congress of Crime Prevention can be called an successful event.

Almost 92% of the surveyed visitors thought that the 18th German Congress of Crime Prevention was very good or good." The German Congress of Crime Prevention has without a question developed into an important forum for the discourse between practice, science, and policy in the field of crime prevention.

In 2013 another field of work started with the "DPT institute for applied prevention research" (dpt-i) in order to strengthen this development and develop it systematically. An important task of this institute could be developing a systematic strategy for crime prevention based on the findings on performance and deficits of the areas of prevention practice, prevention policy, and prevention science as well as on the demands and challenges.

Literature

Albrecht, Hans-Jörg (2013): On the situation of criminology in Germany – An introduction. Mschr- Krim 96. Volume - Issue 2/3 2013, pp. 73-80.

Albrecht, Hans-Jörg (2013 b): Recidivism statistics in international comparison. MschrKrim 96. Volume - Issue 5 – 2013, pp. 400-410.

Albrecht, Hans-Jörg et. al. (publ.)(2013): On the situation of criminology in Germany. Contributions of the conference from June 28 - 30, 2012 at the Max-Planck Institute for foreign and international penal law, Freiburg i. Br. MschrKrim 96. Volume - Issue 2/3 – 2013.

Albrecht, Hans-Jörg et. al. (Publ.)(2012): Freiburg Memorandum. On the situation of criminology in Germany. Also reprinted in MschrKrim 95. Volume - Issue 6 – 2012, pp. 385-391.

Arbeitsstelle Kinder- und Jugendkriminalitätsprävention [Office for Children's and Juvenile Crime Prevention] (Publ.)(2007): Strategies of violence prevention in children and adolescents. An interim result in six fields of action. Munich.

Bannenberg, Britta et. al. (Publ.)(2005): Communal crime prevention. Selected contributions of the

9th German Congress of Crime Prevention. May 17-18, 2004 in Stuttgart. Godesberg.

Bannenberg, Britta/Rössner, Dieter (2002): Effect research in crime prevention. Forum Crime Prevention 1/2002, pp. 5-8.

Becker, Monika (2013): Questions to criminology ... from the perspective of criminal policy. MschrKrim 96. Volume - Issue 2/3 2013, pp. 207-211.

Report on living situation of young people and the services of the children's and youth organizations in Germany – 11th Children's and Youth Report – with statement by the federal government. Deutscher Bundestag. 14th legislative period. Printed material 14/8181 dated 04.02.2002.

Boers, Klaus/Seddig, Daniel (2013): Criminological research and teaching at German Universities in 2012. MschrKrim 96. Volume - Issue 2/3 2013, pp. 115-126.

Boers, Klaus et. al. (Publ.)(2013): Criminology – criminal policy – penal law. Commemorative publication on the 70th birthday of Hans-Jürgen Kerner. Mohr Siebeck Tübingen.

Bühler, Anneke/Groeger-Roth; Frederick (2013): Do we need a "Red list prevention"? What is not recommended in prevention? In: Kerner, Hans-Jürgen/ Marks, Erich (Publ.): Internet documentation of the German Congress of Crime Prevention. Hanover 2013 (www.praeventionstag.de/Dokumentation. cms/2361).

Federal Ministry of the Interior/Federal Ministry of Justice (Publ.)(2006): Second PSR [Periodical security report]. Berlin.

Federal Ministry of the Interior/Federal Ministry of Justice (Publ.)(2001): Second PSR. Berlin.

Dialog on Germany's future. Results report of expert dialog of Federal Chancellor
    2011/2012. Publ. from press and information office of the federal govern-
    ment. Berlin.

Dölling, Dieter et. al. (2006): Meta-analysis of empirical deterrent studies. Study
    approach and first empirical findings. Darmstadt discussion papers in econo-
    mics, No. 170 (http://hdl.handle.net/10419/32076).

DVJJ – Deutsche Vereinigung for Jugendgerichte and Jugendgerichtshilfen [German
    Association for Youth Courts and Youth Court Aid] (Publ.)(2007): Together
    with distributed roles. Position on youth crime prevention. Hanover.

Eisner, Manuel/Ribeaud, Denis/Bittel, Stéphanie (2006): Prevention of youth vio-
    lence. Paths to an evidence-based prevention policy. Publ. by the Confedera-
    te Commission for Foreigners EKA. Bern-Wabern.

11th Children's and Youth Report, see Report on living situation of young people ...

Entorf, Horst (2013): Criminology, economy, and economy of crime: common
    contents, different approaches. MschrKrim 96. Volume - Issue 2/3 2013, pp.
    164-171.

EUCPN – European Crime Prevention Network (2013): Crime prevention activities
    at the EU, national and local level. Thematic Paper No. 4. EUCPN Secreta-
    riat. Brussels.

Feltes, Thomas (2012): The role of police in crime prevention. ZJJ 1, pp. 35-39.

Fontanille, Elsa (2013): European visions on the future of prevention. Forum Crime
    Prevention 1/2013, pp. 64-66.

Freiburg Memorandum (2012) see Albrecht, Hans-Jörg et. al. (Publ.)(2012)

Frevel, Bernhard (Publ.)(2012): Fields of action of local security policy. Networks,
    policy design, and perspectives. Frankfurt.

Frevel, Bernhard/Kober, Marcus (2012): Perspectives of cooperative security policy.
    In: Frevel, Bernhard (Publ.)(2012), pp. 337-358.

Frevel, Bernhard/Miesner, Christian (2012): The research project cooperative secu-
    rity policy in cities – KoSiPol. In: E. Marks/W. Steffen (Publ.)(2012), pp.
    215-219.

Frevel, Bernhard et. al. (2009): Citizen involvement in communal crime prevention:
    Contributions from current research (Part I) on concept and reality. In: E.
    Marks/W. Steffen (Publ.) (2009), pp. 143-160.

Fuchs, Marek et. al. (2005): Violence in schools 1994 – 1999 – 2004. Wiesbaden.

Görgen, Thomas (2013): Field of tension science and practice: Where is crime
    prevention going? 3rd Symposium – German sponsorship award Crime Pre-
    vention. Bielefeld (unpublished manuscript; a brief excerpt can be found in
    Forum Crime Prevention 3/2013, p. 41).

Groeger-Roth, Frederick (2012): "Communities That Care – CTC" in practice.
    Results and experiences from the model trial SPIN in Lower Saxony. Forum
    Crime Prevention 3/2012, pp. 2-6.

Groeger-Roth, Frederick/Hasenpusch, Burkhard (2011): The "Green List for Prevention" – a look at effective and promising prevention programs. Forum Crime Prevention 4/2011, pp. 52-58.

Hahlen, Johann (2012): Policy consulting – an experience report from both sides with a look at the two Periodical Security Reports. In: Hilgendorf, Eric/Rengier, Rudolf (Publ.)(2012), pp. 109- 123.

Hanke, Ottmar (2007): Strategies of prevention of violence at schools. In: Office (Publ.)(2007), pp. 104-130.

Heinz, Wolfgang (2013): What legislators should want to know? or: For what subjects should legislators have current and reliable information from crime and penal law statistics? In: Boers, Klaus et. al. (Publ.)(2013), p. 345-357.

Heinz, Wolfgang (2011): New lust for punishment in justice – reality or myth? NK 1/2011, pp. 14-27.

Heinz, Wolfgang (2007): "cause for concern", "dramatic" ... Some current data for classification and assessment of crime policy discussion. ZJJ 1/07, pp. 65-72.

Heinz, Wolfgang (2006): On the status of unreported crime research in Germany. In: Commemorative publication on the 65th birthday of Helmut Kury, p. 241-263.

Heinz, Wolfgang (2005): Communal crime prevention from a scientific point of view. In: Bannenberg, Britta et. al. (Publ.)(2005), pp. 9-30.

Heinz, Wolfgang (2003): The contribution of the "1st PSR" to crime prevention. In: Kerner, H.-J./Marks, E. (Publ.): Internet documentation German Congress of Crime Prevention. Hanover.

Heinz, Wolfgang (1998): Crime prevention. Comments on an overdue course correction in criminal policy. In: Kerner, Hans-Jürgen et. al. (Publ.)(1998), pp. 17-59.

Hermann, Dieter/Jantzer, Vanessa (2012): School social work – crime prevention effects and improvement possibilities. In: E. Marks/W. Steffen (Publ.)(2012), pp. 207-229.

Hilgendorf, Eric/Rengier, Rudolf (Publ.)(2012): Commemorative publication on the 70th birthday of Wolfgang Heinz. Baden-Baden.

Holthusen, Bernd/Glaser, Michaela (2013): Office positions as new project type of DJI. DJI Impulses – 50 years of DJI. 2/2013, 71 -72

Holthusen, Bernd/Hoops, Sabrina (2012): Crime prevention in childhood and adolescence. On role, contribution, and significance of children's and youth organizations. ZJJ 1/2012, pp. 23-28.

Holthusen, Bernd et. al. (2011): On the need for professional and reflective prevention. DJI Impulses 2.2011, pp. 22-25.

Holthusen, Bernd/Schäfer, Heiner (2007): Strategies for the prevention of violence in children's and youth aid for young people. In: Office (Publ.)(2007), 131-168.

Jasch, Michael (2003): Communal crime prevention in crisis. MschrKrim, 86th Volume, Issue 6/2003, pp. 411-420.

Jerke ,Viktoria: Success factor cooperation in police crime prevention. Forum Crime Prevention 4/2013, 40-41.

John, Tobias/Schulze, Verena (2012): Cooperative security policy in cities (KoSi-Pol). Report on research project. Forum Crime Prevention 3/2012, pp. 4-6.

Kahl, Wolfgang (2014): European network for crime prevention (EUCPN). Forum Crime Prevention 1/2014, pp. 36-37.

Kahl, Wolfgang (2013): Editorial for Forum Crime Prevention 4/2013, pp. 2-3.

Kahl, Wolfgang (2013 a): 19th German Congress for Crime Prevention. May 12-13, 2014 in Karlsruhe. Forum Crime Prevention 4/2013, pp. 39.

Kahl, Wolfgang (2012): "Good social policy is the best criminal policy" and prevents the road to a surveillance society – On the (mis)understanding of the prevention idea. Forum Crime Prevention 2/2012, pp. 26-27.

Kahl, Wolfgang (2011): 10 years of DFK – interim report on the road "to a better tomorrow". Forum Crime Prevention 3/2011, pp. 4-6.

Kahl, Wolfgang/Kober, Marcus (2009): Citizen involvement in communal crime prevention: Contributions from current research (Part 2) On the possibilities for development. In: E. Marks/W. Steffen (Publ.)(2009), pp. 161-170.

Koop, Gerd (2013): Questions to criminology ... from the perspective of the penal system. MschrKrim 96th Volume - Issue 2/3 2013, pp. 202-206.

Kerner, Hans-Jürgen (2013): Application-oriented criminological research: opportunities and risks. MschrKrim 96th Volume - Issue 2/3 2013, pp. 184-201.

Kerner, Hans-Jürgen (2012): 10 years Foundation German Forum for Crime Prevention (DFK). Congratulatory words of a companion, with review of historical development of prevention in legislation and practice. In: Annual report 2011 of the Foundation German Forum for Crime Prevention. Bonn, pp. 28-44.

Kerner, Hans-Jürgen et. al. (Publ.)(1998): The development of crime prevention in Germany. At the same time documentation of the 3rd German Congress of Crime Prevention in Bonn on May 5-7, 1997. Godesberg.

Coalition agreement between CDU, CSU, and SPD: Shaping Germany's future. 18th legislative period.

Kober, Marcus/Kahl, Wolfgang (2012): Impulses for communal prevention management. Insights and recommendations for the organization and work of crime prevention commissions at the communal level. Foundation German Forum for Crime Prevention (DFK)(Publ.), 2nd completely revised edition 2012. Bonn

Koop, Gerd (2013): Questions to criminology ... from the perspective of the penal system. MschrKrim 96th Volume - Issue 2/3 – 2013, pp. 202-206.

Kreuzer, Arthur (2013): Commonplaces, populist but also sensible projects. The criminal policy program of the coalition agreement – a critical review. Guest contribution for the Gießener Allgemeine dated 4.12.2013.

Kunz, Karl-Ludwig (2013 a): Historical foundation of criminology in Germany and its development to an independent scientific discipline. MschrKrim 96th Volume - Issue 2/3 2013, pp. 81-114.

Kunz, Karl-Ludwig (2013 b): On the concept "punitive" and its development in international comparison. In: Klaus Boers et. al. (Publ.)(2013), pp. 113-125.

Kunz, Karl-Ludwig (2011): Criminology. 6th, completely revised and updated edition. Haupt Verlag Bern et. al.

Kury, Helmut (2013): More punishment - less crime: do (harsher) punishments work?
In: Kerner, Hans- Jürgen/Marks, Erich (Publ.): Internet documentation of the German Congress of Crime Prevention. Hanover 2013 (www.praeventions-tag.de/Dokumentation.cms/2339).

Lamnek, Siegfried (1990): The problem of crime reporting in the mass media. MschrKrim 73th Volume, Issue 3 – 1990, pp. 163-176.

State parliament North Rhine-Westphalia (2010): Report of the enquete commission to develop proposals for an effective prevention policy in North Rhine-Westphalia. Düsseldorf,

State Council for crime prevention Mecklenburg-Western Pomerania (LfK)(Publ.) (2011): impulse. prevention works. Business report of LfK 2010/2011. Schwerin.

State Council for crime prevention Mecklenburg-Western Pomerania (LfK)(Publ.) (o.J): impulse. EUROs for prevention. The support program of the State Council for crime prevention. Schwerin.

State Council for crime prevention Mecklenburg-Western Pomerania (LfK)(Publ.) (o.J.): 10 GOOD REASONS. Why and how communal prevention councils should be installed. Schwerin.

Lösel, Friedrich (2013): Criminology and psychology – development and status with special reference to Germany. MschrKrim 96th Volume - Issue 2/3 2013, pp. 153-163.

Marks, Erich (2014): On some crime prevention developments between 1978 and 2013. In: Dirk Baier/Thomas Mößle (Publ.)(2014): Criminology is a social science. Commemorative publication on the 70th birthday of Christian Pfeiffer. Baden-Baden, pp. 443-466.

Marks, Erich (2013): The German Congress of Crime Prevention – an interim report 1993-2013. In: Boers, Klaus et. al. (Publ.)(2013), pp. 128-142.

Marks, Erich (2011): The International Center for Crime Prevention ICPC. In: Kerner, Hans-Jürgen/Marks, Erich (Publ.): Internet documentation of the German Congress of Crime Prevention. Hanover (www. praeventionstag.de/ Dokumentation.cms/1671).

Marks, Erich/Schairer, Martin (2010): New German-European Forum for Urban Security (DEFUS). In: Kerner, H.-J./Marks, E. (Publ.): Internet documentation of the German Congress of Crime Prevention. Hanover 2010, www. praeventionstag.de/Dokumentation.cms/1030.

Marks, Erich/Steffen, Wiebke (Publ.)(2013): Living safely in cities and the country-
    side. Selected contributions of the 17th German Congress of Crime Preventi-
    on 2012. Forum Verlag Godesberg.
Marks, Erich/Steffen, Wiebke (Publ.)(2012): Education – prevention – future. Selec-
    ted contributions of the 15th German Congress of Crime Prevention 2010.
    Godesberg.
Marks, Erich/Steffen, Wiebke (Publ.)(2011): Living (in) solidarity – ensuring diver-
    sity. Selected contributions of the 14th German Congress of Crime Preventi-
    on 2009. Godesberg.
Marks, Erich/Steffen, Wiebke (Publ.)(2009): Involved citizens – safe society. Selec-
    ted contributions of the 13th German Congress of Crime Prevention 2008.
    Godesberg.
Melzer, Wolfgang (2013): Crime prevention at schools – between individual projects
    and school development (Presentation 18th DPT, Bielefeld 2013, in print).
Melzer, Wolfgang et al. (2012): Bullying and violence at schools. Development
    trends from 2002 to 2010. Healthcare system 2012; 74 (Suppl 1), pp. 76-83.
Melzer, Wolfgang/Schubarth, Wilfried/Ehninger, Frank (2011): Prevention of vio-
    lence and school development. 2nd, revised edition. Bad Heilbrunn.
Melzer, Wolfgang/Schwind, Hans-Dieter (Publ.)(2004): Prevention of violence in
    school. Foundations – practical models – perspectives. Documentation of
    the 15th Mainz Victim Forum 2003. Mainz writings on situation of crime
    victims. Volume 38. Baden-Baden.
Meyer, Anja (2012): Professionalism through qualification: New Master's degree
    "Preventive social work with emphasis on criminology & crime prevention".
    Forum Crime Prevention 1/2012, pp. 2-3.
Meyer, Anja (2019): Quality through competence. The Beccaria qualification
    program. In: Kerner, Hans-Jürgen/Marks, Erich (Publ.): Internet documen-
    tation of the German Congress of Crime Prevention. Hanover 2010 (www.
    praeventionstag.de/Dokumentation.cms/1031).
Meyer, Anja (2008): Qualification in crime prevention. ZJJ 3/2008, pp. 368-370.
Mielenz, Ingrid (2013): The DJI between science and practice – possibilities and li-
    mits of policy consulting. DJI Impulses – 50 years of DJI. 2/2013, pp. 78-79.
Mischkowitz, Robert (2013): Questions to criminology ... from the perspective of
    the police. MschrKrim 96th Volume - Issue 2/3 2013, pp. 212-221.
Müller, Thomas (2010): Requirements for an optimal support of communal preventi-
    on commissions. In: Kerner, H.-J./Marks, E. (Publ.): Internet documentation
    of the German Congress of Crime Prevention. Hanover 2010, www.praventi-
    onstag.de/Dokumentation.cms/1110
Müller, Thomas (2004): Communal prevention commissions in Lower Saxony
    (http://www.lpr.niedersachsen.de/Landespraeventionsrat/Module/Publikatio-
    nen/Dokumente/20050606_2_F87.pdf).
Ohder, Claudius (2010): A look back to the future. In: Evaluation and quality deve-

lopment in violence and crime prevention. Documentation of the 10th Berlin prevention congress 2009. Berlin. pp. 14-20.

Ostendorf, Heribert (2005): Critical reflections on crime prevention. Hanover (www. dvjj.de; Conference: Prevention at any cost?).

Ostendorf, Heribert (2002): Opportunities and risks of crime prevention. In: Berliner Forum Crime Prevention. Special edition 5. Documentation of the 2nd Berlin Prevention Congress on October 10, 2001. Berlin, pp. 16-24.

Pfeiffer, Christian et. al. (2004): The media, evil and us. MschrKrim 87th Volume: Issue 6/2004, pp. 425-435.

Pluto, Liane/van Santen, Eric/Seckinger, Mike (2014): Life situations of juveniles as starting point of communal policy design. An expert opinion on participation-oriented survey of youth policy needs. DJI Deutsches Jugendinstitut. Munich.

Program Police Crime Prevention of the States and the Federation (Publ.)(2012): Annual report 2012. Commission for Police Crime Prevention of the States and the Federation. Stuttgart.

Program Police Crime Prevention of the States and the Federation (Publ.)(2009): Quality assurance in police work. Work aid for planning, implementation, and assessment of projects. Stuttgart.

PSR (2006): Second PSR see Federal Ministry of the Interior/Federal Ministry of Justice (Publ.)(2006)

PSR (2001): First PSR see Federal Ministry of the Interior/Federal Ministry of Justice (Publ.)(2001)

Redo, Slawomir Marek (2012): Blue Criminology. The power of United Nations ideas to counter crime globally. A monographic study. Helsinki.

Remschmidt, Helmut (2013): Criminology and forensic children's and youth psychiatry: The significance of the developmental perspective. MschrKrim 96th Volume - Issue 2/3 2013, pp. 172-183.

Reuband, Karl-Heinz (2013): Criminology and sociology. Position in scientific system and scientific public. MschrKrim 96th Volume - Issue 2/3 2013, pp. 140-152.

Reuband, Karl-Heinz (2010): Dimensions of punitive measures and social change. NK 4/2010, pp. 143- 148.

Scheerer, Sebastian (1978): The political-publicistic amplification cycle. On the influence of mass media in the process of penal law norm genesis. KrimJ 10, Issue 3, pp. 223-227.

Schneider, Hans-Joachim (2010): European criminology at the start of the 21st century. Crime, criminology, and criminal policy in Europe. MschrKrim 93th Volume - Issue 6/2010, pp. 475-501.

Schöch, Heinz (2013): Applied criminology. In: Boers et. al. (Publ.), pp. 207-220.

Schöch, Heinz (1994): General prevention from a criminological perspective. In: The Attorney General of the State of Schleswig-Holstein (Publ.)(1994):

What insights in the social sciences can penal law practice implement? Educational event on September 29-30 in the Evangelical Academy Bad Segeberg, pp. 76-83.

Schöch, Heinz (1985): Empirical foundation of general prevention. In: Theo Vogler et al. (Publ.)(1985): Commemorative publication on the 70th birthday of Hans-Heinrich Jescheck. Berlin, pp.1081-1105.

Schreiber, Verena (2007): Local prevention commissions in Germany. Forum Human Geography 2. Frankfurt.

Schubarth, Wilfried (2010): Violence and bullying at schools. Possibilities of prevention and intervention. Stuttgart.

Schubarth, Wilfried (2001): Juvenile violence as economic topic in the media. New criminal policy 3/2001, pp. 24-29.

Schwind, Hans-Dieter (2013): Criminology. A practice-oriented introduction with examples. 22nd, revised and updated edition. Criminology Heidelberg et. al.

Schwind, Hans-Dieter (2000): Has the (anti) violence commission worked in vain? Crime prevention 2/2000, 45-54.

Schwind, Hans-Dieter/Baumann, Jürgen (Publ.)(1990): Causes, prevention, and control of violence. Analyses and suggestions of the independent government commission for the prevention of and fight against violence (Violence Commission). Volume I. Final expert opinion and interim opinion of work groups. Berlin.

Schwind, Hans-Dieter/Steinhilper, Gernot (2014): Memories of the genesis of the KFN. In: Baier, Dirk/Mößle, Thomas (Publ.)(2014): Criminology is a social science. Commemorative publication on the 70th birthday of Christian Pfeiffer. Baden-Baden, pp. 593-603.

Sessar, Klaus (2011): Editorial: Thoughts on the future of criminology in Germany. MschrKrim 94th Volume - Issue 5/2011, pp. I-V.

Spiess, Gerhard (2012): Three test pieces for the assessment of juvenile penal law diversion practice - a study using recidivism statistical findings. In: Hilgendorf, Eric/Rengier, Rudolf (Publ.)(2012), pp. 287-305.

Steffen, Wiebke (2013 a): Security as a basic need of humans and responsibility of the government. Report for the 17th German Congress of Crime Prevention. April 16 & 17, 2012 in Munich. In: E. Marks/W. Steffen (Publ.)(2013), pp. 47-119.

Steffen, Wiebke (2013 b): Prevention is too important to be left just to the police. Thoughts on the significance of police crime prevention in the context of crime prevention as a general social responsibility. In: Boers, Klaus et al. (Publ.)(2013), pp. 485-498.

Steffen, Wiebke (2013 c): Communal crime prevention – an interim report. Presentation at the Seminar 8/2013 of the DHPol on 14.02.2013 (unpublished).

Steffen, Wiebke (2012 a): Security as a basic need of humans and responsibility of the government. Report for the 17th German Congress of Crime Prevention, April 16 & 17, 2012 in Munich. In: E. Marks/W. Steffen (Publ.)(2012), pp. 47-119.

Steffen, Wiebke (2012 b): Learning and living situation of children and juveniles as places of education and prevention of violence. Report for the 15th German Congress of Crime Prevention, May 10 & 11, 2010 in Berlin. In: E. Marks/W. Steffen (Publ.)(2012), pp. 39-104.

Steffen, Wiebke (2012 c): Communal crime prevention in Germany – Comments on the successes and deficits, risks and side-effects (http://www.kriminal-praevention.bremen.de/sixcms/ media.php/13/01%20-%20Wiebke%20 Steffen.pdf).

Steffen, Wiebke (2011): Modern societies and crime. The contribution of crime prevention to integration and solidarity. Report for the 14th German Congress of Crime Prevention June 8-9, 2009 Hanover. In: E. Marks/W. Steffen (Publ.)(2011), pp. 45-116.

Steffen, Wiebke (2009): Involved citizens – safe society. Citizen involvement in crime prevention. Report for the 13th German Congress of Crime Prevention June 2-3, 2008 in Leipzig. In: E. Marks/W. Steffen (Publ.)(2009), pp. 25-72.

Steffen, Wiebke (2006) a: Crime prevention in Germany: A success story? In: Feltes, Thomas et al. (Publ.)(2006): Criminal policy and its scientific foundations. Commemorative publication on the 70th birthday of Dr. Hans-Dieter Schwind. C.F.Müller Verlag Heidelberg, pp. 1141-1154.

Steffen, Wiebke (2006 b): Police work close to citizens and community-oriented in Germany. In: Berg, Manfred et al. (Publ.)(2006): Penal law in the US and Germany. History and recent developments. Heidelberg, 117-128.

Steffen, Wiebke (2005): Commissions of communal crime prevention – inventory and perspective. In: Bannenberg, Britta et. al. (Publ.)(2005), pp. 156-167.

Steffen, Wiebke (2004): Communal crime prevention in Germany: A success story? Forum Crime Prevention 4/2004, pp. 18-21.

Steffen, Wiebke (2002): Community policing or police work close to citizens: A new challenge? Forum Crime Prevention 1/2002, 11-13.

Steffen, Wiebke (1995): Changes in the perception of police responsibility – Community orientation as a modern target perspective? In: 50 year of police education in Münster. Series of police leadership academy No. 3/4/1995, 107-122.

Steffen, Wiebke/Hepp, Reinhold (2007): Strategies of police prevention of violence in childhood and adolescence. In: Office (Publ.)(2007), pp. 169-195.

Foundation German Forum for Crime Prevention (Publ.)(2013): Development support and violence prevention for young people. Quality criteria catalog of the DFK expert panel for the selection and implementation of effective programs.

Foundation German Forum for Crime Prevention (Publ.)(2013): Development support and violence prevention for young people. Impulses of the DFK expert panel for the selection and implementation of effective programs – a guideline for practice.

Stolpe, Oliver (2009): An Overview of Crime Prevention at the International Level. In: Coester, Marc/ Marks, Erich /Eds.): International Perspectives of Crime prevention 3. Contributions from the 3rd Annual International Forum 2009. Godesberg, pp. 39-46.

Uhle, Ria (2012): Changes, paradigm shifts, crises – prevention of violence in schools in change. In: E. Marks/W. Steffen (Publ.)(2012), pp. 301-313.

van den Brinck, Henning (2012): A look behind the scenes of communal prevention commissions. Conference report on final symposium of research project "Cooperative security policy in cities" (KoSiPol). Forum Crime Prevention 4/2012, pp. 4-7.

Waller, Irvin (2012): Balanced investments into proven crime prevention. Kriminalistik 7/2012, pp. 415-419.

Waller, Irvin (2011): More law and order! Or rather less crime? Publ. at request of German Congress of Crime Prevention by Burkhard Hasenpusch and Erich Marks. Godesberg.

Welsh, Brandon C./Farrington, David P. (2012): Science, politics, and crime prevention: Toward a new crime policy. Journal of Criminal Justice 40 (2012), pp. 128-133.

Wijckmans, Belinda (2013): European Crime Prevention Network (EUCPN): Crime prevention activities on EU, national, and local level. In: Kerner, Hans-Jürgen/Marks, Erich (Publ.): Internet documentation of German Congress of Crime Prevention. Hanover 2012 (www.praeventionstag.de/Dokumentation.cms/2256).

Ziercke, Jörg (1998): Requirements for a future-oriented, integrated social crime prevention – Need for a federal prevention commission. In: Kerner, Hans-Jürgen et al. (Publ.)(1998), pp. 281-292.

Erich Marks

Prevention requires practice, policy, and science and new concentrated and systematic initiatives

Opening address for the 19th German Congress of Crime Prevention on May 12, 2014 in Karlsruhe

1. Welcome to the 19th German Congress on Crime Prevention

For the start of the 19th German Congress of Crime Prevention I would like to welcome all present Congress participants, guests of honour, and media representatives to the Baden metropolis Karlsruhe. I would especially like to welcome all those people interested in prevention who are connected to the Congress via the internet live or with a time delay.

The German Congress of Crime Prevention and its partner organisations are very gratified about the unwavering support that Europe's biggest annual prevention congress again enjoyed this year.

I ask for your understanding once again this year if I am only able to mention a few persons by name from the large group of this year's prominent Congress participants and guests of honour. The guests of honour include representatives of the Bundestag [German Parliament] and the State Assembly of Baden-Württemberg, the Parliamentary Secretary of State for the Federal Minister for Family, Seniors, Women, and Youth, Ministers and State Secretaries of different departments from several Federal States, numerous mayors, State Administrators, a large number of high-ranking representatives from the areas of Justice, Police, Science, and NGOs, foreign diplomats, numerous Presidents and Directors of Federal and State Agencies, and high-ranking representatives of the partner organisations of the Congress of Crime Prevention. I would like to welcome the following persons by name at this point:

*Jadesola A. **Adesuyi***, Minister, Embassy of the Republic of Nigeria in Germany

*Serhat **Aksen***, Consul General of the Republic of Turkey

*Dr. Nadine **Bals***, Managing Director of the German Association for Juvenile Courts and Juvenile Legal Aid (DVJJ)

*Bianca **Biwer***, Federal Managing Director WEISSER RING

*Prof. Dr. Reihard **Böttcher***, President of the OLG retd., Honorary Chair WEISSER RING

*Prof. Dr. Gerd **Brudermüller***, Honorary Chair of the German Family Court Committee (DFGT)

Arne **Busse**, scientific consultant of the Federal Centre for Political Education (bpb)

Stefan **Daniel**, Managing Member of the Board of the Foundation German Forum for Crime Prevention (DFK)

Thomas **Dittmann**, Assistant Secretary of State in the Federal Ministry of Justice and Consumer Protection (BMJV)

Günther **Ebenschweiger**, President of the Austrian Centre for Crime Prevention

Prof. Dr. Rudolf **Egg**, Director of the Criminological Centre (KrimZ)

Prof. Dr. Manuel **Eisner**, Deputy Director of the Institute of Criminology, University of Cambridge

Saskia **Esken** Member of Bundestag (SPD), member in the Commission for Education, Research, and Technology Impact Assessment and in the committee Digital Agenda of the German Bundestag

Dr. Johannes **Fechner** Member of Bundestag (SPD), member of the Commission for Verification of Credentials, Immunity, and Rules of Procedure as well as the Commission for Justice and Consumer Protection

Prof. Dr. Dean L. **Fixsen**, President of the Global Implementation Initiative, University of North Carolina, USA

Reinhold **Gall** Member of State Assembly, Minister of the Interior of the State Baden-Württemberg

Prof. Dr. Christian **Grafl**, University Vienna and representative of the German Congress of Crime Prevention in Austria

Prof. Dr. Ulf **Gundlach,** Secretary of State in Ministry of the Interior and Sports of the State Saxony-Anhalt

Dr. Wolf-Dietrich **Hammann,** Assistant Secretary of State of the Ministry for Integration Baden- Württemberg

Thierry **Hartmann**, Police Attaché, French Embassy in Germany

Melissa **Hathaway**, Belfer Center for Science and International Affairs, USA

David **Hermanns**, Managing Director CyberForum

Peter **Holzem**, President of the Federal Police Direction Stuttgart

Elizabeth **Johnston,** Secretary General EFUS and Chair of the International Centre for the Prevention of Crime, Paris/Montreal

Eva **Kühne-Hörmann** Member of State Assembly, State Minister of Justice Hessen

Javad **Kazemi**, Ambassador, Embassy of the Islamic Republic of Iran in Germany

Prof. Dr. Hans-Jürgen **Kerner**, Chairman of the German Foundation for Crime Prevention and Aid to Offenders (DVS)

Uwe Leest, Chairman Alliance against Cyber-mobbing

Tina **Mahler**, German Society for international Cooperation (GIZ)

Michel **Marcus**, Secretary General of the French Forum for Urban Security

Caren **Marks,** Parliamentary Secretary of State at the Federal Minister for Family, Seniors, Women, and Youth

Gisela **Mayer,** Chairwoman of the Foundation against Violence at Schools

Prof. Dr. Viktor **Mayer-Schönberger**, Oxford Internet Institute

Dr. Frank **Mentrup**, Mayor of the City of Karlsruhe

Roswitha **Müller-Piepenkötter,** Federal Chairwoman of WEISSER RING

Jürgen **Mutz**, Chairman of the Curatorship of the German Foundation for Crime Prevention and Aid to Offenders (DVS)

Daniel Hark-Mo **Park,** Director of the Delegation of the Korean Institute for Criminology, Seoul

Norbert **Pieper,** Senior Expert, Deutsche Post AG

Guilherme **Pinto**, President of the European Forum for Urban Security (EFUS)

Dr. Elisabeth **Pott,** Director of the Federal Centre for Health Education

Peter **Reckling**, Federal Managing Director of the Professional Association for Social Work, Criminal Law, and Criminal Policy (DBH)

Alexander **Salomon** Member of State Assembly, member of the faction Bündnis 90/ Green party in the State Assembly of Baden-Württemberg

Dr. Martin **Schairer,** Chairman of the German-European Forum for Urbane Security (DEFUS)

*Dr. Uwe **Schlosser**,* Attorney General, Karlsruhe

*Dr. Christoph **Schnaudigel**,* State Administrator of the District of Karlsruhe

*Dieter **Schneider**,* President of the State Criminal Police Baden-Württemberg

*Dr. Hans-Dieter **Schwind**,* President of the Foundation Council of the German Foundation for Crime Prevention and Aid to Offenders (DVS)

*Walter **Staufer**,* consultant of the Federal Centre for Political Education (bpb)

*Dr. Wiebke **Steffen**,* German Congress of Crime Prevention (DPT)

*Katrin **Stüllenberg**,* Chair of the Foundation for Crime Prevention

*Frank **Tempel*** Member of Bundestag (Die Linke party), deputy Chairman of the Interior Commission of the German Bundestag

*Gerd **Thielmann**,* vice president of the German University of the Police

*Matthieu **Tsangu*** Makukula, Embassy Council, Embassy of the Democratic Republic of Congo in Germany

*Florencia Eugenia **Vilanova de von Oehsen**,* Consul General of El Salvador

*Jörg **Ziercke**,* President of the Federal Criminal Police

*Dr. Herbert O. **Zinell**,* Assistant Secretary of State of the Ministry of the Interior, Baden-Württemberg

I would like to extend a special welcome, connected with heartfelt gratitude for your great personal commitment, to the many hundreds of active members who made this "grand opus" of the 19th German Congress of Crime Prevention in Karlsruhe possible in the first place. Your commitment, in many cases on a volunteer basis, covers a very wide area, from presentations and moderation to technical and organisational support. Already at the start of the Congress, I would like to thank our hosting event partners, the State of Baden-Württemberg, and especially the City of Karlsruhe for 9 months of intensive, successful, and very pleasant joint preparation work. The Karlsruhe section of the Congress has set new standards in many ways and I will certainly remember them under the category of "shared attention" (in the best sense) due to their attentive and shared work for a common goal.

2. The Congress - an overview

The 19th German Congress of Crime Prevention is segmented into four central sections with several sub-sections. All presentations are documented in the Congress catalogue with abstracts and additional supplemental materials and are also available in digital form on the website www.praeventionstag.de:

1. Plenary events

- Opening of Congress
- Evening event in Garden Hall at the invitation of the State of Baden-Württemberg and the City of Karlsruhe
- Final plenary
- Presentations
- on the main topic and current prevention topics
- Project spots
- Forum Youth Aid (DJI)
- Media forum (bpb)
- Congress opinion
- 8th Annual International Forum (AIF)
- Special events

2. Exhibit

- Actions
- Campus
- Info booths
- Posters
- Special exhibits

3. Workshop

- Accompanying events
- Stage
- Film forum
- Presentation on demand
- Student university

Overall, the 19th German Congress of Crime Prevention offers more than **200 presentations**. Parallel to the Congress, ca. **250 professional organisations** will present themselves with exhibits, on the Congress stage, and in the film forum.

Leading up to the Congress, the mentioned criminologist, **Dr. Wiebke Steffen**, again presented a **scientific opinion** on the main topic of the 19th German Congress of Crime Prevention "Prevention requires practice, policy, and science" which was already widely noted and discussed in the time leading up to the Congress. The opinion is also the basis for the **Karlsruhe Declaration** of the German Congress of Crime Prevention and its organising partner, which will be published on May 13.

During the opening event, the renowned Director of the Violence Research Centre at the University of Cambridge, **Prof. Dr. Manuel Eisner**, will hold a talk on the topic **"50% less violence worldwide by 2050 — approaches to a global strategy"**.

The closing speaker of the Congress is the internationally renowned researcher and author **Prof. Dr. Viktor Mayer-Schönberger** with a talk on the topic "**Big Data – Opportunities and risks in prevention**": "Big Data" not only promises new insights into reality but also better predictions. But what is so special about "Big Data", especially in terms of prevention? Where are its strengths and what are its limitations?

The International Forum of the 19th German Congress of Crime Prevention will feature numerous reports from **international experts and specialised organisations** about their experiences in the areas of prevention policy, prevention research, and prevention practice from more than 20 European and non-European countries. In total, about **150 foreign guests from 30 countries** will participate in this year's Congress.

As part of the 19th German Congress of Crime Prevention, the **European Forum for Urban Security (EFUS)** will hold this year's General Assembly with a Congress-public programme under the subject "Europe and prevention: positions and needs of the local actors and decision makers" with simultaneous interpretation in English, French, and German.

For the first time, the programme of the 19th Congress in Karlsruhe will also include a **series of special events**: Symposium on internal security; Karlsruhe forum for cyber-safety; US Juvenile Justice. From the first Juvenile Court of the US in Chicago in 1899 via the Chicago School to the Model Courts for Change; Barometer Security in Germany (BaSiD) – results from the joint project; Transition management between juvenile law enforcement and follow-up care: How can we reduce the high recidivism rates?; Parent-LAN – Together. Games. Experience (event by spielbar.de of bpb with partners); Protection of the constitution and prevention - a contradiction?; NEST – Material for early help; Restorative Circles (RC) – Healing instead of punishment. A form for conflict transformation, developed in the violent world of Brazilian favelas; ways to sustainable prevention (of violence). From theoretical concept to communal networking work.

The 19th Congress is supported by more than **40 partner organisations**. I would once more like to thank all partners and supporting institutions and their employees for their generous support in terms of content, ideas, and materials.

3. Main topic: Prevention requires practice, policy, and science

The following idealised interdependence model is supposed to provide a few suggestions for the development of criminal policy prevention initiatives for the coming years for the main topic of the 19th German Congress of Crime Prevention "Prevention requires practice, policy, and science":

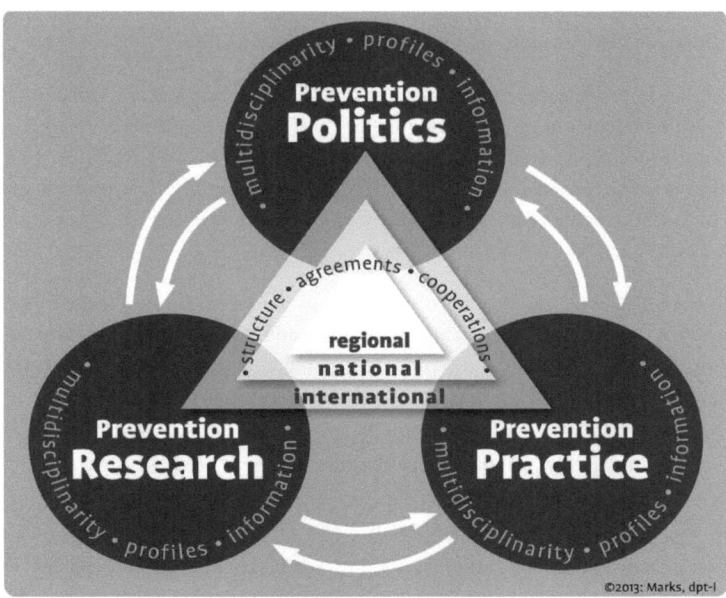

The three central fields of work of prevention: practice, policy, and science

Prevention practice, prevention policy, and prevention research should be considered the central fields of work for an integrated and sustainable prevention orientation. In the coming years we will need to develop a stringent development and differentiation within these three central fields of work. We also need to develop clearly structured cooperation and networks between these three central fields of work. Corresponding agreements concerning responsibilities, work load distribution, cooperation structures should be found both at the communal, national, and international levels. In addition, improved communication agreements between these vertical levels are necessary and must be developed.

Three central requirements for each field of work:

Interdisciplinary: Interdisciplinary cooperation should be organised and ensured systematically in each field of work of prevention. Representatives of the youth and social work agencies and the police should be represented in the field of work of prevention practice, as should NGOs and volunteer organisations. Representatives of political parties, legislation, the various departments of the executive and judiciary should be involved in the field of work of prevention policy. Public, state, and private research institutions in the applicable disciplines and sub-disciplines (e.g. sociology, psychology, biology, medicine, political science, legal studies, economy, criminology, victimology, etc.) should participate in the field of work of prevention research, as should organisations of research support and scientific associations.

Competent: An important prerequisite for a successful social prevention orientation is a clear self-understanding of the individual fields of work. Definitions, self-understanding, and responsibilities should be formulated in the respective fields of work of prevention practice, prevention policy, and prevention research. Clear profiles and portfolios of the three fields of work will also include clear descriptions of the existing resources, capabilities, and service structures.

Informative: In particular, the profiles of the fields of work prevention practice, prevention policy, and prevention research should be communicated better and more aggressively in the future. Each field of work should make its profiles available to the public proactively for free, with a large measure of common sense.

The three central tasks for joint action in the three central fields of work:

Structures: At the three central communication levels - the communal/regional level, the national level, and the international/global level - the prevention fields of prevention practice, prevention policy, and prevention research should cooperate equally in permanent commission structures and possibly include even further partner organisations. Such a fixed commission structure can realise mutual information, basic agreements, and specific cooperation in a transparent and sustainable manner.

Agreements: In addition to working communication paths within and between the respective prevention fields and prevention levels, it is becoming increasingly important to reach an understanding concerning terminology, definitions, objectives, criteria, methods, different profiles and responsibilities, as well as areas of focus, strategies, and specific projects and programmes.

Cooperation: A formalised and continuous communication between the fields of work of prevention practice, prevention policy, and prevention research can help publish common positions and prepare, realise, and evaluate specific projects.

In addition to the technical-methodical solutions from the respective perspectives of the involved disciplines and prevention actors, more fundamental and farther-reaching structural changes are necessary if we want to actually develop, realise, and evaluate prevention and intervention measures successfully. It is essential to find a new communication culture between the three involved central prevention fields of prevention practice, prevention policy, and prevention research which are mutually very interdependent .

The main topic of this Congress "Prevention requires practice, policy, and science" is at the centre of numerous presentations and consultations of the 19th German Congress of Crime Prevention. Based on the scientific Congress opinion by the criminologist Dr. Wiebke Steffen, a few specific requirements have emerged in the time leading up to the Congress. The spectrum ranges from requirements to strengthen communal prevention strategies and improved integration of existing research insights to a bolder prevention-oriented social and criminal policy.

In my view, I would like to mention the establishment of interdisciplinary and inter-departmental prevention centres as a central requirement – at all political levels – communal, state, and federation. This way, crime prevention and other prevention areas could work together more effectively and thus form the basis for a systematic, social, and especially sustainable prevention strategy/policy. It has been shown that investments into effective prevention measures pay off in the form of lower crime numbers as well as lower costs for the tax payer. Practice, policy and science must work together here. I would like to end this address with a plea to the field of policy; it is for these reasons that policy should finally begin investing more purposefully in effective prevention programs and inter-departmental prevention centres.

I wish us all a stimulating and insightful Congress with great results in the prevention city of Karlsruhe.

Claudia Heinzelmann and Daniela Köntopp

Prevention Work in Germany in the Face of the Exhibition Accompanying the German Congress on Crime Prevention (GCOCP)

Exhibition stands serving the purpose to present recent developments, to facilitate an exchange of expert information and to establish contacts constitute an essential part of large exhibitions and congresses. While the first four German Congresses on Crime Prevention featured brochure display tables only, the 5th Congress in Hoyerswerda, Saxony, heralded the start of an additional involvement of exhibitors. A documentation of this Congress in 1999 already registered a number of 68 information stands. This number increased steadily during the next years as the following diagram illustrates.

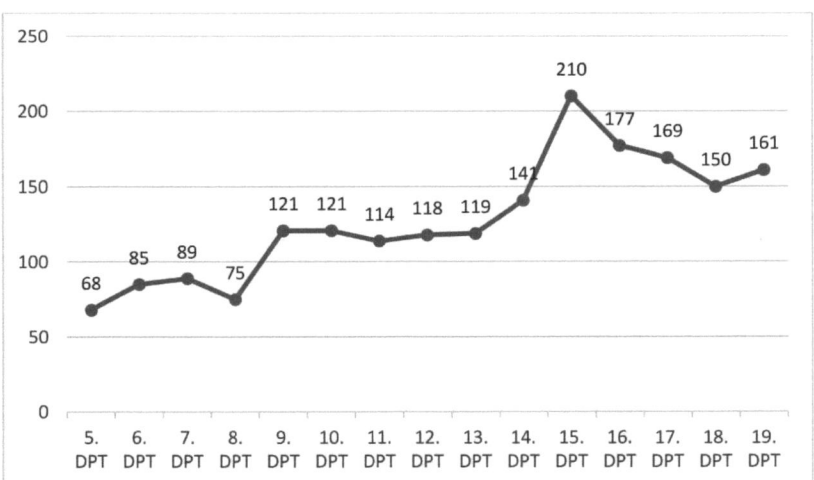

Fig. 1) Number of exhibition stands present at the German Congresses on Crime Prevention

The organizations' interest in applying for an exhibition stand at the GCOCP seems undaunted. By now, the Congress usually comprises a total area of 5000 m². Besides information stands presenting diverse projects, organizations and institutions, the annual Congress comprises special exhibits, poster presentations as well as mobile presentations in motor vehicles in the outdoor area. For an adjuvant visual impression of this Congress area, please consider the film and picture material on the homepage of the GCOCP[1].

---

[1]   Film and sound material on the Congress are assigned to the respective Congress (see www. gcocp.org).

The exhibition area of the German Congress on Crime Prevention reveals in a particular way the diversity of the topics and approaches of action in the field of prevention. A tour of the exhibition shows this in an immediate and vivid manner. Cities and countries present their preventive activities, associations introduce themselves, initiatives show their approaches, organizations have their brochures on display, projects provide samples of their work, and many more. The host federal state and partially the respective city as well appear in a special way with, for instance, a so called "*Ländermeile*", which refers to an area or hall where all local information stands are grouped together.

Evaluation reports of the GCOCP prove that the exhibition area is highly appreciated by the congress visitors. 89,5 % of the respondents rated the information stands of the last GCOCP "good" or "very good". On an evaluation scale of five levels, the Congress accompanying exhibition reached an average value of 1,8[2]. This evaluation remained constant over the years[3]. In their commentaries, Congress visitors highlighted the range of variation of the exhibition stands. However, others felt slightly overwhelmed by their richness[4].

The Congress accompanying exhibition should therefore by no means be considered an "accessory decoration" to the various topics thoroughly propounded and discussed in talks and speeches. It is on the contrary core element of the German Congress on Crime Prevention since it renders the activities visible and provides an opportunity for direct contact and exchange.

Thus, it makes sense to render this part of the exhibition more easily accessible to a foreign audience as well, which becomes increasingly involved in the GCOCP via the Annual International Forum (AIF). This was realized for the first time within the framework of the 19th German Congress on Crime Prevention in Karlsruhe, which offered guided tours through the exhibition area in English and French. These tours visited exhibition stands especially relevant for international guests, where reference persons were primed to provide further information and answer questions. The guided tours were well acknowledged; there was room for many contacts and exchanges.

As further service for the international audience, a translation of the overview of the exhibition stands at the congress could be realized. On the one hand, this English

---

[2]   cf.: Rainer Strobl, Christoph Schüle, Olaf Lobermeier: Evaluation des 19. Deutschen Präventionstages, in: Kerner, Hans-Jürgen u. Marks, Erich (Hrsg.), Internetdokumentation des Deutschen Präventionstages. Hannover 2014, www.praeventionstag.de/dokumentation.cms/2882, S. 15.

[3]   Evaluations according to the evaluation reports of previous congresses: 18th GCOCP: 1,8; 17th GCOCP: 1,7; 16th GCOCP: 1,8; 15th GCOCP: 1,9; 14th GCOCP: 1,8; 13th GCOCP: 1,8 (see section "congresses" on the following website: www.praeventionstag.de).

[4]   cf.: Rainer Strobl, Christoph Schüle, Olaf Lobermeier: Evaluation des 17. Deutschen Präventionstages, in: Erich Marks & Wiebke Steffen (Hrsg.): Sicher leben in Stadt und Land. Ausgewählte Beiträge des 17. Deutschen Präventionstages 16. und 17. April 2012 in München, Forum Verlag Godesberg GmbH 2013, S. 144.

synopsis facilitates an easier identification and localization of information stands relevant to international congress visitors. On the other hand, the written overview offers a good insight into current activities in the field of crime and violence prevention in Germany and into which actors are involved in this field. It shows the range of variety of activities that mark prevention work in Germany as well as the diverse organizations that are concerned with the topic.

For this reason, the English overview of the information stands at the 19th German Congress on Crime Prevention is added to this book. The following 161 information stands (besides 9 special exhibitions, 26 performances in the section "Campus and Activities" and 19 poster presentations) were present at the Congress accompanying exhibition. The information stands are listed in alphabetical order by the name of the exhibiting institution and are described by a brief outline of their contents.

Overview of Exhibitors

AGJ-Fachverband – Konflikt-KULTUR

"Konflikt – KULTUR" [Conflict – CULTURE] is an extensive, scientifically sound prevention and training programme for all types of schools and youth welfare institutions. The "AGJ-Fachverband" [AGJ-professional association] is part of the Catholic charitable services "Caritas" and is concerned with a fight against poverty, health promotion and youth protection.

Aktion "Sportler setzen Zeichen" – WEISSER RING e.V.

"Sportler setzen Zeichen – für eine gewaltfreie Jugend" [Sportsmen take a stand – for a non-violent youth] is a nationwide prevention campaign initiated by "WEISSER RING e.V." whose aim it is to decrease youth violence by providing children and adolescents with an access to recreational and sports activities.

Aktionsbündnis Amoklauf Winnenden – Stiftung gegen Gewalt an Schulen

The coalition for action "Amoklauf Winnenden" [school shooting Winnenden] was founded by relatives of the school shooting's victims and was transferred into the ecclesiastical foundation under public law "Stiftung gegen Gewalt an öffentlichen Schulen" [Foundation Against Crime at Public Schools] in November 2009.

Ambulanter Justizsozialdienst Niedersachsen

The "Ambulanter Justizsozialdienst Niedersachsen" [ambulant judiciary social services of Lower Saxony] employs 450 workers engaged in offender support, court assistance, supervision of conduct and "AussteigerhilfeRechts" [support for drop-outs of right-wing extremism].

Arbeitskreis Aktiv gegen Frauenhandel und Ausbeutung

The counselling centres for those affected by human trafficking in Baden-Wuerttemberg, *"Fraueninformationszentrum Stuttgart"* [Women's Information Centre Stuttgart], *"FreiJa Freiburg and Kehl"* as well as the *"Mitternachtsmission Heilbronn"* [midnight mission Heilbronn] offer free and confidential counselling and accompaniment.

AWO Karlsruhe gemeinnützige GmbH

"AWO" provides help for children, adolescents and their parents in a variety of ways via a network of institutions, which are part of its Socio-Therapeutic Child and Youth Welfare Association.

Baden TV

Exhibition stand and interview platform of the current media partner Baden-TV.

B.B.W. St. Franziskus Abensberg, Träger: Kath. Jugendfürsorge der Diözese Regensburg e.V.

The "B.B.W. St. Franziskus Abensberg" is a leading institution in the field of occupational rehabilitation for young people with handicaps and disadvantages.

Beccaria Fachkräfte Kriminalprävention

The information desk provides the possibility for participants of the "Beccaria Qualifikationsprogramm" [Beccaria qualification programme] (2008-2014) to exchange views, get to know each other and inform visitors about the programme.

Behandlungsinitiative Opferschutz (BIOS-BW) e.V.

"BIOS-BW e.V." is concerned with providing convicted sex offenders and violent criminals with the possibility of attending a therapy that is aimed at reducing the risk of re-offending and thereby protecting victims.

Bewährungshilfe Stuttgart e.V. / PräventSozial Justiznahe Soziale Dienste gemeinnützige GmbH

"Bewährungshilfe Stuttgart e.V." [probation service Stuttgart] and "PräventSozial Justiznahe Soziale Dienste gemeinnützige GmbH" [social services closely related to the judiciary] are private social service providers who work collaboratively in supporting the criminal justice.

Buchhandlung Büchergilde

The "Buchhandlung Büchergilde" [bookshop Büchergilde] is a local bookshop run by its owner which offers among others art exhibitions, readings and bookstands.

Bündnis gegen Cybermobbing e.V.

The association will provide information about its work and cyber-bullying.

Bund Deutsche Kriminalbeamter

The "BDK" [Association of German Detective Constables] exclusively represents the social and professional concerns of the members of the criminal investigation department, officers and pay scale employees, and supports their economic, occupational and cultural interests.

Bundesamt für Justiz

The "Bundesamt für Justiz" [Federal Agency of Justice] decides on the grant of money for the emergency relief of victims of extremism ("Härteleistungen").

Bundesamt für Migration und Flüchtlinge – Präventionskooperation

The federal agency combines a counseling centre for people concerned about the radicalisation of a relative or acquaintance with a clearing house promoting an exchange between police authorities and Muslim organisations in Germany.

Bundesarbeitsgemeinschaft für Straffälligenhilfe (BAG-S) e.V.

This specialised organisation is concerned with improving and expanding the support of delinquents and moreover represents the concerns of offender support on a national level.

Bundesarbeitsgemeinschaft Prävention & Prophylaxe e.V.

This non-profit organisation offers workshops on the topic "Sexualised Violence" for pedagogical personal at schools, kindergartens and sports clubs.

Bundesarbeitsgemeinschaft Täterarbeit Häusliche Gewalt e.V.

The national association is an umbrella organisation for institutions which offer work with perpetrators in the field of domestic violence in inter-institutional cooperative associations.

Bundeskriminalamt

The "Bundeskriminalamt" [Federal Criminal Police Office] will inform about the organised deception via telephone of especially the elderly population by false promises of winning money and will present its prevention actions against it.

Bundesministerium für Justiz und Verbraucherschutz / Bundesamt für Justiz

The "Bundesministerium für Justiz und Verbraucherschutz" [Federal Ministry of Justice and Consumer Protection] will offer material informing about its work and general crime prevention.

Bundespolizei

The "Bundespolizei" [Federal Police] wil inform about the dangers and risks of geocaching on railway facilities.

Bundeszentrale für gesundheitliche Aufklärung (BzgA)

The "Bundeszentrale für gesundheitliche Aufklärung" [Federal Centre for Health Education] informs about its various addiction -prevention campaigns whose particular target groups are children, adolescents and young adults.

Bundeszentrale für politische Bildung

The main objective of the "Bundeszentrale für politische Bildung" [Federal Agency for Civic Education] is to enhance an understanding of political issues, to increase a democratic awareness and to foster a willingness for cooperation.

Courage – Sicherheit fördern e.V., Kehl

The counseling team "Kommunale Kriminalprävention" [Municipal Crime Prevention] introduces itself and presents its methods and projects, which have been successfully implemented for a couple of years now. The association "Courage – Sicherheit fördern e.V." [Courage – Promoting Safety] has been founded in 2004 in order to support the counseling team.

DBH-Fachverband für Soziale Arbeit, Strafrecht und Kriminalpolitik

The "DBH-Fachverband" is a nationally and internationally active professional association for social work, criminal law and policy. It consists of associations and organizations with altogether 10.000 members working in the fields of probation service, support for delinquents and help for victims.

Der PARITÄTISCHE Sachsen-Anhalt – Landesweites Netzwerk für ein Leben ohne Gewalt

The nationwide network for a life without violence accomplishes extensive prevention work and consolidates the victim protection with respect to violence in close social relationships through regular skilled work.

Deutsche BOB-Initiativen – BOBBayern Initiative

The target objective of the BOB-initiative is to raise young people's awareness for the topic of drink-driving and to thereby reduce or prevent car accidents caused by driving under the influence of alcohol. In Bavaria, BOB is implemented in nine rural districts.

Deutsche BOB-Initiativen – Pfalz-BOB

The police headquarters Westpfalz and the "Bund gegen Alkohol- und Drogen im Straßenverkehr" [Association Against Alcohol and Drugs in Road Traffic]" inform about their work.

Deutsche BOB-Initiativen – Polizeipräsidium Mittelhessen

The concept of BOB has been implemented by the police headquarters of Mittelhessen since 2004 and has been complemented through further measures.

Deutsche BOB-Initiativen – Polizeipräsidium Trier

BOB Trier is a campaign that raises awareness for the risks and dangers of driving under the influence of alcohol or drugs and thereby aims at reducing traffic accidents.

Deutsche Sportjugend im Deutschen Olympischen Sportbund e.V. (dsj)

The "Deutsche Sportjugend" is the umbrella organisation of children and youth sport in Germany and comprises 80 member organisations. The organisation offers preventive concepts, trainings and tools which are targeted at helping coaches, group leaders and pedagogues in dealing with problems of right-wing extremism, homophobia, bullying et al. in the sports sector.

Deutsche Stiftung Mediation

The "Deutsche Stiftung Mediation" [German foundation mediation] aims at a sustainable establishment of mediation in the field of politics, economy and society in Germany, which should in turn serve to strengthen an autonomous conflict resolution, improve the culture of dispute and support the German judicature.

Deutsche Vereinigung für Jugendgerichte und Jugendgerichtshilfen e.V. (DVJJ)

The German professional association for "Jugendkriminalrechtspflege" [juvenile justice system] enhances an interdisciplinary co-operation of professions involved in the "Jugendstrafverfahren" [youth penal procedure] and promotes a professional discourse between the sectors of practice, science and politics.

Deutscher Familienverband Landesverband Sachsen-Anhalt e.V.

The counseling centre "ProMann" [ProMan] in Magdeburg (founded in 1999) is concerned with advising boys and men and is specialized on working with men having problems with violence.

Deutscher Ju-Jutsu Verband e.V.

The ju-jitsu association initiated a nationwide project under the heading "Nicht-mit-mir!" [Not-with-me!] which provides a national concept for prevention, self-assertion and self-defense for children and adolescents and is designed for currency and sustainability.

Deutsches Forum für Kriminalprävention

The non-profit foundation was established by the Federal Government and the Federal States in 2001. Target objective of the forum is to reduce the risk of crime via preventive measures, to limit harm and damage caused by crime and to enhance a feeling of security among the population.

Deutsches Jugendinstitut e.V.

The "Deutsches Jugendinstitut e.V." [German youth institute] is the biggest social-scientific institute for research and development with respect to the fields of childhood, youth and family and the respective practical and political subject areas in Germany.

Deutsch-Europäisches Forum für Urbane Sicherheit e.V. (DEFUS)

The "Deutsch-Europäisches Forum für Urbane Sicherheit" [German-European Forum for Urban Security] provides the possibility for an exchange and cooperation of the various actors in the field of safety work. It actively contributes to the enhancement of public security in cities and municipalities, especially in the field of communal crime prevention, crime fighting and traffic safety.

Deutschland sicher im Netz e.V. (DsiN)

The association "Deutschland sicher im Netz" [Germany safe on the Internet] is the central address for consumers and middle-class companies in all concerns of IT security. The association enhances the level of trust in new technologies via understandable and straight-forward messages on how to safely use the Internet and information technology.

Die Kinderschutz-Zentren

The union of "Kinderschutz-Zentren" [child-protection centres] in Germany is aimed at reducing and preventing violence against children, child abuse, child neglect and sexual abuse. The child-protection centres conduct own conventions and offers further training.

DKSB Ortsverband Karlsruhe Stadt und Landkreis e.V.

The "Deutscher Kinderschutz Bund" [German association for child protection] presents its projects on crime prevention: classes for parents "Starke Eltern – Starke Kinder" [Strong parents – Strong children] and group training social skills "Mach dich stark" [Stand up for yourself].

Drogenhilfe Köln

"Drogenhilfe Köln" is engaged in addiction prevention and works in a target-group-specific and cause-oriented way.

EJF gAG

The "Evangelisches Jugend- und Fürsorgewerk" [Protestant youth and welfare foundation] supports social institutions and services for people of all ages looking for personal and social care and companion. It unites charitable children-, youth- , and family welfare organisations, institutions for the support of disabled or elderly people, for hospic care, for further training, hotels and conference venues.

ESM Jugendbüro / Jugendamt Stadt Marl

Information on the concept "Präventions- und Handlungskonzept gegen Gewalt in Marl" [concept on the prevention of and action against crime in the city of Marl] including its network and accompanying modules will be provided at the information desk.

European Forum for Urban Security (EFUS)

The European Forum for Urban Security is an association of more than 250 European cities and municipalities jointly working in the field of crime prevention and security.

Evangelische Gesellschaft Stuttgart e.V.

The Protestant association is present with two information desks:
1. The "Yasemin-mobile Beratungsstelle" [Yasemin-mobile counselling centre] is concerned with the support of young migrants between 12 and 27 years old who are subject to or threatened by violence in the name of honour and forced marriage.
2. "Fit für mein Kind" [Fit for my child] is a preventive project for parents with migrant background offering intercultural workshops for parents and outreach work with regard to family advisory services.

Fachkräfteportal der Kinder- und Jugendhilfe

The "Fachkräfteportal der Kinder- und Jugendhilfe" [Web portal for professionals of child and youth services] is an online platform providing the possibility of an exchange of information and facilitating a cooperation and communication of professionals in the field of child and youth services.

Fairplayer e.V.

The non-profit association "Fairplayer e.V." aims at promoting social commitment and civil courage and moreover supports a development of sustainable strategies for an enhancement of social competencies in childhood and youth.

Förderung der Bewährungshilfe in Hessen e.V.

The association maintains and fosters institutions and projects aimed at offender support and probation service in different cities in the federal state of Hessen.

Förderverein "Sicherer Landkreis Böblingen e.V. "

The support association "Sicherer Landkreis Böblingen e.V." [Safe administrative district Böblingen] presents its structure and methods for working in the field of crime prevention with a particular focus on the permanently implemented offers in the district.

FREIE HILFE BERLIN e.V.

Since 1990, "FREIE HILFE BERLIN e.V." [Free Help Berlin] has been offering social services inside and outside the prisons of Brandenburg and Berlin, including among others a support of homeless people or those threatened by homelessness, prisoners and their relatives and citizens wishing to engage in charitable services.

Freikirche der Siebten-Tags-Adventisten K.d.ö.R.

The congregational chapel, department women, in collaboration with the development aid organisation "ADRA International" advocates fighting against any form of violence. Thereby, different projects in Germany are implemented and supported.

Galli Präventionstheater und Lichtmädchen e.V. "Märchen helfen heilen"

The "Galli Präventionstheater" [Galli theatre for prevention] conducts nationwide projects in kindergartens, schools and troubled areas and offers a number of prevention plays all written by Johannes Galli. A display wall as well as a number of movie examples will illustrate the projects of the association "Lichtmädchen e.V."

Gegen-missbrauch e.V.

The association "gegen – missbrauch e.V." [against – abuse] fights against the sexual abuse of children. The aim is to not only serve as a platform for victims of sexual child abuse but to moreover actively provide help.

Gemeinde Unfallversicherungsverband Hannover / Landeskriminalamt Niedersachsen

The project "PaC – Prävention als Chance" [PaC – Prevention as Chance] will be presented. This is a multi-layoured programme implemented in an entire municipality which involves all institutions and sections of the population engaged in socialising and educating children and adolescents.

Gewaltstopper e.V.

The "GewaltStopper e.V. Verein für konfrontative Pädagogik, AAT/CT" [Association stop violence; association for confronting pedagogy] is aimed at supporting children and youth services, at-risk adolescents and a distribution of confronting pedagogy in youth work.

Gewerkschaft der Polizei

The "Gewerkschaft der Polizei" [trade union police] organises about 173.000 employees - officers and pay scale employees - and is hence the biggest and most influential trade union in the police sector.

Gewinnsparverein der Volksbanken und Raiffeisenbanken in Baden-Württemberg e.V.

"Schütze dein BESTES" [Safe Your BEST] is an initiative by the interior ministry of Baden-Württemberg, "GIB ACHT IM VERKEHR" [Pay attention in traffic], and the "Gewinnsparverein der Volksbanken und Raiffeisenbanken in Baden-Württemberg e.V." and further partners, which is aimed at protecting the BEST – the human brain.

GSJ – Gesellschaft für Sport und Jugendsozialarbeit gGmbH / Berliner Polizei Dir. 5 Stab 4 – Prävention und Öffentlichkeitsarbeit

A series of photographs, a Power Point presentation and a video documentation will provide information on the work and training of "Konfliktlotsen" [guides in conflict situations].

Haus des Jugendrechts Stuttgart

Since June 1, 1999, the "Haus des Jugendrechts Stuttgart" [House of juvenile justice Stuttgart] has joined the work of police, prosecution and child protective services under one roof in order to fight and prevent child and youth delinquency.

Hessisches Landeskriminalamt / Polizei Hessen

The "Informations- und Kompetenzzentrum Ausstiegshilfen Rechtsextremismus" [centre for the support of people wanting to exit right-wing extremism] presents its current programme on exiting right-wing extremism.

Hessisches Ministerium der Justiz, für Integration und Europa

The exhibition will give an overview of the work of the Crime Prevention Council Hessen, particularly on the work of its 10 working groups. Moreover, the Coordination Centre against domestic violence established in the "Hessisches Ministerium der Justiz, für Integration und Europa" [ministry of justice, for integration and Europe] will be presented.

Hessissches Kultusministerium – Projekt Gewaltprävention und Demokratielernen

The project "Gewaltprävention und Demokratielernen" [violence prevention and democracy learning] is aimed at supporting schools in implementing programmes targeted at violence prevention and a facilitation of democracy.

Hilfswerk der Deutschen Lions e.V. – Lions-Quest "Erwachsen werden"

"Lions-Quest 'Erwachsen werden'" [Lions-Quest – growing up] is a further training programme for all pedagogues and multipliers working with children and adolescents. Central focus of the programme is the development and support of general social and life competencies of 10- to 14-year-olds.

International Centre for the Prevention of Crime (ICPC)

The International Centre for the Prevention of Crime (ICPC) was founded in 1994 and is the sole international organization dedicated exclusively to crime prevention and community safety. The German Congress on Crime Prevention is member of ICPC.

IN Via Kath. Verband für Mädchen- und Frauensozialarbeit i.d. Erzdiözese Freiburg e.V.

The Catholic association for social welfare for girls and women in the archdiocese of Freiburg is connected to the caritas association [Catholic charitable services] of the archdiocese of Freiburg and registered voluntary youth welfare organisation.

Initiative Sicherer Landkreis Rems-Murr e.V.

The "Initiative Sicherer Landkreis Rems-Murr e.V." [Initiative safe administrative district Rems-Murr] is one of the main pillars supporting crime prevention in the district of Rems-Murr. It will present some of its projects as well as its prevention films on the topics of civil courage, stalking and binge drinking.

Internationaler Bund

A main focus of the "Internationaler Bund" [International Association] in Baden is, among others, working with young people in the field of crime prevention in the urban and rural districts of Karlsruhe and Mannheim. The work is realised in three different projects.

Jugendförderwerk Villingen Schwenningen e.V.

The interactive prevention puppet theatre "Tims Abenteuer" [Tim's adventure] is concerned with the topics of bullying, violence and theft and was developed by social workers, teachers, the police and affected children.

Jugendstationen Gera und Jena / Saale-Holzland-Kreis

The youth centres of Gera, Jena and Saale-Holzland-Kreis as well as the cooperative work of prosecution, police and "Jugendgerichtshilfe" [juvenile legal support agency] will be presented.

Junge Menschen im Aufwind (JuMA), Speyer

Presentation of the socio-pedagogical work project "Junge Menschen im Aufwind, Speyer" [young people on the rise] – a project for adolescents and young adults who became offenders.

Junges Staatstheater Karlsruhe

Limits and discovering ways for their transcendence in an active exchange – that is the "Junges Staatstheater Karlsruhe" [young state theatre Karlsruhe].

Justizvollzugsanstalt Wiesbaden

The prison of Wiesbaden, on behalf of the "Hessisches Ministerium der Justiz, für Integration and Europa" [ministry of justice, for integration and Europe], presents the various aspects of re-offending prevention in the light of current political and economic changes in society.

juuuport – www.juuuport.de, die Selbstschutz-Plattform von Jugendlichen für Jugendliche im Web

The website www.juuuport.de serves adolescents to help each other in case of trouble in or with the web. Questions concerning cyber-bullying, rip-off, or data privacy may be asked either publically in the "fooorum" or privately via e-mail. The questions will be answered by same-aged juuuport-scouts.

Katholische Bundes-Arbeitsgemeinschaft Straffälligenhilfe im Deutschen Caritasverband (KAGS)

More than 100 Catholic organisations, services and institutions offering support for offenders, their relatives and victims of crime, have joined together in the "Katholische Bundes-Arbeitsgemeinschaft Straffälligenhilfe" [Catholic Federal Association for Offender Support].

Kinder- und Jugendamt Heidelberg

"Wir helfen Kindern" [we help children] is a project between urban day-care facilities of the "Kinder- und Jugendamt" [child and youth welfare office] of Heidelberg, the prevention section of the police headquarters and the "Verein Sicheres Heidelberg e.V." [Association for a safe Heidelberg].

klicksafe

Main task of the EU-initiative "klicksafe" is to show internet users how to critically and competently use the internet and new technologies and to facilitate an awareness of the chances and risks of these media. Clicksafe develops concepts and materials for pedagogues, teachers and parents as well as for children and adolescents.

Kolping-Bildungswerk Württemberg e.V. – "Schule ohne Rassissmus – Schule mit Courage" Landeskoordination BW

"Schule ohne Rassissmus – Schule mit Courage" [School Without Racism – School With Courage] is the biggest German pupil network system counting more than 1300 schools involved. Since its adoption from Belgium in 1995, it has developed into a vivid and creative youth movement in Germany.

Koordinierungs- und Entwicklungsstelle Verkehrsunfallprävention (KEV) beim Landeskriminalamt Baden-Württemberg / Bund gegen Alkohol und Drogen im Straßenverkehr (B.A.D.S.)

The project "Gib Acht im Verkehr" [Pay Attention in Traffic] in the federal state of Baden-Württemberg provides a forum and platform for mutual prevention work with respect to traffic. Police departments as well as various other organisations participate in the project.

Koordinierungsstelle Gewaltprävention und Verein Verantwortung statt Gewalt e.V.

The "Koordinierungsstelle Gewaltprävention" [coordination centre for the prevention of violence] has conducted prevention work in schools for more than 20 years now. It conducted, among others, six pilot experiments on the topic of violence prevention and an EU-project for the fostering of better relations between schools and parental homes.

Kreis Lippe, Kooperationsgremium "Für Lippe gegen Häusliche Gewalt"

The "Koordinationsgremium 'Für Lippe gegen Häusliche Gewalt'" [cooperation committee "For Lippe against domestic violence"] joins all institutions in the district of Lippe working in the field of domestic violence: police, women's counseling centre, other counseling centres, justice, youth welfare offices, women's centre, medical association et al.

Kriminologische Masterstudiengänge der Ruhr-Universität Bochum

The "Ruhr-Universität Bochum" offers two extra occupational master courses: "Kriminologie und Polizeiwissenschaft" [criminology and police science] and the international course "Criminal Justice, Governance and Police Science."

Landesamt fürVerfassungsschutz Baden-Württemberg

An intellectual and political engagement with extremism of all kinds is an obligatory part for the permanent protection of our social fundamental values. Central focus of the prevention work of the "Landesamt für Verfassungsschutz" [state office for the protection of the constitution] is the information and advising of state actors like government, parliament and public authorities.

Landesarbeitsgemeinschaft Mobile Jugendarbeit / Streetwork Baden-Württemberg e.V. und Mobile Jugendarbeit Karlsruhe

"Mobile Jugendarbeit" [mobile youth work] in the federal state of Baden-Württemberg joins streetwork, individual support, working with groups and gangs as well as community work. More than 130 institutions nationwide work with the concept of the mobile youth work.

Landesinstitut für Präventives Handeln

The "Landesinstitut für Präventives Handeln" [State Institute for Preventive Action] presents its project on risk- and harm-reduction with respect to 'recreational' consumption ("Freizeitkonsum") of addictive substances.

Landeskriminalamt Baden-Württemberg, Geschäftsstelle "Förderprogramm Prävention alkoholbedingter Jugendgewalt (PAJ)"

The programme "Prävention alkoholbedingter Jugendgewalt" [prevention of alcohol-related youth violence] is aimed at engaging adolescents in non-violent communal life and in a responsible dealing with alcohol.

Landeskriminalamt Mecklenburg-Vorpommern

The "Landeskriminalamt Mecklenburg-Vorpommern" [state bureau of investigation of Mecklenburg-Vorpommern] presents the county-wide school competition "Wir in Mecklenburg-Vorpommern – fit und sicher in die Zukunft" [We in Mecklenburg-Vorpommern – fit and safe into the future]. Aim of the project is to prepare the next generation via age- and time-appropriate offers for a health-conscious and safe way of life.

Landeskriminalamt Niedersachsen

The "Landeskriminalamt Niedersachen" [state bureau of investigation of Lower Saxony] presents the topic "Gemeinsam für ein sicheres Zuhause" [Together for a safe home]. Main focus will be an exemplary presentation of the cooperative work of police, municipalities and real estate.

Landeskriminalamt Rheinland-Pfalz und Verbraucherzentrale Rheinland-Pfalz

The citizens of the federal state of Rheinland-Pfalz are confronted with increasingly more professional and constantly changing methods used by fraudsters and hustlers. Preventing and prosecuting such crimes is of mutual interest to the "Verbraucherzentrale Rheinland-Pfalz" [consumer advice centre of Rheinland-Pfalz] and the "Landeskriminalamt Rheinland-Pfalz" [state bureau of investigation of Rheinland-Pfalz].

Landeskriminalamt Sachsen-Anhalt

The "Landeskriminalamt Sachsen-Anhalt" [state bureau of investigation of Sachsen-Anhalt] will present prevention projects on the topics of potential dangers on the Internet (media package "Ich bin online" [I am online]) and addiction and drugs (media package "Vollrausch – Verlorene Lebenszeit" [Drunken stupor – lost life time]).

Landespräventionsrat Niedersachsen

The "Landespräventionsrat Niedersachsen" [Crime Prevention Council of Lower Saxony] has been a proficient contact name for crime prevention in Lower Saxony since 1995. The Council understands crime prevention as an extensive task, which needs the support of various social forces. Hence, 270 member organisations are joined together in the Council and are represented by a non-profit board.

Landespräventionsrat Nordrhein-Westfalen

The "Landespräventionsrat Nordrhein-Westfalen" [Crime Prevention Council of North Rhine-Westphalia] and the ministry of justice will cooperatively present different projects on the topic of prevention: "Projekt Sichere Netzwelten" [project safe spaces on the internet], "Verfahren beschleunigen, kriminelle Karrieren beenden, Sicherheit verbessern" [hastening proceedings, ending criminal careers, improving security] and "Gemeinschaftsinitiative B5" [community initiative B5].

Landespräventionsrat Sachsen

The "Landespräventionsrat Sachsen" [Crime Prevention Council of Sachsen] will present its work together with the "Landesprogramm 'Weltoffenes Sachsen für Demokratie und Toleranz'" [country programme "cosmopolitan Sachsen for democracy and tolerance"] and the "Landeskriminalamt Sachsen" [state bureau of investigation of Sachsen].

Landespräventionsrat Sachsen-Anhalt

The "Landespräventionsrat Sachsen Anhalt" [Crime Prevention Council of Sachsen-Anhalt] in cooperation with other institutions from Sachsen-Anhalt will present preventive activities for various subject areas.

Landesprogramm Weltoffenes Sachsen für Demokratie und Toleranz

The "Landesprogramm 'Weltoffenes Sachsen für Demokratie und Toleranz'" [country programme "cosmopolitan Sachsen for democracy and tolerance"] has supported regional and municipal projects encouraging a democratic culture and fostering the democratic constitution since 2005. Main focus lies on the support of projects and initiatives advocating democracy, tolerance and cosmopolitan attitudes in the free state of Sachsen.

Landratsamt Breisgau-Hochschwarzwald

In Breisgau-Hochschwarzwald, institutions actively engaged in preventive work have jointly developed a "HANDBUCH ZUR PRÄVENTION" [guide on prevention] which contents principals and recommendations on prevention with regard to children and adolescents.

Landratsamt Karlsruhe

Family centres are open encounter and counseling centres for young families, children, parents and seniors. There are 22 family centres in the administrative district of Karlsruhe. They promote a social togetherness in city and municipality, work independently and self-organised and are mostly supported by voluntary workers.

Landratsamt Karlsruhe

The "Landratsamt Karlsruhe" [administrative district office of Karlsruhe] will present its programme "Wegschauen ist keine Lösung" [Looking the other way is no solution], which is aimed at reducing an abuse of addictive substances by young people.

Landratsamt Karlsruhe – Frühe Hilfen

"Frühe Hilfen" [Early support] is a preventive special service offered by the youth welfare office in cooperation with the public health office. The assessment of counseling and social support for families takes place on a voluntary basis and is free of costs.

Lebenswertes Murgtal e.V. – Verein für Prävention und Sicherheit

The association for prevention and safety "Lebenswertes Murgtal e.V." [Murgtal - a place worth living] will present its "Niedrigseilparcours" [low ropes course], which serves as an action-oriented learning and training field for young and old. Moreover, it will inform about its prevention project "Mut statt Wut" [Courage instead of anger], which is aimed at school children from grade two to three showing problems in their social behaviour, a high readiness to use violence, and a low frustration tolerance.

Ministerium des Innern, für Sport und Infrastruktur

The information desk of the "Ministerium des Innern, für Sport und Infrastruktur" [Ministry of the Interior, for sport and infrastructure] will be occupied by the central office for crime prevention, the crime prevention council of Rheinland-Pfalz and the foundation crime prevention Rheinland-Pfalz.

Ministerium für Inneres und Kommunales des Landes NRW

Information desk presenting the crime-preventive initiative "Kurve kriegen" [Get one's act together] by the "Ministerium für Inneres und Kommunales des Landes NRW" [ministry of the interior and municipal affairs of North Rhine-Westphalia].

Ministerium für Kultus, Jugend und Sport Baden-Württemberg

The "Ministerium für Kultus, Jugend und Sport Baden-Württemberg" [ministry of education and cultural affairs of Baden-Württemberg] informs about school prevention work, especially about the prevention concept "stark.stärker.WIR" [strong.stronger.WE] for schools in the federal state. The concept has been developed as a consequence of the school shootings at Winnenden and Wendlingen.

Netwerk Straffälligenhilfe in Baden-Württemberg

The 47 member associations of the "Netzwerk Straffälligenhilfe in Baden-Württemberg" [network offender support in Baden-Württemberg] implement different nationwide projects in the field of offender support. Moreover, many member associations maintain advice and counseling centres and assisted living arrangements for offenders, and conduct various work projects and programmes on crime prevention.

Netzwerk gegen Gewalt

"Netzwerk gegen Gewalt" [Network against violence] is an inter-agency crime prevention initiative of the federal state government of Hessen. Since 2002, a nationwide networking and exchange of information on current topics has been fostered and nationwide projects have been promoted.

Netzwerk Gewaltprävention und Konfliktregelung Münster

The "Netzwerk Gewaltprävention und Konfliktregelung Münster" [network violence prevention and conflict resolution Münster] was founded in 1999 and consists of 20 actors. The network is actively engaged in 9 subject fields: cyber-bullying, social competencies, conflict resolution, prevention of sexual violence, et al.

Netzwerk Zuhause sicher e.V.

The "Netzwerk Zuhause sicher e.V." [Network safe at home] is a crime preventive project advocating a prevention of burglary and home fire. It has been generated out of a police initiative so that the network is conceived from and designed for police practice.

Netzwerkarbeit für nachhaltige Gewaltprävention: Konzept: MIT-EIN-ANDER in Kita und Schule

The "Konzept: MIT-EIN-ANDER in Kita und Schule" [concept: together at day-care facility and school] was evolved by partners from the sectors of school, municipality, police, science and support associations of prevention work. It is used in the microcosm of municipality, day-care facility and school.

Neustart gGmbH

"Neustart gGmbH" [association restart] is responsible for the implementation of the probation service, court assistance and victim-offender mediation in Baden-Württemberg.

Niedersächsisches Ministerium für Inneres und Sport

"White IT – alliance for children" is an association aimed at contributing to the fight against child abuse and its representation. Technical as well as social methods and strategies should be determined, evaluated and implemented.

Oberzent-Schule Beerfelden

The school of Beerfelden will present its "Mediencoachprojekt" [media coach project] which is a peer project aimed at instructing pupils of secondary education in dealing with new media. The pupils are trained by various project partners so as to improve their media competency and be able to help younger pupils with their problems.

Odenwald-Regional-Gesellschaft (OREG)mbH

The "Odenwald-Regional-Gesellschaft (OREG)mbH" [Odenwald regional subsidiary], the police department Odenwald and the Odenwald public transport companies have cooperatively trained voluntary bus- and train attendants since 2004. These voluntary helpers are pupils from grade 8 onwards who are educated by qualified trainers in a professional training lasting several days.

Ortspolizeibehörde Bremerhaven

The "Ortspolizeibehörde Bremerhaven" [local police office Bremerhaven] is the last municipal office in the Federal Republic of Germany which is autonomously responsible for the assessment of police tasks. It will present a chosen number of crime and traffic preventive measures from 2013.

Papilio e.V.

"Papilio" is a programme for kindergartens which is aimed at enhancing socio-emotional competencies and thereby preventing a development of addiction and violence. "Papilio" reduces early behavioural problems and thus prevents addiction and violence in adolescence.

PHINEO gAG

The non-profit organisation "PHINEO gAG" developed a guide under the headline "KURSBUCH WIRKUNG" [Guide Effect] which informs about effect-oriented working and planning strategies in prevention projects. With a number of easily understandable illustrations, proper advice and a practical example, it moreover demonstrates how to analyse the effects of preventive projects.

Polizei Sachsen

The "Landeskriminalamt Sachsen" [State Office of Criminal Investigations] and the "Handwerkskammer Dresden" [Chamber of Crafts Dresden] jointly developed the prevention programme "Sicheres Handwerk" [Safe Handcraft] which is particularly concerned with a preventive fight against robbery in craft businesses in Sachsen.

Polizeiinspektion Schwerin

The "Polizeiinspektion Schwerin" [police station of Schwerin] presents its cooperative project "ZIVICO – Schwerin zeigt Gesicht" [civil courage – Schwerin takes a stand] via a number of posters, the evaluation of a citizen survey on the topic of the citizen's personal sense of security in their hometown, and three spots on civil courage.

Polizeiinspektion Stralsund

The police station of Stralsund presents its anti-violence project "Eh Alter" ['Hey Dude']. Target group of the project are pupils at "Förder- und Sonderschulen" [special needs schools], who have already experienced violence in various forms and who have often been in trouble with the law.

Polizeiliche Kriminalprävention der Länder und des Bundes (ProPK)

The "Polizeiliche Kriminalprävention der Länder und des Bundes (ProPK)" [Police Crime Prevention of the Federation and the States] is an institution of the "Innenministerkonferenz" [Conference of the Ministers of the Interior] that publishes media like e.g. leaflets, broschures and films on a nationwide basis. It thereby informs about different forms of crime and shows how these might be prevented.

Polizeipräsidium Aalen – Haus der Prävention

The police of the Rems-Murr-district provides an advice centre connected to the criminal investigation department that has been available to all citizens needing advice and support since 1987. Since 2007, the "Haus der Prävention" [house of prevention] has provided a wide range of offers regarding prevention in the field of traffic and crime for individuals, schools, networks and a great number of other sections of the population.

Polizeipräsidium Bochum – Kriminalprävention

"Seniorensicherheitsberater" [volontary workers adivising elderly people on safety issues] trained by the police headquarters of Bochum will present the "Seniorensicherheitsprojekt" [project on the safety of elderly people] and their work. Main focus of the work lies on criminal acts to the detriment of elderly people.

Polizeipräsidium Heilbronn

The "Polizeipräsidium Heilbronn" [police headquarters of Heilbronn] will present its new prevention structure with a responsibility for four districts, its cooperation with prevention associations and a number of chosen projects on current topics.

Polizeipräsidium Karlsruhe, Haus des Jugendrechts Pforzheim und Enzkreis – "Anti-Graffiti-Mobil"

In the "Haus des Jugenrechts" [house of juvenile justice], police, prosecution and the "Bezirksverein für soziale Rechtspflege" [county union for the social administration of justice] jointly work together. The youth welfare offices of the city of Pforzheim and the Enzkreis are also part of the cooperation. The concept allows for quick, individual reactions to criminal acts by adolescents.

Polizeipräsidium Karlsruhe, Referat Prävention, Schutzengel Pforzheim-Enzkreis

The project "Junge Fahrer – gib Deinem Schutzengel eine Chance" [Young drivers – give your guardian angel a chance] has been initiated by the Pforzheim-Enzkreis in 2008. The guardian-angel concept relies on the influence of the peer group – voluntary participants are informed about the impact of drugs, alcohol and the main causes of traffic accidents and are thereby qualified as 'guardian angels' who may exert direct influence on the potential driver on the spot.

Polizeipräsidium Ludwigsburg / Referat Prävention

The project "Mit Spaß und Spiel gegen Drogen und Gewalt" [Fun and game against drugs and violence] considers the fact that the social behaviour of children and adolescents is strongly oriented at role models. Since sportsmen and football players in particular exert an important exemplary function, the "VfB Stuttgart" [football club of Stuttgart] actively participates in the project in order to positively influence the thinking and behaviour of children and adolescents with respect to violence and/or the consumption of drugs.

Prävention im Blick – im Landkreis Diepholz

The project "Bürgermut tut allen gut – Nachbarschaften gegen Häusliche Gewalt" [Civil courage is beneficial for everyone – neighbourhoods against domestic violence] will be presented. What is special about this project is that it directly addresses the civilian population in the rural area and thereby aims at a sensitising them and strengthening their own ability to take action when it comes to dealing with domestic violence.

Präventionsnetzwerk Karlsruhe

The "Präventionsnetzwerk Karlsruhe" [prevention network of Karlsruhe] consists of 14 non-profit full-time organisations from Karlsruhe and its district. The network serves as a communication platform independent of all departments and agencies.

Projekt Chance im CJD Creglingen

The "Projekt Chance" [Project Chance] established in the "CJD Creglingen" [Christian association of youth villages in Creglingen] is an extensive pedagogical education and training programme for young men who became offenders. Instead of an imprisonment, the adolescents absolve a temporary training programme that is specifically designed for them.

Rat für Kriminalitätsverhütung Schleswig-Holstein (RfK)

The "Rat für Kriminalitätsverhütung Schleswig-Holstein" [council of crime prevention of Schleswig-Holstein] has been established in 1990 in order to contribute to the reduction of crime and its effects in Schleswig-Holstein via the establishment of a network of governmental and non-governmental organisations and institutions. Moreover, the factual security situation as well as the citizen's subjective sense of security should thereby be enhanced.

Regiestelle TOLERANZ FÖRDERN – KOMPETENZ STÄRKEN und Initiative Demokratie Stärken / BIKnetz – Präventionsnetz gegen Rechtsextremismus

"TOLERANZ FÖRDERN – KOMPETENZ STÄRKEN" [Encourage tolerance – reinforce competence] supports projects for tolerance and democracy and against right-wing extremism. "Initiative Demokratie Stärken" [initiative reinforcing democracy] is a preventive programme against left-wing extremism and Islamic extremism. "BIK-netz – Präventionsnetz gegen Rechtextremismus" [BIK-net – prevention network against right-wing extremism] is a nationwide information and competence network for the support of preventive pedagogical work against right-wing extremism.

Rheinisches Präventionsinstitut gegen Gewalt

The interdisciplinary institute is concerned with the following tasks: research in the field of prevention regarding protection concepts against social, domestic and sexual violence; expert talks on the topic; prevention trainings against social, domestic and sexual violence; establishment of a network with European prevention partners.

Schillerschule Brühl / Baden

The "Schillerschule Brühl /Baden" [school of Brühl/Baden] has been teaching the special subject "TrosT – EIN REDESTABRITUAL" [consolation – a ritual with a talking stick] that is aimed at effective prevention work since 2009/10.

SDNA Technology GmbH

SDNA is part of a consortium located in Schriesheim near Heidelberg which started to make prominent high-value marking products including artificial DNA (kDNA) under the trade name SelectaDNA, SelectaMark and Microdust as a prevention strategy in the fight against theft and robbery in Germany at the end of 2009.

Seehaus e.V.

The project "Seehaus e.V." [Lake house] offers an alternative to the conventional penal system – remote from prison walls and the negative influence of other prisoners. Adolescent offenders willing to refine themselves may apply for the project and may, with the approval of the prison director, spend their prison term within the project.

Sicheres Freiburg e.V.

The association "Sicheres Freiburg e.V." [Safe Freiburg] has been founded on the instigation of the "Freiburger Koordinationsrat Kommunale Kriminalprävention" [municipal crime prevention coordination council of Freiburg] in 2002. Since then, the association has prompted and implemented a great number of projects particularly aimed at crime prevention and the encouragement of civil courage.

SKM – Katholischer Verein für soziale Dienste in der Erzdiözese Freiburg e.V.

The "SKM – Katholischer Verein für soziale Dienste in der Erzdiözese Freiburg e.V." [SKM – Catholic association for social services in the archdiocese of Freiburg] is an umbrella organisation comprising 14 "SKM-Vereine" [association for social services for Catholic men] which are engaged in offender support and assistance to the homeless.

Stadt Esslingen in Kooperation mit dem Polizeirevier Esslingen

The project "Wilde Pause" [Wild break] allows children from age three to 13 to scramble, struggle and wrestle during their break. Being supervised by a pedagogue or teacher, the children learn to realistically estimate themselves in a playful way. Thereby, prejudices and fears of contacts are reduced, frustration tolerance and empathy are enhanced and aggression is dissipated.

Stadt Karlsruhe

Prevention is an important topic for the municipality of Karlsruhe: Many offices are engaged in preventing violence, racism and drug abuse via counseling services and a variety of projects. The city will together with its partners inform about this engagement.

Stadt Karlsruhe – Kulturbüro

The "Kulturbüro Karlsruhe" [cultural office of Karlsruhe] presents two types of events annually realised with a number of partners in Karlsruhe; firstly, the "Karlsruher Wochen gegen Rassismus" [Weeks against racism in Karlsruhe] and secondly "KiX+JuX – Das Kulturfestival der Kinder und Jugendlichen" [Culture festival for children and adolescents].

Stadt Karlsruhe Gleichstellungsbüro ZJD

The "Gleichstellungsbüro ZJD" [office for equal oppprtunities] presents information on the project "Häusliche Gewalt überwinden" [Defeating domestic violence].

Stadt Karlsruhe, Sozial- und Jugendbehörde / Hauptabteilung Beratung

The municipal counseling and advice centres of Karlsruhe will present a number of chosen core themes and projects, e.g. burnout prevention concepts for employees and the project "Jugendschutz Karlsruhe" [Youth protection Karlsruhe] initiated by the addiction prevention division.

Stadt Karlsruhe, Sozial- und Jugendbehörde / Jugendgerichtshilfe

The involvement in the youth penal procedure is legal task of the youth welfare office. A team of social workers advise and support adolescents during the entire proceedings.

Stadt Karlsruhe, Sozial- und Jugendbehörde / Sozialer Dienst

Information on social work at schools as well as on the cooperation of social work at schools and child protection will be provided.

Stadt Karslruhe – Ordnungs- und Bürgeramt

Karlsruhe is a safe city – for this to remain the case, the city highly relies on its "Kommunaler Ordnungsdienst" [municipal security service]. Via the continual presence of this municipal security service in the streets, the citizen's sense of security should be increased.

STEP – Verein zur Förderung von Erziehung und Bildung e.V.

"STEP – Verein zur Förderung von Erziehung und Bildung e.V." [STEP – Association for the support of upbringing and education] is among others concerned with a material and immaterial support of nationwide projects promoting a partnership in the field of education via the programme STEP.

Stiftung Opferhilfe Niedersachsen

The "Stiftung Opferhilfe Niedersachsen" [foundation under public law for victim support in Lower Saxony] was founded in 2001 by the Federal Government of Lower Saxony. The foundation grants victims of criminal acts material support besides the statutory claims and in addition to material benefits provided by victim support offices and promotes victim support as a general social responsibility.

Stiftung Pro Kind

"Pro Kind" [Pro child] is a pilot project in the context of which a home visit programme for financially and socially charged expectant mothers was tested. Specially trained family attendants visited the families from the time of pregnancy until the child's second birthday. Accompanying research with a control group evaluated the pilot project.

Täter-Opfer-Ausgleich im Justizvollzug und LAG TOA Baden-Württemberg

The project "TOA im Justizvollzug" [victim-offender mediation in law enforcement] establishes the possibility for a clarifying communication between victim, perpetrator and their respective relatives and as far as possible for a compensation.

theaterpädagogische werkstatt gGmbH

The "theaterpädagogische Werkstatt gGmbH" [theatre education workshop] has developed prevention programmes on the topics of sexual abuse, addiction, violence, right-wing extremism, civil courage and general concerns about education since 1994.

Triple P Deutschland GmbH

"Liebend gern erziehen mit Triple P" [Educating with affection with Triple P] is a scientifically valid and prevention-oriented approach aimed at strengthening child-raising competencies and further competencies regarding the establishment of parental relationships.

Unfallkasse Baden-Württemberg

The "Unfallkasse Baden-Württemberg" [accident insurance company of Baden-Württemberg] is statutory accident insurance institution for the municipalities and the federal state of Baden-Württemberg. All employees working for municipal or governmental institutions, as well as kindergarten children, pupils and students rank among the company's insurants.

Universität Erlangen – EFFEKT

"EFFEKT: EntwicklungsFörderung in Familien: Eltern- und KinderTraining" [Development support in families: training for parents and children] consists of a behavioural training for parents and a social-cognitive training for children. The trainings are targeted at emotionally charged families.

Verein Programm Klasse2000 e.V.

"Klasse2000 e.V." [Class2000] is the nationally most widespread programme aimed at health promotion as well as at violence and addiction prevention at primary schools. 18.300 classes with more than 420.000 pupils from all federal states participated in the programme in 2012/13.

Verein zur Förderung der Methode Puppenspiel in der Kriminal- und Verkehrsprävention e.V. (VPKV)

The puppet show is a scientifically proven method in the field of crime and traffic prevention. The puppet theatre is nationally mostly applied by police officers who have joined together in the "Verein zur Förderung der Methode des Puppenspiels in der Kriminal- und Verkehrsprävention e.V." [association for the promotion of the method of the puppet show in crime and traffic prevention].

Verkehrsbetriebe Karlsruhe GmbH (VBK)

Prevention work is a very important issue for the "Verkehrsbetriebe Karlsruhe" [transport services of Karlsruhe]. The transportation company therefore published a short film last year, aimed at demonstrating to young people the danger of listening to music via headphones while being on the road.

Verlagsgruppe Hüthig Jehle Rehm GmbH

The "Verlagsgruppe Hüthig Jehle Rehm GmbH" [publishing group Hüthig Jehle Rehm GmbH] offers professional literature on criminological science, practice and training.

WEISSER RING e.V.

Crime prevention is of central importance to the "WEISSER RING e.V." [association 'white ring']. The nationwide non-profit aid organization has supported victims of criminal acts and their relatives for more than 35 years now.

Zartbitter e.V.

"Zartbitter e.V." [Association bittersweet] is a contact and information centre against sexual abuse of girls and boys which provides a number of very different prevention and intervention offers on the topic of sexualized violence.

„Zentrale Beratungsstellen" der freien Straffälligenhilfe mit Förderung durch das Justizministerium NRW

The projects „Zentrale Beratungsstellen" in offender support [central advice centres], which are promoted by the ministry of justice of North Rhine-Westphalia, will report about the practical work within and outside of prisons and will provide information on the offers of the advice centres and the networking in North Rhine-Westphalia.

Zusammenhalt durch Teilhabe

The programme "Zusammenhalt durch Teilhabe" [Solidarity through participation] initiated by the Federal Ministry of the Interior promotes a confident, vivid and democratic community culture in rural and structurally weak areas.

Frank Buchheit, Ruža Karlović

Prevention connects! The Twinning-light Project 'Strengthening Capacities of the Ministry of Interior for Crime Prevention' (Croatia – Baden-Württemberg)

This contribution to the miscellany elucidates the Twinning-light project IPA 2008 which was a cooperation of the Police of the German state Baden-Württemberg and Croatia during a nine-month period in 2012/2013. The article[1] follows the presentation at the 8th International Forum on the 19. German Congress on Crime Prevention but reflects also some later developments – because the cooperation between Croatia and Baden-Württemberg in the field of Crime Prevention continues.

The purpose of the project was (just) to strengthen the capacities of the Ministry of Interior for Crime Prevention. But the purpose is broader than its goals. From the Croatian point of view it was e.g. a big success to implement a large amount of recommendations made by the mixed team of German prevention experts and their Croatian colleagues. Furthermore the development of a Crime Prevention manual was a big step forward, as was the update of the Crime Prevention curriculum for police development and education. Finally changes into the education of police officers at all levels were proposed. But Crime Prevention isn't only a police issue. The claim „Prevention connects" was chosen because prevention improves the quality of life for each individual within the community and it links formal and informal mechanisms of social control. Prevention also connects all levels of the community and fosters its continual evaluation and improvement.

First we would like to introduce the two partners with their structures and recent changes in policing general and police (crime) prevention in particular, then present the components of the project – some only at a glance, some a little broader – and then draw a conclusion on the outcomes of the project.

The first partner: Croatia

It should be stated what Crime Prevention means from a police aspect. In Croatia there is no national strategy for Crime Prevention. There are national strategies and programs in which the Ministry of the Interior participates as the leader or sub-leader in the implementation of measures and activities, based on which the Prevention Department within the General Police Directorate has been undertaking prevention activities. Namely, there is a National strategy for protection against domestic violence, National Road Safety Program, the National Roma inclusion strategy, National Strategy for the Prevention of Drug Abuse etc.

---

[1] The Authors would like to thank Christiane Honer for her support on the preperation of this written version.

As Croatia had a major transition of the political system it is important to prepend a brief overview of the development of modern Croatian police. The most important moment of democratisation within the Croatian police was the passing of the Law on Police in 2000. It made the Croatian police forces step out of the old political regime into a new, democratic one. Another important event came to practice in 2003. The beginning of a formal development within this system began by implementing the community policing approach.

In 2004 community police officers were introduced to police organisations, to be more precise there were added two positions to the police work force i.e. the "community police officer" and "police officer for prevention". This affected the way and methodology of work within the territorial sector. In 2009 a Law on Police Duties and Powers has come into force. This law, in addition to the Law on Police and the Croatian constitution, became the basic legal framework for preventive policing.

In 2011 a new Law on Police came to force and has significally enforced the democratisation within the police in the direction of transparent police career development and introductions of new competition for employing officers to executive positions via public tender.

The history of Croatian Crime Prevention as a symbol for the democratisation process is linked with Baden-Württemberg for a long time. This ranges from the top-management level with the mixed Croatian-Baden-Württemberg government committee to pragmatic solutions on a regional level in Croatia. The Twinning-light project also included the work of prevention information centers. The German partners in the project had equipped centers for Crime Prevention in: Zagreb, Varaždin, Bjelovar and Karlovac and were involved in the opening of centers in the recent years. In the meantime two more Informative Preventive Centers were opened in Osijek last year and Rijeka this year. They were also involved in an analysis of the service rendered as part of the continual development for a better efficiency.

General Police Directorate and Police Administrations		Police Officers for Prevention
General Police Directorate	1 (Department)	5
Bjelovarsko - Bilogorska	/	2
Brodsko Posavska	/	2
Dubrovačko-Neretvanska	/	2
Istarska	1 (Division)	4
Karlovačka	/	2
Korivničko-Križevačka	/	2
Krapinsko-Zagorska	/	2
Ličko-Senjska	/	2
Međimurska	/	2
Osječko-Baranjska	1 (Division)	4
Požešk-Slavonska	/	2
Primorsko-Goranska	1 (Division)	4
Sisačko-Moslovčka	/	2
Splitsko-Dalmatinska	1 (Division)	4
Šibensko-Kninska	/	2
Varaždinska	/	2
Virovitičko-Podravska	/	2
Vukovarsko-Srijemska	/	2
Zadarska	/	2
Zagrebačka	1 (Department)	7
total	6	58

The chart shows the organisational structure for Crime Prevention within the Ministry of Interior, which plays a leading role in Crime Prevention. Within the General Police Directorate there's a Prevention Department that employs five police officers for prevention. Also in the biggest, Zagrebačka County police Administration, there's a Prevention Department. Prevention divisions were founded in the police administrations of the second category (the police administration is divided into four categories). Meaning that on the Croatian territory there are six organisational Crime Prevention units that employ 58 police officers for prevention within the police administration.

These administrations are Zagreb, Rijeka, Osijek, Split and Pula county police administrations, while within the other 15 police administrations there are no Crime
Prevention units, but prevention police officers are organisationally linked to the head
of Police Administration Office.

Depending on the category of police administration there was founded a Department,
Division or Section of Public order under which the work of Crime Prevention is
being done by prevention officers who are also coordinators for community police
officers at the level of police administrations. As such on the national level there
are 692 community police officers (uniformed officers), and 21 community police
officers coordinators.

The developed support of the prevention system is the merit of community police. In other
words, community police and police prevention officers in other police stations unite their
work efforts with the work of the organisational prevention units within the police administrations, and are under the superintendence of the Directorate police administration.

With the purpose of sustainability of the prevention system, Croatian and German
police have continued cooperation through the mixed committee. It is however important to mention that Croatia already had a productive cooperation with the Austrian
police department and the UNDP. The topics of these cooperations were problematic
local areas and the EUCPN accession process. Actually Police Crime Prevention in
Croatia is focused on early prevention and situational oriented Crime Prevention with
an emphasis on property crimes. Crime Prevention in the Croatian police is strategi-
cally evaluated, for this is the key planning criteria of the police work on a national,
regional or local level. The process is developed on the basis of security assessment,
i.e. the evaluation of probability for an event to cause harm.

The second partner: Baden-Württemberg

The second partner within the project is Baden-Württemberg. It makes little sense to
describe the structure of the police in Baden-Württemberg and the prevention landscape already at the beginning of the project. On January 1st, in 2014, the new police
structure came into effect. As for a start: In 2012 Baden-Württemberg was divided
into 38 police departments.

Meanwhile, Baden-Württemberg is divided into only 12 police departments. As part
of the reform has been set, the nearly 500 officers, or more specific "full-time equi-
valents" are available to work for the field of prevention. The heads of prevention
belong organisationally to the headmaster´s office and so even the structure shows
that prevention has a top priority!

With this organisation, the tradition of prevention should be continued seamlessly. It
started in the 1980s, in the 1990s followed the focus of Crime Prevention at commu-

nity level. From 2000 onwards the Baden-Württemberg prevention-officers spread their knowledge and experience throughout south-eastern Europe. Not least because of migratory movements and the flow of „Gastarbeiter", Croatia was also long before the EU accession process a perceived neighbour-country to Baden-Württemberg. The cooperation with Croatia started already 10 years before the Twinning-light project. Particularly the leader of the German delegation, Joe Schneider, had many close and personal contacts.

So it is not surprising to read in the Baden-Württemberg proposal responding to the Croatian Project Fiche:

> „The federal Republic of Germany is particularly interested in supporting the Croatian partner when it comes to strengthening the capacities of public administration. An enhanced administrative and policy making system in Croatia is a precondition for efficiently and effectively transposing and implementing the Acquis Communautaire and the accession to the European Union."

The further expectation was, of course, to continue to benefit from the experience of the international exchange.

Just to give an example: The structured approach to the design of preventive projects using the "Beccaria-Standards" was presented at many missions in Croatia, Romania, Bulgaria, Moldova and further as a useful way. With the promotion to the outside, the procedure developed internally as an exemplary practice and relevant help for project management in the field of Crime Prevention. The basic idea of learning from each other and the systematic development of the existing practice was the general approach of the project. The participating Short-term Experts from Baden-Württemberg have never considered themselves as those who know how prevention in Croatia works. Prevention officers in Croatia are the most distinguished experts of their practice – the German officers could only make a contribution to develop their know-how further. According to this idea the „claim" for the Twinning-light project was selected: „Prevencija spaja! Prevention connects!" It was the conviction of all colleagues that the emergent outcome of the project may be more than the sum of its parts.

Components of the Twinning-light project

To illustrate this, the components of the project shall now be presented. They have evolved from the Croatian Project Fiche and the Baden-Württemberg proposal. To give an overview they will be introduced first in coarse steps and later on a bit more subtle.

The „Component 0" included the management and control tasks as well as the measures for ensuring the visibility of the project. The aim of „Component 1" was to analyze the existing system of Crime Prevention - in theory and practice - and to develop recommendations for the further development. A similar starting point had the „Component 2", which developed a handbook together with Croatian prevention officers. „Component 3" referred to the education & training system to create with competent teachers curricula and teaching materials for Crime Prevention. Finally, it was the task of the „Component 4" to make the created approaches, materials and aids widely known in order to increase the sustainability of the project. The approach of the project was thus both „top-down" and „bottom-up".

It was the idea to promote the second part with an additional measure even further: to obtain a current picture of the orientation of the Crime Prevention in Croatia, a questionnaire was created by the Baden-Württemberg side, which was distributed to all prevention officers and the deputy head of the police headquarters, who are responsible for Crime Prevention on a regional level. The openness of the Ministry of Interior for this step - the data were analyzed in Baden-Württemberg and reported back only in aggregated ways - deserves a special honorable mention! In addition to the hard facts of education & training and the practice of Crime Prevention in Croatia, questions were asked about attitudes and opinions of the Crime Prevention officers - and also answered in a very open way. The aim was both to have a broad and current data base that could be fed as soon as possible in the sub-projects. In addition, the Crime Prevention on base-level should be given a voice and thus their participation will be fostered to the process.

The enumeration of the single measures and activities carried out are presented here only at a glance - some activities shall be explained closer. In activity 1.2, different officers of the Croatian police of different hierarchical levels discussed in a two-day workshop on Crime Prevention in Croatia - including the use of a SWOT analysis. The comparative analysis of Crime Prevention in Belgium, Croatia and Baden-Württemberg provided the insight that there can't be one best system. The relevant context - of civil society actors, from scientific to political support and national prevention councils - is extremely different and requires appropriate solutions. The manual created in activity 2.4 is therefore less on individual model projects, but rather to the structured design of preventive approaches. Fostering Crime Prevention to the state of evaluability is a big step forward to foster effectiveness and efficiency.

Before the Twinning-light project there existed an education for police officers within the basic and advanced degree education. As such from 2005 the Police College has added Crime Prevention into its curriculum. It is still an elective course at the bachelor level and the graduate level. However, the plan is to make it obligatory starting next term, according to German expert recommendation. The will to implement this change was there for a longer time but the hands of the police were tied in deciding the curriculum as these matters are specifically entrusted to the Croatian Ministry of Science, Education and Sports. In the program of basic education there was developed a module in the area of prevention lasting 27 school hours. In the field of police employee specialization, prevention is added into the program for all police officers. Also, there were adopted five new seminars for prevention and community police officers consistent with the recommendations, for example: New technologies, cybercrime, prevention against violence towards children and youth, prevention of drug abuse, and technical security and protection that was verified by the general police director. In the end a program of in-service training which is aimed at police officers in the police stations up until the level of shift supervisor was achieved, and was organized in several modules. One of the modules talks about prevention and during this module uniform, traffic and riot police officers will have a chance to informatively listen about prevention. The lecturers will be prevention police officers that are pedagogically trained.

In publications there were found materials developed by the Croatian police which have preceded the bilateral agreement. The Publishing Department within the PA regularly publishes the journal "The Police and Security" with articles dealing with Crime Prevention. Once the whole publishing was devoted to Crime Prevention[2].

Three years ago, the same Department published the course book: Situational Crime Prevention-from theory to Practice-based evidence. But as a result of the cooperation the new Crime Prevention handbook and a lot of other educational material for police officers at all levels were released.

Prevention Department at the General Police Directorate has deepened the international police cooperation. As a new EU member, Croatia has become an active and rightful member of EUCPN and it is to mention that Croatia has applied to a preventive project and received the European Crime Prevention award. The project is titled "Living life without violence" and it won within the early prevention category last year in Lithuania. Croatian police representatives were a part of the EFUS conference in 2012 in Paris. The Croatian city of Solin is a member of EFUS and is currently the only one in Croatia.

As a result of this Twinning-light project the Beccaria standards were implemented. These have been accepted as guidelines for quality assurance. Preventive projects that are being applied on the national level have been built and transformed with the binding Beccaria standard, while the police administrative projects are being seen and condoned from the side of the Prevention Department. As a result of the stated team work, the General Police Directorate developed a strategic document called "Guidelines for Crime Prevention." This document defines directions for preventive policing; it also defines the leaders of preventive work, their responsibilities, financial assets, international police cooperation and several more topics. This document has been forwarded for implementation and action to all belonging units last year.

Regarding the financing of police preventive work, it is common practice for Prevention programs to be financed with the support of partners outside the Ministry of the Interior, i.e. the UNDP that had been financing most of the preventive police activity.

---

[2]   cf.: Ruža Karlović / Frank Buchheit (2013): Stavovi policijskih službenika o modelu koncepcijske određenosti uloge I organizacije policije. In: Policija i Sigurnost, 1-2013, ISNN: 1848-428X. Available online: www.mup.hr/mobile/default.aspx?id=161858.

There is also a way of financing activities with the help of local councils for Crime Prevention. However, in line with the recommendations, in the future we will practice financing through resources from the budget of the Ministry of Interior and we will encourage the formation of trusts through the work of the council for Crime Prevention of the local government for a more transparent way of financing. Last year there was developed one trust in Međimurska County by the police administration.

Putting the prevention units at a high level within police hierarchy gives importance to police prevention and aids its implementation. As a conclusion it is to state that prevention of crime is the priority task of managers.

A recommendation that has not yet been implemented has to do with the establishment of the National Coordination Group for Prevention of Crime. However, this coordination group within Croatia is formed according to specific project thematics, meaning that if a project is recognized as useful on a national level; interests and duties of local and regional prevention upholders are being followed through the work of this national coordination group. Stronghold of action for this group is the ministerial decisions of cooperations. An example of that would be the project called "High five healthy life" where four ministries were involved with their representatives who overlooked the joint project on a national level.

When, comparing the two pictures, i.e. before and after bilateral cooperation we can notice an apparent growth in duties and the last implementation element, which is evaluation, seems to connect the steps in a nice project systematic. Exchange of relevant data and monitoring of preventive activities is currently executed through the OZI base. OZI is a public map within the system which is connected to all organisational units for prevention within the police. Currently a database inspired by the German model is to be developed. It'll be used as a checklist to monitor prevention officers a more objectively. The performance of each employee is assessed once a year.

As part of the „Component 4" the four regional workshops should be mentioned, in which the results of the efforts were presented. They experienced a very positive feedback from colleagues. According to the motto „Prevencija spaja!" there are certainly many photographic proofs of this alignment. Beside the official „family photos" the support of administration and politics deserves a particular and thankful mention. Both the kick-off and closing event experienced brisk attention of the Croatian Ministry of the Interior and afterwards from the official representatives as well as by the press. On the final „family photo" also representatives of science are mapped so that the theme of the 19th "German Congress on Crime Prevention" has already been anticipated: prevention needs practice, science and policy!"

The closing event was accompanied by the police inspector of the riot police of the German countries, Mr. Wolfgang Lohmann, the President of the Police of Baden-Württemberg, Mr. Gerhard Klotter, next to Mr. Erich Marks, whom you may have heard at the opening of the congress. From all the parties, the conclusion was drawn that after the „hot phase" of the Twinning-light project the good cooperation should be continued steadily. The everyday life in the project consisted of countless conversations, conferences, workshops and informal talks - sometimes even late in the night in our non-official representation: a Pub in the heart of Zagreb. The pictures point out, what „Prevencija spaja!" means: The joint development of results on a level playing field with the Croatian colleagues.

Conclusion

The Twinning-light project consisted – to mention some hard facts – of additional 200,000 euros, it had been implemented within eleven months, in five components, 18 activities and 25 measures as well as 152 working days. Eleven colleagues were called as Short-term Experts for the Twinning-light project, eight of them were actively involved in the project activities. The vast majority was able to hark back to years of experience in ISEC missions in Croatia and other countries in Southeast Europe. It would be appropriate to name here all project participants and to mention their contributions with praise. However, since there are at least 43 names, it's easier to refer to the mentioning in the manual on page 75. You will find the participants involved in alphabetical order of their first names - what is to be regarded as an expression of the close cooperation of colleagues.

But it wouldn't be possible to run this project with only these resources. Both partners brought in staff and resources, which are not included on this list. Based on the Baden-Württemberg experience, presumably there was for every business day in Croatia at least two at home. Finally the immense efforts of the Croatian partners should be mentioned here.

In the original plan, the components were organized in a clear sequence as logical structure. The real implementation ran for several reasons somewhat less clearly structured. On the one hand, the holidays had to be put into consideration. The complete month of August needed to be excluded from project activities, as the Croatian police was busy with other tasks (specially with tourism-related tasks on the Mediterranean coast). The same was to be pointed out for the Christmas period, in which all participants had to recharge from the first half of the project – and were celebrating Christmas with their families.

Another challenge was the Croatia police-reform-induced change of the Croatian project manager - from Mato Blažanović to Sandra Veber. Although there were no substantial breakages, many agreements already achieved had to be re-discussed and clarified. The fact that the handover of the baton went so smoothly was a performance of the entire project, but especially the Croatian and German project management, which had to carry a lot of conversations during those days.

There's a question with a good cause to an only eleven month project, which wanted to change a lot – was there a sustainable change realized? We have observed that the process of Crime Prevention is of the goals noted in the main document indicating the strategic plan of the Ministry of Interior and other institutions whose responsibilities encompass the work of preservation within public security. Within this strategic plan, the first goal is to reduce the risk of criminal behavior as well as to improve the prevention of crime. The ways of implementation can be recognized in the same way as the results of this project. These ways are, as previously noted: project development and implementation, strengthening networks of councils for Crime Prevention (Croatia holds 216 councils) and adoption of good practices of other nations in Crime Prevention. In other words, the results of this project can even be recognized in this strategic document. It is visible that both sides have profited from this project.

We are very satisfied with all the project outcomes and want to thank our partners for their effort and cooperation in making this project a success. We are looking forward to further cooperation. As someone said teamwork divides the task and multiplies the success, we can truly see the result of that within this project and all of our presentations. We would like to put an emphasis on the outcome, as the effect beyond the project itself, is specially to be seen in the common learning and the associated harmonization and further development of the prevention of both partner countries. This was reflected in a, to use a little exaggerated formulation, "jealous" remark of a Baden-Württemberg colleague, not involved in the project: „If you make all these cool things in Croatia - what do you actually offer to us?" This wasn't only jealousy, but also the desire for a more structured development of preventive approaches (think of the Beccaria standards), the professional implementation of projects (for example with the help of project management measures) and ultimately the focus on effective and thus resource-saving, efficient approaches in Crime Prevention. With this knowledge the colleague told: "Hey, I also want these cool tools that you were presenting in Croatia!"

To put this a little more sophisticated: the project showed that procedures and methods of evidence-oriented Crime Prevention can be implemented in the daily routines of Police Crime Prevention. The positive example can lead to the desire of non-participants to go this route as well. We are not yet at the end of this road, rather at the beginning, but we are together in this way: Prevention connects! Prevencija spaja!

Jörg Ziercke

Cybercrime - the darker side of the digital society

1. Introduction

Ladies and Gentlemen,

Thank you very much for giving me the opportunity to open today's special event on Cybersecurity as part of this year's German Congress on Crime Prevention.

First some preliminary remarks on the objectives of my presentation.

1. Reports on cybercrime are aimed at clarification, not demonization.
2. Knowledge of cybercrime aims at raising user awareness, protecting the user.
3. Trust in the internet is to be strengthened.

My aim today is to look at prevention, not legal aspects arising from encryption and anonymisation.

The internet has permeated nearly all areas of life; for many it has become an integral part of their lives. "Always on" is the catchphrase. Terms such as "smart home", "internet of things" or "industry 4.0" are synonyms which underline the fact that modern IT, data processing and the internet will influence our everyday lives and economic activities to an even greater extent in the future.

During the time it took me to give this brief introduction, around the world:

- about 1.3 million videos were watched on Youtube,
- more than 2 million enquiries were googled,
- 6 million Facebook entries were viewed,
- 100,000 twitter messages[1] and over 200 million emails were transmitted, though over 90% of these were SPAM mails.

But like all aspects of life, there is an up and a downside! In order to protect yourself from cybercriminals, you have to know more about the phenomena of cybercrime.

Cybercrime is a new dimension of crime which changes each day. Perpetrators have access to countless potential victims and targets worldwide. The potential risk for the individuals, business enterprises and financial institutions, as well as for the state and its institutions, is considerable and omnipresent. For the perpetrators, the risk of being caught is small compared to the analogue world. Cybercrime's growth potential is boundless, as

---

[1]   Other sources estimate this number at roughly 300,000

is the potential damage it can wreak. The internet has done away with national borders, which means that there are no criminal-geographic areas in the cyber world. Terrorism and organised crime do not recognise any borders and are constantly growing.

One thing is for certain: the internet and modern means of communication have decisively influenced our communication behaviour and social life. On the one hand, they have found their way into traditional forms of crime, especially in the field of fraud; on the other hand we see the emergence of new forms of crime – forms of crime that would not be possible without the use of modern information and communication technology. In almost all areas of crime, perpetrators avail themselves of sophisticated technology and use the internet as an instrument of crime. Throughout the world, people become the victims of fraud, extortion, property crime, phishing, theft of their digital identity, Scareware, Ransomware, cyber grooming and cyber bullying. They allow themselves to be radicalised and recruited, are duped into believing criminal scams of ostensibly online shops or call centres, unknowingly become part of a botnet, the instrument of modern crime. It is not only citizens who are the victims of cybercrime. Enterprises are also the focus of criminal activities.

The objective is to compromise data, to use the digital identity of someone else for one's own criminal purpose, to access know-how and protected information.

But it is also about attacks on critical infrastructures, states or companies.

All users, but especially companies, must actively address the issue of cybersecurity if we are to meet the challenges posed by cybercrime. According to a security study carried out by Corporate Trust, "Industrial espionage 2012", less than half the companies surveyed had a security management with clear regulations for information protection. And only every fifth company had even defined know-how worthy of protection. Studies have repeatedly demonstrated the reluctance of companies to report attacks. Surveys carried out at chambers of commerce and industry have highlighted the fact that only 20% of companies in Germany lodge a complaint following a cyber attack. This means that undetected crime is at least 5 times higher than the official figures!

Why are such attacks not reported to the police?

- Filling a complaint is too time consuming,
- companies are skeptical that investigation by the authorities will be successful,
- or the companies do not know who to contact within the authorities.

And there is another reason: they fear damage to their reputation. However, as long as enterprises fail to recognise the danger or refuse to report identified attacks, the authorities cannot become active and cannot draw up a comprehensive picture of the threat posed. There have always been cases of victims who for various reasons did not report crimes. Many people are unaware of the fact that they are the victim of a crime, many crimes go undetected!

Data theft is a particularly good example: 2.0 theft is a case of copying, i.e. the stolen data is never removed from where it is stored. The "loss" is frequently only noticed when the damage has already been done, for example, a copyright violation or product piracy.

2. Current Forms of Cybercrime

A brief look at current forms of cybercrime

2.1 Phishing

One of the best known forms of cybercrime is probably phishing in connection with online banking. The number of reported cases has fallen, but is still at between 3000 and 4000 incidents.

In 2012, the number of such cases in Germany fell sharply by 46% to about 3,400 (3,440; 2011:6,422). The number of undetected incidents is unknown. The average loss incurred was around 4000 euro per incident. An explanation for this lies in the fact that, in addition to a greater awareness on the part of the users, in 2012 many German banks improved their security systems, especially with the introduction of the so-called mobile TAN (mTAN) procedure. With the mTAN procedure the transaction number required for authorisation for online transactions is sent to the bank customer's mobile telephone. The introduction of this second, independent communication channel improves security. We saw a similar drop in the number of incidents in 2008 when German banks introduced the iTAN procedure throughout Germany. However, in the following year the figures rose again and in 2010 had increased well above the all-time high of 2007. It remains to be seen how long the new security system will be an obstacle to criminals.

The phishing tools used develop at the same pace that security measures are introduced. The procedure used by offenders in the early days, when they sent unsolicited bulk emails in which the recipients were called upon to reveal their online banking access data, is almost a thing of the past. Malware is invariably used. The volume of new malware has increased sharply. Every one to two seconds a new malware programme is created somewhere in the world. In order to circumvent the functionality of virus protection programmes, these are normally only active for a few days and are then replaced by new versions.

Currently, phishers favour the following variations to spread their malware.

1. „Drive-by infection": Unwitting downloading of malware simply by visiting a website which offenders have compromised.

2. The malware is spread via social networks[2] in which the subsequent victim trusts the offender and then either opens infected attachments in good faith or follows links.

3. "Spear infection" Specific individuals targeted with personalised phishing or infection mails with the aim of infecting the computer or obtaining data required to carry out other actions. One reason for this modus operandi is that many internet users have become increasingly wary of opening anonymous emails. However, they are less cautious if the email is addressed to them personally.

Meanwhile, two thirds of the malware is spread by means of drive-by infections. According to the IT sector[3], each day 13,000 infected websites are uploaded on the internet worldwide[4]. Additionally, hackers target frequently visited websites in an effort to manipulate these websites with a view to spreading the malware much faster and reaching a larger group of users. In this way offenders can, for example, disseminate Trojans which are capable of "interposing" themselves between online banking transactions in order to manipulate transfer details.

In spite of a recent fall in numbers, online banking continues to be one of the main targets. Offenders have already responded to the introduction of the mTAN process and have achieved initial successes.

They go about this in the following way:

1. Using traditional phishing methods attackers extract access data used for online banking.

2. Without the bank customer being aware of this, they then set up the mTAN procedure. The offenders provide a mobile number for receipt of the mTAN.

3. The activation code provided by the bank per mail is intercepted by the offenders.

4. The offenders are now able to transfer money from the bank customer's account.

But even this scam is now a thing of the past. In the meantime we can see a technically more sophisticated attack scenario. Here the offenders use malware to attack the mTAN procedure on Android smartphones, making it is no longer necessary to infect a computer. The offenders are not only responding to the introduction throughout Germany of the mTAN procedure by the German banks, but also the increasing use of smartphones and tablet computers for online banking.

---

[2]   E.g. Facebook, Studi-VZ, Wer-Kennt-Wen

[3]   IT service provider Symantec

[4]   dpa press release dated 2 March 2010

This development demonstrates that the offenders are constantly endeavouring to keep pace with security applications on the market. The extent to which the offenders are market oriented is demonstrated by the fact that devices using the Android operating system are attacked. 75% of all mobile terminals worldwide are run on the Android operating system, which means it holds a dominant market position.

- The "Google play store" alone offers almost 1 million apps for this operating system, not to mention apps offered by third parties. There is a real possibility of coming up against a "black sheep", and possibly malware.

- Almost 700,000 malware variations have been identified on Android devices since the beginning of this year.

Many Android devices use even older versions of this operating system. There are usually no support contracts and thus no obligation on the part of the manufacturer to provide updates. The consequences: security vulnerabilities which are identified after a device has been purchased are not fixed. The devices are often poorly protected.

2.2 Digital Identity

Cyber criminals are interested in all types of access data which ultimately enables them to conduct internet transactions at the expense of third parties and for their own benefit. The digital identity is the sum of all possibilities and rights of the individual users and their activities within the overall structure of the internet. In concrete terms: All kinds of user accounts including passwords.[5]

The German authorities are currently dealing with a case where investigations into cyber criminals resulted in the discovery of a data collection of about 16 million German and other e-mail addresses with passwords. It is not yet known how the offenders obtained the data, whether the data has already been fraudulently misused and, if so, what possible losses have been incurred. You have doubtlessly heard that in connection with this the Federal Office for Information Security set up the website "www. sicherheitstest.bsi.de" at the beginning of 2014. Internet users were able to check if data associated with them was listed. Some 30 million people made use of the service. There were about 1.6 million hits directly linked to the requesting parties, i.e. the email in question was amongst the 16 million stolen data files.[6] Recently, another case of 16 to 20 million stolen email account data became known.

---

[5]   Examples: E-mail and messenger services, social networks, e-commerce (online banking, online brokerage, sales portals such as eBay, reservation systems for flights, hotels, etc.), home office accounts with access to internal company resources, e-government, cloud computing

[6]   As of 12 February 2014: 29.7 queries, 1.58 million hits

2.3 Carding

Credit card data in particular, including payment addresses and further information, is also a part of one's digital identity. Our estimates indicate that over the last few years at least 200,000 credit card holders in Germany were victims of fraudulent credit card transactions – a trend that is on the increase. We are talking here about „carding".

We estimate that the financial losses incurred by the German financial sector alone were in the mid three-digit million euro range – approximately 70 % of these losses were the result of Internet transactions! According to Interpol, more than 160 million lost credit card data with a purchasing power of over 5 billion USD was recorded throughout the world in 2010 alone.

Let me give you an example of the profitable use of credit card data by cyber criminals:

One of the largest modern-style bank robberies was committed exactly one year ago. Following successful hacking attacks, offenders used forged credit cards to make 17,000 withdrawals totaling about 40 million USD in 23 countries around the world within two days. 2.3 million euro was withdrawn in eight cities in Germany.

2.4 Scareware, Ransomware

A further example of the perpetrators' inventiveness is the use of what is referred to as Scareware – software that is meant to generate fear. The user is guided onto a web site where he is led to believe that a system scan for viruses, trojans etc, has been conducted on his computer and a large amount of malware identified. The user is then offered a tool to remove the malware. During the execution of the tool on the computer a purported anti-virus solution is installed. This has to be paid for and registered following installation. Because he is concerned about the security of his data, the customer discloses his credit card details for the payment. Whilst providing this data the customer is called upon to supply further information in respect of his address and/or email address. What the customer does not know is that the tool installed for the purpose of helping him avert supposed threats to his computer in fact ensures that malware is installed on his system.

With regard to the number of offences committed using Scareware: Microsoft reports that in one year they alone purged over 13 million computers of Scareware. Such "digital extortion", in different variants, is an increasing phenomenon to which both private individuals and companies can fall victim. Some examples:

- Compromised data that was "stolen" from the original owner is offered for re-purchase.
- The attacker threatens to make public the successful attack on the data or IT infrastructure of a company. The company in question is told to pay "hush money".

- The exaction of protection money, for example by threatening to carry out a DDoS attack on the company's IT infrastructure. Should the company refuse to pay, an attack is indeed carried out. But more on this later.

Ransomware works in a similar way. Ransomware infects, for example, the computer of victims while they are surfing the internet. A pop-up window appears claiming that the computer has been used for criminal acts and has therefore been locked. To unlock the computer the user has to pay a "fine" of €100 by means of a digital payment system. He is advised that the hard disk will be deleted if he fails to make the payment. Relatively small sums are demanded with a view to motivating as many infected victims as possible to make a payment. To create the impression that this is a police measure, the offenders use logos of police authorities and various well-known antivirus software vendors. In one particular case, over a period of only two days an offender in Germany attempted to infect 200,000 computers and was successful in 32,000 cases.

Numerous countries all over the world are meanwhile affected by this phenomenon. Adapted versions of Ransomware are now also circulated, for example, in North and South America. The reason for this is that the malware source code can be bought in the so-called underground economy (since late 2011).

2.5 Botnets

Cybercriminals often use so-called botnets to carry out their offences these are computers of usually unsuspecting victims which cybercriminals have infected with malware and gained control over. Once infected, the victim's computer is used to carry out attacks; it becomes an instrument of crime!

The dimensions botnets can take on can be seen from an example in Spain. A 23-year-old „bot herder" had control over a global botnet („Mariposa") with 12 million infected computers.

Early in June 2013, the United States carried out measures directed at the infrastructure of the so-called Citadel botnets.

Approximately 1,000 of an estimated total of 1,400 Command &Control Servers, servers to control bots, were deactivated in more than 80 countries. According to Microsoft, up to 5 million personal computers all over the world are thought to be infected by the Citadel malware.[7]

Following on from PC systems, cyber criminals are now increasingly focusing their attention on smartphones. These are infected by manipulated Apps. When a smartphone is infected it becomes part of a botnet and malware with other functions can be ins-

---

[7] Reuters, 06 June 2013

talled at any time. From the perpetrators' point of view the smartphone is the better bot! Modern smartphones are high-performance devices which are "always on" and permanently connected to the internet via modern high-speed networks.

It is examples like this which show that criminals analyse new technologies for potential illegal application, identify flaws and within a very short period develop methods to exploit these for their own purposes.

2.6 Underground Economy

A separate market has been established on the internet which provides everything cyber criminals require to carry out offences. The products available in the underground economy range from:

1. malware to
2. server capacity,
3. anonymous or encrypted communication channels,
4. services for creating false identities,
5. credit card data right up to
6. anonymous payment systems.

This illustrates how professionally organised and lucrative cybercrime is.

2.7 Attacks on Critical Infrastructures

For quite some time now the internet, and other services available on the internet, have themselves become critical infrastructures. As already mentioned, attacks can have fatal consequences for the economy and society. The borderlines between crime, espionage and terrorism are diffuse.[8]

A series of attacks directed at industrial facilities and critical infrastructures worldwide since 2010[9] has been a powerful reminder of the far-reaching consequences a cyber attack which exploits the flaws in a system can have.

Or: The consequences of a mass DDoS attack in March 2013 on the SPAMHAUS group, an organisation combating unwanted internet advertising, can be regarded as collateral damage. SPAMHAUS creates, among other things, real-time blacklists of spam senders in order to enable internet providers to filter out such authors. However, the attack not only blocked access to the SPAMHAUS website, but also resulted in a temporary breakdown of the UK's central internet node and slowed down large parts of the entire internet.

---

[8]   FAZNET, 07 February 2011; DE MAIZIÈRE on the occasion of the Munich Security Conference

[9]   The stuxnet trojan was first discovered in July 2010

2.8 Cyber bullying

However, let us not forget commonplace cases such as cyber bullying.

Cyber bullying is the use, mostly by pupils, of the internet or mobile phone to deliberately insult, threaten or harass over a long-term period. The perpetrators use the internet and mobile telephone services to humiliate and harass their victims. A whole range of internet services are used for this purpose such as emails, online communities, microblogs, chats, (chat rooms, instant messenger), discussion forums, guest books and boards, video and photograph platforms, web sites, and other applications. Mobile telephones are used for such bullying whereby calls, text messages, MMSs or emails are sent to the victim to tyrannize him or her. Today, mobile phones are equipped with cameras and video cameras, digital voice recorders and access to the internet, all of which facilitate bullying by means of easy-to-use technology.

The internet seems to lower the inhibition threshold for bullying activities. Many people seem to find it easier to attack, insult and humiliate someone in the apparently anonymous virtual world. The psychological face-to-face inhibition threshold no longer exists. There is a smooth transition from „fun" to violence in terms of bullying. Statements such as, „I was only joking" highlight the fact that such „practical jokers" frequently have no sense of right and wrong and lack sufficient awareness of the consequences of their actions.

The fact that the internet never forgets, and by this I mean that even deleted contents can come to the surface again and again, means that the victim can be repeatedly confronted with the material even though the conflict with the perpetrator has been resolved. Cyber bullying can at times have tragic consequences. There are cases of pupils who committed suicide as a result of cyber bullying.

In 2011, 25,000 European children and teenagers between the ages of 9 and 16 were interviewed as part of the EU Kids Online study. They were asked about their experience with cyber bullying. Spread throughout Europe, 6% of the children and teenagers interviewed stated that over the last 12 months they had been the victim or perpetrator of cyber bullying. Five percent of children in Germany have had such experience with bullying, which means that Germany is slightly below the European average.

3. Suppression strategies

The threats posed by cybercrime are manifold. The Internet provides perpetrators with numerous opportunities to commit offences, innumerable potential victims and points of attacks. There is a significant potential for risks and extensive damage and, in our estimation, this is expected to increase over the coming years. Technical developments towards an „always on" society will reinforce the effect. In this context the increasing popularity of smartphones and mobile computers such as tablets will play a decisive role.

3.1 Global Player Initiative

New forms of crime underline clearly that there is no alternative to a holistic suppression strategy.

Besides consistent operational action across agencies, it is essential to integrate the business sector in a network of information. In recent years the Bundeskriminalamt has increased its co-operation with the private sector. We have taken the initiative to start an intensive direct dialogue with the private sector, in particular with German global players who do business throughout the world. In the meantime, 58 companies have decided to enter into co-operation with our office.

Often, enterprises possess important information which can supplement intelligence held at our end and which can be incorporated in our early detection strategies. In return we can raise the business community's awareness of security risks. Businesses are then able to take the necessary protective measures.

3.2 IPPP

We believe that the expertise available in companies, research institutes, industry and science will have to be fully exploited in the fight against cybercrime to a much greater extent than has been the case so far. Moreover, we want to comply with the request made by numerous business enterprises and associations to establish a central point of contact for all questions related to cybercrime.

As a first step in the area of cybercrime, we entered into an institutionalised Public Private Partnership (iPPP) with the key actors of the banking sector.[10] This new co-operation platform with its "German Competence Centre for Cybercrime" (G4C), set up by major German banks, has an operational orientation. Cybercrime specialists from the BKA are attached to this centre. The aim here is to strengthen all aspects of efficient criminal prosecution in this area of crime.

3.3 Response recommendations in cases of cybercrime

The following applies to the private sector.

Anyone can be the victim of cybercrime. A study has shown[11] that small and medium-seized businesses are a favoured target for cyber criminals. 50 percent of all cyber attacks target companies with fewer than 2,500 staff, a third of the companies affected have fewer than 250 staff.

Such companies are easy prey for cyber criminals precisely because they think they are of no interest to cyber criminals and have therefore failed to establish adequate security

---

[10]   Signing of co-operation agreement with G4C planned for 21 January 2014

[11]   Symantec Corporation: Internet Security Threat Report 18/2013

precautions. At a first glance, the reasons given by the companies for not reporting attacks may seem plausible. Nevertheless, the consequences of such a policy are very counter-productive. As long as companies continue to conceal attacks they have identified, the authorities in charge will remain in the position that they will neither have an opportunity to carry out an investigation nor have an accurate overview of the true situation. The potential to cause damage increases if offences are not reported!

It is against this background that one should view the obligation to report cyber attacks, which policymakers are considering and which business circles reject

State police authorities and the BKA have drawn up "Response recommendations for the private sector in cases of cybercrime". These guidelines are intended to provide targeted companies with concrete information on how they should respond to cyber attacks and remove any uncertainty they may have in connection with reporting such criminally relevant incidents. The interests of the law enforcement authorities and the companies are therefore given due consideration. The following are just some aspects:

- statutory basis is presented,
- recommendations for senior management and system administrators are provided,
- possibilities and principles of police investigative work are presented,
- and central contact points at the federal and state police are provided.

These recommendations are available in printed form or online at the BKA's homepage www.bka.de.

But the principle applies that one can protect oneself from internet attacks.

1. PC protection: Computer protection using anti-virus programmes and a firewall should always be your first priority. As data carriers such as CDs and USB memory sticks are increasingly being used to spread malware, it is advisable to check these for viruses before use.
2. Emails and chat: Only open emails from senders you trust. Suspicious emails from people you do not know should be immediately deleted. Malware is often concealed in graphics or email attachments. Under no circumstances should you open suspicious data files!
3. Software: Be careful about which software or plug-ins you install. A healthy distrust helps: If you have any doubts regarding authenticity, then it is better to forgo the download or installation.
4. File sharing network: Anyone who shares files with people they do not know risks infecting his/her computer with malware programmes. Moreover, sharing music, films or software which is protected by copyright is a criminal offence and can, in addition to a fine and imprisonment, lead to a compensation claim on the part of the owners of the rights.

5. Online shopping: Numerous businesses are evaluated on shopping, auction and price-comparison sites. A positive evaluation can be an indication of professional business practices. In any case, a good portion of honest mistrust is advisable - especially with regard to web sites offering goods well below the market price.

6. Payment on the internet: One should be particularly careful when purchasing goods on the internet, especially where payment in advance is required. When making a payment, account and credit card details should be transmitted via an encrypted connection.

7. Online banking: The connection to the computer used for banking purposes must, as is the case when making online payments, be encrypted. There are frequent new protection processes such as iTAN, eTAN and HBCI. You should contact your bank and select the latest process.

8. Private information and passwords: Do not use the same password for multiple services - for example email accounts, online shops and communities. The longer a password is, the more difficult it is to crack.

9. Offers to become a goods or financial agent: Any offers received on the internet or by email to work as a goods or money agent should be strictly rejected. If you comply with dubious offers and forward goods or money, you are aiding and abetting fraud or money laundering and will have to face criminal proceedings and claims for compensation.

10. Apps and subscription tricks: You should be aware of the fact that apps involve costs and can transmit sensitive data. You should be wary of any apps which are free of charge. Caution is called for with online services which require registration. Amongst the mass of serious promotion offers there are cases where people are unconsciously duped into ordering goods or entering into subscription contracts.

I therefore appeal to you: The responsible use of the internet lies in your hands!

4. Conclusion

The internet has become an indispensible pillar of global economic, political and social information and communication processes, but also provides the breeding ground for all sorts of criminal activity.

We must not allow the internet to become an area where the law does not apply. Crime suppression must be possible here too in order to bolster confidence in the internet and maintain its advantages.

In order to be able to successfully counter internationally active and networked cybercrime, a culture of trusting co-operation between the security authorities is required. We are facing joint challenges which we have to tackle in a concerted and coordinated way and on which we need to share our knowledge.

Companies, and ultimately also the general public, must raise their awareness of the situation and take responsibility for their own actions. I therefore welcome this special event on cybersecurity within the framework of the German Congress on Crime Prevention.

Wolfgang Kahl

Developmental support and violence prevention for young people: Prerequisites for success and sustainability

Perspectives for a systematic development and dissemination of effective violence prevention programmes in Germany

1. Introduction: ... the question of designing projects sustainable (?)

This article explains the approach of complementary developmental support and violence prevention for young people and describes the efforts of the Foundation German Forum for Crime Prevention (DFK) and its partners as well as the involvement of staff of its office, aimed at improving the quality of developmental support and violence prevention work in the relevant fields of activity of social policy (such as youth, family, social affairs, education, interior affairs, judicial affairs) and at strengthening it in the long term. "Gelingensbedingungen für die Prävention von interpersonaler Gewalt im Kindes- und Jugendalter" [Prerequisites for the successful prevention of interpersonal violence among children and young people] (2008/2012) and "Impulse zur Entwicklungsförderung und Gewaltprävention für junge Menschen" [Impulses on developmental support and violence prevention for young people] (2013) are two booklets that have given practitioners specialised principles for a developmental understanding of support and prevention. In these works, experts in the field have compiled scientific and practice-related findings and make recommendations for educational work. In spring 2014, the DFK and the Lower Saxony Crime Prevention Council presented their joint web portal "Wegweiser Entwicklungsförderung und Gewaltprävention" [directory on developmental support and violence prevention], an interactive range of information that links programme recommendations of Lower Saxony's "Green List Prevention" with information and advice on implementing prevention concepts. In a further step, training courses are to be developed that support those in positions of responsibility in educational institutions to successfully design sustainable processes of change and implementation.

2. Conceptual approach: To support the positive development of young people

Nearly one young person in five in Germany temporarily exhibits problematic experience and behaviour. As well as introverted forms, such as fears and depression, aggression, delinquency, violence, criminality and substance abuse in particular are widespread. Many such behavioural problems are not very serious and are overcome through a stabilising social environment and other positive influences as well as through developmental support. That applies, for example, in the case of so-called typical juvenile delinquency and violence. However, a small proportion of each year group develops serious, long-term problems from childhood that can last into adulthood. Among young people who have behavioural problems only later, these problems often do not disappear by themselves. As a result of serious behavioural problems in particular, victims, the family and the social environment suffer. It is not infrequently the case that offenders themselves are also victims, e.g. as a result of abuse, family neglect or adverse life circumstances. Social behavioural problems are also associated with greater difficulties in education, gaining vocational qualifications, health and social integration. Considerable costs are incurred to society, which can amount to more than a million euro in individual cases.

Both with regard to victims and offenders and to society as a whole, it is therefore necessary to take counter-action through preventive measures as early and as effectively as possible. This takes place within the context of prevention that is related to and supports development.

Developmental violence prevention is based on the assumption that dissocial behavioural problems and serious forms of criminality are often manifestations of a development history. Particularly when serious problems occur at an early stage, it is not infrequent for problematic long-term careers to continue into adulthood. Extensive research into the causes in recent years has shown that many biological, psychological and social factors are responsible for problems of violence and criminality.

The approach of developmental violence and crime prevention is based on the understanding that it is worth promoting the healthy social development of children and youngsters and to nip in the bud any imminent negative developments. Prevention measures that are related to or support development are based on systematic forms of social training and education in the context of the family, school and local community and are directed at different target groups (children, young people, parents, teachers, the social environment and entire municipalities) with a view to reducing the risk factors that cause adverse developments and to strengthening protective factors.

The developmental approach is not in competition with other measures (e.g. situation-related crime prevention), but is a central consistent part of integrated, cross-cutting prevention concepts. Priority is to be given to its development, without devaluing or neglecting other prevention concepts. Developmental support in general social contexts overlaps with work in the field of primary prevention and the effects are mutually supplementary.

The major individual, family and social risk factors for behavioural problems among young people are known, whereas less research has been done into the influence of protective factors. The development risks can have differing effects in individual cases and also vary according to the person's age and stage of development. The respective prevention programmes should be designed accordingly. In Germany, there are now many approaches that aim to prevent behavioural problems among children arising in the first place and establishing themselves, and to support positive development. These include early social and cognitive support, social competence training, parenting advice, courses in child education, home visits by family helpers, all-day childcare, anti-mobbing programmes in schools, measures to prevent school failure, parent meetings in socially disadvantaged neighbourhoods, integration programmes for migrants, neighbourhood help and youth delinquency treatment measures.

International research indicates that developmental prevention is promising and that effective programmes are also worthwhile from the point of view of their cost-benefit ratio. It is therefore necessary that this area be developed in Germany as a matter of urgency, not only in terms of quantity, but above all also with regard to the quality of interventions. The work of the German Forum for Crime Prevention and the resulting knowledge base serve this end. They contain basic considerations and criteria for the successful development, implementation, evaluation and dissemination of develop-ment-related prevention programmes. The information can help practitioners, politici-ans, administrators and other interested persons to appropriately judge the relevance and quality of existing prevention programmes and to take well-founded decisions. The available knowledge base, which is continually expanding, also serves to support the sustainable dissemination of effective and practicable approaches to prevention.

A review of the DFK's work to date shows a continual process of compiling and trans-ferring scientific expertise for social and pedagogical fields of activity for children and young people.

3. Impulses of the DFK for the further development of violence prevention in Ger-many in the period from 2001 to 2011

From its beginnings in 2001, the DFK's work has focused on the question of how vio-lence prevention can be systematically and sustainably designed. The following presen-tation shows the thread running through its activities to date.

3.1 Project "Primary prevention of violence towards group members" (2001-2006)

In August 2001, the Federal Ministry of Justice commissioned the Foundation to dis-cuss the criminological concept of "hate crimes" developed in the USA with a view to the German situation and to draw conclusions for prevention.

The manifestation of violence stemming from prejudice is characterised by the motive of humiliating, intimidating and violently attacking people on account of their group-related characteristics, such as skin colour, nationality, religion, political attitudes, disabilities, lifestyle, social status or sexual orientation. Brute force is often involved, whereby offenders select the particular victim facelessly at random in order to sym-bolically hit an entire population group.

The main result of this work, which was carried out over several years, was to make recommendations on the primary prevention of "violence towards group members".

The final report, published in 2006, drew the following conclusions concerning the general criteria contributing to the effectiveness of primary prevention: *"The earlier social standards and behaviour are learned and the more intensive personal relationships and attentiveness in the process are, the more effective prevention is. Thus, in addition to basic socialisation within the family, kindergarten and school have an important role to play. The aim is to form or change the person's inner attitude to dealing with "different-ness". Constantly addressing the issue of violent actions and isolating and sanctioning offenders are antidotes to a general willingness to use violence and foster prejudice."*

3.2 Information of the Conference of State Premiers and the Federal Chancellor on the situation concerning violence prevention and on central needs to take action to ensure its sustainable design (2003-2006)

In a decision of 26 June 2003, a year after the shooting at Gutenberg Grammar School in Erfurt, the *Conference of the 16 State Premiers and the Federal Chancellor (PM-Conference)* underlined that the alliance of the whole of society to outlaw violence and its glorification had to be supported at a high political level.

In this decision, the PM-Conference made reference to the report by the working group on violence prevention it commissioned immediately after the Erfurt killings in spring 2002, which was submitted to it in March 2003, *"Proscription of violence and enhancement of the pedagogical competence in families and schools – The need for political action in relation to the emergence, use and spread of violence in various areas of our society"*.

The *Heads of State-Government (PM-Conference)* called for close cooperation and coordination between all relevant facilities and institutions; in particular, the *German Youth Institute (DJI)* and the corporate *Police Crime Prevention Programme (ProPK)* were to be comprehensively involved. The *German Forum for Crime Prevention (DFK)* was asked to liaise as necessary and to initiate and coordinate networks and the pooling of resources (the further-reaching organisational proposal by the working group on violence prevention of March 2003 that the DFK be used as the central networking and coordination centre for violence prevention was not followed, however).

In spring 2004, the DFK sent a questionnaire to all the relevant Federal departments and conferences of specialist ministers, all the umbrella organisations of independent welfare organisations, and other central organisations. The evaluation of this questionnaire revealed a remarkably wide variety of projects, measures and programmes. Some of these were nation-wide or region-wide programmes, and some were regional or local initiatives. Some projects were connected only to individual institutions. Reference was made to model programmes and to further developments of regular practice.

In summer 2006, the *Federal Chancellor and the PM-Conference* were informed in a report for which the DFK had primary responsibility on the findings concerning the situation regarding violence prevention in Germany and on central requirements for action for its ongoing organisation. The developments in specialist practice described should not obscure the fact *"that knowledge concerning the sustainability, transferability of procedures and experiences and the conditions required for the strategies to be successful is currently extremely sparse. Thus, reinforced efforts are required in the field of evaluation, particularly in the form of follow-up studies in the field of violence prevention among children and young people. It would be helpful and a relief for all concerned to pursue realistic objectives and not to hold excessively high expectations (e.g. in the form of simple, universally applicable "recipes")".*

Concerning the necessary social framework conditions, the report states that *"All efforts for the further development of violence prevention among children and young people would be ineffectual if they were not embedded in appropriate institutional conditions and social-policy endeavours. Conflict mediation efforts are soon made ad absurdum unless there is a correspondingly supportive atmosphere in the immediate environment of those involved, e.g. kindergartens, schools, youth groups and districts. [...] In addition, as opposed to orientation to spectacular acts of violence, there should be more conscious appreciation of and support for those who are not violent. For adults, children and youngsters alike, there should be an ethic and culture of non-violence and pro-social interaction and this should be made into a political and social maxim. Reference should be made more frequently to positive examples and successes in dealing with violence rather than repeatedly referring to shortcomings. In general, families and schools are not hotbeds of violence, but in the overwhelming majority of cases fulfil social tasks of education and integration which are what make civil society possible in the first place. [...] In order for violence prevention to be successful, it has to be accompanied and backed by social policies that are effective in the long term. Thus, enabling children and youngsters to have real opportunities for the future, supporting their education and qualification, opening up opportunities for them to have a stake and participate, and countering the increasing social divide in the cities and between the regions remain essential challenges, also in connection with preventing violence among children and young people."*

3.3 Report by the German Youth Institute (DJI): Strategies for violence prevention among children and young people – An interim evaluation in six areas of activity (2007)

In order to be able to obtain in-depth statements on the situation concerning violence prevention in view of the diversity highlighted by the DFK questionnaire, the *DJI* was commissioned with preparing an extensive report with the participation of the *DFK* and the *Police Crime Prevention Programme (ProPK)*.

The further work concentrated on six areas of activity: the family, children's day-care, extra-curricular provision by youth welfare, schools, the police and the judiciary. If relevant in the individual fields of activity, the issues of migration and gender were pursued as cross-cutting issues.

In compiling the report, experts in the field were asked to describe the current state of the discussion in the relevant fields of activity in accordance with comparable parameters and to identify challenges. In mid-2007, the German Youth Institute (DJI) published a comprehensive report on violence prevention strategies among children and young people, entitled "*Strategien der Gewaltprävention in Kindes- und Jugendalter*", in which it gave a detailed presentation of the challenges involved in further developing specialised professional practice and the necessary supporting framework conditions.

The report focuses on violence prevention strategies on which the many practical on-site projects, measures and programmes are based. This provides an overview of the situation concerning the conceptual and methodological bases and likely challenges in the field of violence prevention among children and young people, regardless of whether they have been realised in specific projects, measures or programmes.

As a result of taking stock of the current situation, a very broad spectrum has developed in Germany, ranging from formalised, extremely standardised programmes to very open, rather general concepts. Many mixed forms may be found between these poles. Only a few programmes appear to have been evaluated on the basis of verifiable criteria, and in particular, little appears to be known about long-term successes. Reference was also made to a problematic tendency to declare individual projects or programmes to be "best practice" or "good practice": *"Usually, what is behind such labels is little more than the experience that participants believed that the programmes had been successful in practice. In the overwhelming majority of cases, these programmes would not stand up to hard criteria of cross-examination from other fields of activity, e.g. sustained success over a lengthy period, the existence of measurable results, programmes' innovative character, observability of recognised positive effects, such as outcome, repeatability, a sufficiently large area of application and independence from regional or other conditions."*

Finally, the report summarises the state of development of violence prevention in Germany as follows:

"The overall picture gained by this summary of violence prevention strategies is a pleasing one. This positive impression of specialist practitioners in the field of violence prevention has to be relativised, however, firstly, when one looks at the dissemination of these strategies in specialised professional practice. It cannot be assumed that the approaches and concepts required are always known wherever there is a corresponding need, let alone that they are available and can be implemented. Secondly, time and again, there is a lack of willingness among policy-makers, the public and specialised professional practitioners to perceive the relevant problems objectively, to address them proactively and to understand them constructively as a task on which they themselves need to take action. In many cases that would mean admitting, at least to themselves and to those directly involved, that previously effective means are no

longer sufficient to control violence among children and young people. Thirdly, it has been shown that in some places, only insufficient institutional conditions and coope- rative structures exist, have been developed or are desired. It is also evident that the necessary specialist competence is only available to a limited extent and the necessa- ry human and financial resources are not available, e.g. because licences have to be obtained or expensive course units completed, or because insufficient staff are availa- ble for additional activities. To sum up, it may be stated that in view of the presented overall view of specialised professional practice in the field of violence prevention, the primary central challenge, with certain provisos, is to secure existing strategies and give them a broader base through improved qualification, and to disseminate and further develop them rather than to develop entirely new approaches. "

3.4 Expert report on *"Prerequisites for the successful prevention of interpersonal violence among children and young people"* (2008)

The realisation that only insufficient criteria exist for describing the likelihood of success of work in the field of violence prevention prompted the DFK to commission Professor Scheithauer and his team at the Free University of Berlin (FUB) to carry out a systematic review, drawing on current international research, to ascertain the prere- quisites for successful violence prevention which constitute a measure for evaluating the effectiveness of prevention programmes. The expert report, published in 2008, presented as its starting point for an improvement in the range of services on offer a developmental understanding of prevention that not only comes into play when child- ren and youngsters already have manifest problems. Rather, it promotes children and young people, on the one hand supporting them systematically in their psychosocial and emotional development and on the other hand helping to balance out possible de- ficits before starting new stages of life and during the transition to new environments (for example, the transition from kindergarten to primary school or from school to job training). In this spirit, particular emphasis is to be given to the importance of universal measures aimed at supporting emotional and social competences at an early age and specifically not directed at individualisable delinquency risks or dangers. Po- sitive effects in the sense of supporting general competence and development are also of benefit to all participants in universal measures and do not cause stigmatisation. Some violent phenomena only arise in groups (e.g. bullying/mobbing in school clas- ses) and can be explained through group phenomena (e.g. according to the social roles approach, according to which there are not only offenders and victims of violence, but also other involved parties who need to be taken into account when carrying out prevention) and interactions so that effective prevention work should also take place in the groups and not only with (possible) offenders and victims.

The effect of developmental prevention is to prevent violence among children and young people who indicate a specific risk of becoming violent later on unless they receive supportive assistance. But effects relating to other risks (e.g. manifest psychological problems, addiction, depression) can also be achieved by means of such prevention. There is a clear connection between the lack of important social-emotional competences and aggressive behaviour, violence and delinquency/dissociality. Selective measures are required for high-risk groups in the course of their further development, and children/youngsters who are already violent require help in the form of special, indicated prevention and intervention.

A comprehensive implementation approach addresses primarily the fields of activity of the family, institutional care (e.g. kindergarten) school and the social environment, if only on account of the existing comprehensive accessibility of the target groups; the actors in these groups should cooperate better with a joint understanding of developmental support. The effects of changing one's perspective from an approach based on deficits to an understanding based on strengths, without disregarding deficits, are already evident in some tested and evaluated programmes to improve competences, self-confidence and the ability to empathise. These measures are available in manualised form and have been supplemented by further training formats for parents and school and kindergarten teachers, and are offered in particular to childcare institutions and schools at primary and lower secondary level.

Prerequisites for successful violence prevention – a brief survey

Following systematic research into the literature on meta-analyses and reviews on aggression
   and violence, Scheithauer and his team were able to identify conditions that increase and
   decrease risk. Constituent parts of prevention programmes were also identified which have
   proved to be effective in reducing and preventing violence. Thus, successful programmes
   may be described as follows: They (are)

- theoretically well-founded,
- centred on the individual and the environment,
- address resources and deficits, development tasks/transitions,
- cross-setting (e.g. school and home),
- often multi-component programmes,
- culturally adaptable, and take into account age and gender differences,
- highly structured (e.g. manualised) and nevertheless
- variable in their didactics (tailoring),
- carried out by trained leaders,
- whereby programmes carried out regularly over a longer period (at least 9 months) in
   particular appear to be useful.
- Set store by cultivating relationships and by stakeholders' willingness to implement the
   programmes,
- are highly implementable and
- ideally both universal and selective/indicated.

As well as being efficient and effective, programmes' quality, and thus success, is also reflected
   in their implementation. As well as the professionalism/competence of the users/trainers, the
   following implementation aspects gain significance:

- duration and intensity of the measures
- sustainability
- support, further training, supervision

Ultimately, the quality and the success of a violence prevention measure, including its
   scientifically-based development, taking implementation structures into account, lies both in
   the hands of programme developers, trainers and supporters and in the hands of users and
   implementers, to whom continuation in keeping with the programme is recommended,
   particularly after introduction of the measure is complete, in order to guarantee the
   sustainable success of the applied measure.

3.5 Promoting the evaluation of violence-prevention programmes (since 2009)

A special form of supporting violence prevention, which began in 2009, is financial
support for evaluations of the implementation of violence prevention programmes in
municipal fields of work (childcare institutions, schools, family welfare, youth welfare) and of the resocialisation of extremist violent offenders. Examples are *"Miteinander an Kita und Schule-EFFEKT / Antibullying"* [Together against bullying in child-

care facilities and schools] in the rural district of Ostprignitz-Ruppin, *"Prävention im Team - PiT – Hessen"* [Teaming up to prevent violence in the Federal Land of Hesse], *"Familien optimal stärken – famos"* [Optimally strengthening families] in Paderborn, *"buddY - Übergänge Kita-Grundschule"* [Transitions from childcare facilities to primary school] in Detmold and Paderborn, *"Violence Prevention Network: Abschied von Hass und Gewalt"* [Goodbye to hatred and violence] and *"PARTS - Programm zur Förderung von Akzeptanz, Respekt, Toleranz und Sozialer Kompetenz"* [Programme to promote acceptance, respect, tolerance and social competence]. The results of the evaluations of the process and effect, some of which have been completed, will be assessed for transferability within the context of knowledge transfer and the findings on the DFK's different transfer formats will be made available.

3.6 Cooperation project of Deutsche Bahn AG (DB), the DFK and the Free University of Berlin on the dissemination of developmental programmes (since 2010)

The realisation that the comprehensive implementation of effective developmental programmes in Germany is only just beginning and in particular that there is a lack of the financial resources required to guarantee a sustainable process of dovetailed modules led the DFK, Deutsche Bahn AG (DB), a member of the DFK's Board of Trustees, and the Free University of Berlin (FUB) to enter into a cooperation in order to start to consolidate developmental prevention work that has proved to be effective, beginning with a prevention programme.

DB earmarked basic financing, initially for five years, for disseminating throughout Germany the anti-mobbing programme *fairplayer.manual*, which was presented with the *European Crime Prevention Award 2011*.

3.7 Knowledge management on developmental support and violence prevention (since 2008)

The DFK provides knowledge for transfer in order to make both the findings gained through its own initiative and through other initiatives researchable and usable by researchers and practitioners. Specialist articles in the journal *forum kriminalprävention* present current criminological and prevention-related research results, discuss strategic and conceptual questions, and present and put up for discussion experiences from specialist practice. The *DFK Newsletter* also refers to new findings and available knowledge. The *DFK Website* brings its own formats together in *"Wissen gegen Gewalt"* (Knowledge against violence) and pools the collections of information and research formats of various institutions and actors in its *"Prävention im Überblick"* [Prevention Survey] portal (www.kriminapraevention.de).

4. DFK project "Developmental support and violence prevention for young people" (since 2011)

The needs for support in dealing with issues such as disruption, mobbing, violent phenomena, addictive behaviour and psychological disorders continue to be articulated in the regular education and training systems. In spite of, or perhaps because of the significant variety of the range of services on offer, the DFK's starting situation was as follows:

Firstly, it is evident that the need to strengthen training competences in childcare institutions, social child and youth work facilities and schools is only taken up systematically to a (very) limited extent by their responsible agencies and administrations.

That is to say that adjustments in basic and further training as well as in organisational development, regarded as necessary by practitioners and experts, are not being introduced, or are being introduced only hesitantly.

Secondly, it has to be stated that the quality of the majority of violence prevention services is problematic, as it is usually unclear.

That is to say that users of violence prevention measures frequently experiment with unassessed or ineffectual programmes.

Thirdly, a great deal of knowledge about effective approaches to preventing violence and the prerequisites for their implementation have existed for a number of years, but these are not sufficiently well known in practice, let alone available to users in the long term and in a quality-assured way.

That is to say that effective approaches are not disseminated systematically and thus long-term.

Fourthly: A variety of efforts to improve, disseminate and assure the quality of programmes (such as project management tools, programme databases, scientific reviews and expert reports) have shown little effect to date.

That is to say that knowledge transfer is not effective and/or there is a lack of will or ability to take up perceived findings.

4.1 DFK Advisory Council and guidelines on *"Developmental support and violence prevention for young people"* (2012/2013)

In autumn 2012, the DFK convened an Advisory Council, consisting of 13 expert academics and practitioners, to further clarify the problems raised (inadequate system adaptation, dissemination of ineffectual programmes, lack of consolidation of effective approaches, limited effect of previous steering instruments). The Council has been working since then, focusing in particular on the following:

- creating greater transparency concerning effective and practicable programmes and their implementation,
- improving dissemination and interlinking of effective and practicable programmes,
- gaining more knowledge about as yet untested programmes, programme implementation and linking/dovetailing programmes.

DFK Advisory Council on "Developmental Support and Violence Prevention for Young People ":	
Professor Dr. Britta Bannenberg: Justus-Liebig-University Giessen	Professor Dr. Siegfried Preiser: University of Psychology Berlin;
Professor Dr. Andreas Beelmann: Friedrich Schiller University Jena;	Professor Dr. Herbert Scheithauer: Free University of Berlin;
Dr. Christian Böhm: *Land* Institute for Teacher Training and Schools Development Hamburg;	Professor Dr. Dr. Christiane Spiel: University of Vienna;
Professor Dr. Thomas Görgen: German Police University Münster;	Elmar Undorf: Schools Psychological Service, Rhine-Sieg District;
Professor Dr. Nina Heinrichs, Braunschweig University of Technology	Professor Dr. Ulrich Wagner: Philipp University of Marburg;
Professor Dr. Dr. Friedrich Lösel: University of Cambridge;	Professor Dr. Andreas Zick: University of Bielefeld.
Erich Marks: Lower Saxony Crime Prevention Council;	

The Council's first result is *"Entwicklungsförderung und Gewaltprävention für junge Menschen (E&G)"* [developmental support and violence prevention for young people], guidelines that were presented and discussed at the *18th German Congress on Crime Prevention* in Bielefeld in 2013. It follows on from the expert opinion *"Prerequisites for the successful prevention of interpersonal violence among children and young people"*, extending the perspective of support and prevention, particularly regarding aspects of effectiveness, measuring effects, implementation quality and implementation in childcare institutions and schools. Finally, questions of transfer and the further dissemination of effective, practicable prevention programmes are discussed. Further impulses are provided by a quality criteria catalogue that helps to judge the quality of prevention and intervention measures or programmes. It can be used as an aid for decision-making in selecting, using and supporting measures. It helps programme providers in optimising the programmes they offer. The guidelines are addressed at professional practitioners but also at those responsible for taking decisions in institutions, administration and, not least, politics.

4.2 Further perspectives: Memorandum on "Promoting quality, structure and cooperation" (2013)

The DFK and the experts were well aware that further steps are required to develop prevention work for young people, for example to improve knowledge transfer and practical implementation: *How can the findings presented in the guidelines be even more successfully disseminated and structurally tangible progress be made in preventive work in all fields of activity, particularly in pedagogical institutions?*

The *DFK Advisory Council* discusses these questions on an ongoing basis and will continue to work on promoting the quality and dissemination of developmental prevention. It recommends that the Foundation and its cooperation partners take the following aspects into account (*Memorandum of the DFK Advisory Council*, situation as of October 2013, with the motto "*Promoting quality, structure and cooperation*", cf. www.wegweiser-praevention.de):

- *Knowledge transfer instruments are to be further developed. For example, information and assistance that may be useful for the various needs of institutions, administrative offices and organisations carrying out social work can be provided on a web portal. High-quality information that is already available should be integrated.*

- *The information provided by a needs-based web portal should not concentrate only on explicitly recommending effective programmes, but should put these in the context of central aspects such as their scientific basis, selection of target groups, setting, timing, intensity, methods, didactics and special framework conditions.*

- *The findings and programme recommendations on the "Green List Prevention" of the Lower Saxony Crime Prevention Council should be taken up and linked with the web portal. Before that is done, its structure, procedures and results should be constructively examined and modifications recommended if necessary.*

- *It is particularly important to announce the conditions and prerequisites for supporting successful implementation of prevention concepts and programmes in the areas of activity of the pedagogical institutions and social assistance system. The provision of supplementary personal advice and services is just as desirable as the creation of relevant further training programmes for professionals, for example in childcare institutions and schools and also for their steering levels.*

- *Relevant standards and framework conditions should enable implementation processes to be examined and the implementation quality to be secured long-term.*

4.3 Project continuation and the "www.wegweiser-praevention.de" [prevention directory) web portal (2014)

The DFK office's project team took up the Advisory Council's recommendations and has already launched further partial projects:

One group, headed by Professor Andreas Beelmann (Jena), is working on systematising, collecting and assessing German-language evaluation studies on prevention programmes and is preparing them for knowledge transfer. The task of a second working group, with the involvement of Professor Christiane Spiel (Vienna), is to create transparency on the theory and practice of implementing preventive services.

With financial support from the Federal Ministry of Justice and Consumer Protection, the design and technical implementation of the recommended internet portal *"Wegweiser Entwicklungsförderung und Gewaltprävention"* [directory on developmental support and violence prevention] have been carried out in coordination with the Lower Saxony Crime Prevention Council. The portal has been available since 12 May 2014 at www.wegweiser-praevention.de and on the websites of its cooperation partners, the DFK and the Lower Saxony Crime Prevention Council, and may be linked with the websites of other actors in the field of prevention, education servers etc. in the future.

The *"prevention directory"* is a comprehensive information portal on *"developmental support and violence prevention for young people"* in cooperation with the *"Prevention Green List"*. It provides information about prevention programmes that have been tested for effectiveness and practicability and are thus recommended by reputed researchers.

This orientation guide is recommended in particular for anyone responsible for or working in childcare institutions and schools who wants to develop their institution and use professional support to that end. As well as making basic recommendations on working with prevention programmes, one finds targeted information on the objectives, quality, dissemination and availability of specific programmes as well as on their implementation. The information is placed in useful categories headed by questions (Why do we need developmental support and violence prevention? Which programmes can be recommended? Where does the information on programme quality come from? Where in Germany have the programmes been distributed? How are the programmes implemented?).

Why do we need developmental support and violence prevention?

Development-orientated prevention measures are based on systematic forms of social education and training in the context of the family, schools and municipalities and are directed at different target groups (children, young people, parents, teachers, the social environment and entire municipalities). The approach aims at the healthy social development of children and young people, aiming to support this and nip in the bud any imminent negative developments. Developmental support in general social contexts overlaps with work in the field of primary prevention and the effects are mutually supplementary.

A selection of texts explains the scientific basis and logic of the approach. The guidelines, prerequisites for success and quality criteria are available for downloading. The strategic considerations for systematic preventive work and the framework conditions they require, as concluded from these, are also presented.

Which programmes can be recommended?

Social learning can be supported through different pedagogical approaches, methods and training that have a good theoretical foundation and have proven their practical effectiveness.

Recommended programmes on *"developmental support and violence prevention"* combine principles and methods in a useful *programme of action* with manuals, materials and other aids in order to be able to achieve the positive effects aimed for among the target groups in a way that is appropriate for their age and taking the respective learning context into account (e.g. childcare institution).

Programmes are not "blueprints" that can be implemented without thought; they rather support and facilitate pedagogical or social work because not every procedural or learning step has to be thought from scratch in each case and use can be made of what has been successful in the past. Work with programmes should be integrated into an overarching pedagogical concept, however, which takes into account the principles explained in the "developmental support and violence prevention" guidelines, chapters 3 and 4 and in the guidelines for effective prevention programmes of the "Green List Prevention".

Starting early and working continuously are important principles of prevention work, but it should be noted that it is neither recommended that as many programmes as possible be included in a concept at the same time, nor that a mere succession of programmes be planned. Combinations are possible, however, for example linking programmes in different learning and life contexts (school, family) or for example in the temporal sequence of childcare facilities and primary school. An indication of such programme compatibility is in preparation.

A *survey of recommendable programmes* leads to individual *programme profiles*. You click on the relevant field of activity and information on the corresponding programme appears. The relevant logo takes you the basic data and more detailed information.

The naming of the programmes is based on the categorisation of the "Green List Prevention" into the following categories: effectiveness proven (level 3) and effectiveness probable (level 2). Information on the significance of most of the evaluations on which these categorisations are based are summarised in a separate evaluation profile.

Additional aspects for inclusion in the survey are as follows: The aims should be related to supporting the development of young people and achieving violence prevention behavioural targets. The recommended programmes in Germany also offer a support service, for example through their own trainers, multiplier training programmes and various advice formats. This makes them particularly practicable, distinguishing them from programmes that can only be implemented autodidactically, for example using a guide book. The survey cannot currently claim to be exhaustive. It is being extended on an ongoing basis as permitted by the DFK office's working capacities. Applications for inclusion in the survey cannot be made directly, but are possible indirectly by making a proposal for inclusion in the *"Green List Prevention"*.

Where does the information on programme quality come from?

Before their dissemination, prevention programmes have to be evaluated, i.e. examined using scientifically recognised methods with regard to their target achievement and effectiveness. In addition, statements on the quality of a measure's implementation are required in order to be able to make programme recommendations. *Programme evaluations* are carried out in methodically different ways and their results are difficult to compare. There are no binding standards.

In the *evaluation profiles*, the design and method of German-language studies are described, their individual characteristics are evaluated in detail and then a summary assessment is made. Finally, records of the results describe the strength and sustainability of the measured effects. The evaluation profiles are not yet available. Access will be given to these in 2014.

Where in Germany have the programmes been distributed?

The *distribution and availability* of effective and practicable developmental support and violence prevention programmes varies greatly in different parts of Germany. The question of the availability of specialist and organisational service provision may play an important role in making a selection decision. A map with pop-up windows gives an idea of the availability of the programmes in Germany.

How are the programmes implemented?

The *implementation* of pedagogical and prevention programmes is a complex and difficult process which involves going beyond individual personal commitment to carry out regular adaptations at system, organisational and practical levels. *Implementation* means adapting a selected programme conceptually to the respective institutional context, e.g. of a school or childcare institution, so that it can achieve the desired effects.

Often, specialist discussions concentrate on questions of the general effectiveness of prevention programmes without sufficiently taking into account the logic of the contexts of application or sufficiently considering the conditions required for pedagogical work to be successful.

The knowledge offered in this section is devoted to the German and international situation in *research into implementation* and presents key findings, a summary of American scientific studies and concepts as well as *abstracts* of the individual publications to which reference is made. Following on from that, specific assistance is provided in the form of checklists, templates and online tools for practical use.

The "Beccaria Steps" of Lower Saxony Crime Prevention Council are already available. This interactive online tool provides support with step-by-step programme planning, implementation and monitoring (cf. also www.beccaria.de).

Further modules are under preparation and are being continually supplemented.

5. Summary: ... and finishing with sustainable answers (?)

The "*directory on developmental support and violence prevention*" project is first of all a good example which shows that cooperation between actors at Federal and State level is possible if the partners have a common understanding of prevention and common objectives, can build trust and share tasks and responsibility within the project. The DFK and the Lower Saxony Crime Prevention Council will continue down this road.

The information portal on crime prevention (www.wegweiser-praevention.de) was activated on 12 May 2014 but was unable to offer all the services planned at that stage. An unplanned advantage is that users' feedback and experiences can be taken into account in further developing the website and its concept. Lengthy work in progress also underlines, however, that professionally substantiated, comprehensive and speedy continuation requires better human and financial resources, which the DFK has been unable to achieve to date.

In a letter of autumn 2013 from the DFK's spokesman, Professor Beelmann, to the Bundestag parliamentary groups in the government, the *DFK's Advisory Council on Developmental Support and Violence Prevention* drew attention to the significance of developmental education / prevention and demanded new political initiatives including "*improving the framework conditions for preventive action and to that end setting up a central agency at Federal level with its own staff and budget.*"

As is shown by scientific findings, DFK project work and the positive response from specialist professional practice, significant effects can be achieved with relatively limited, but only with sufficient, funding. Comparison with the resources used for repressive concepts need not be shunned.

It is to be hoped that the constructive dialogue within the Federal Government will be continued and that the *National Prevention Centre* proposed by an expert commission deployed by the Federal Chancellor can be realised with the inclusion of the resources and expertise of the DFK office – particularly with the objective of earmarking appropriate resources for the work already begun on *"developmental support and violence prevention for young people"*. Only then can the further impulses, for example in the Standing Conference of the Ministers of Education and Cultural Affairs of the States in Germany and the competent Federal and State departments, succeed, for example in establishing a further-training programme on the implementation of prevention programmes.

"Developmental support and violence prevention" is a concept based on long-term effectiveness which has a good theoretical basis, has been frequently successfully tested in practice and is increasingly attracting attention and gaining relevance in Germany. A corresponding knowledge and support service has been created at State and Federal level in recent years – as shown in this article - and it can largely satisfy the diverse information needs. To what extent the efforts to transfer knowledge can have any major impact on the qualification and long-term dissemination of the approaches and services of *"developmental support and violence prevention"* is not yet foreseeable. Clearer political support at all levels of action is just as necessary as creating further training formats that supplement knowledge transfer as practised to date, particularly for pedagogical fields of work.

We cannot tell at the moment whether this development will ultimately lead to a "National Strategy" such as that in Austria, Switzerland or Scandinavian countries, but it should be kept in mind and demanded as a strategic objective. After extending, completing and improving knowledge transfer services, ways should thus be found for entering into a specialist policy discussion in the competent political departments and their conferences.

The standard of prevention work in Germany to be aspired to here should be as follows (comparable with the *International Standards for the Prevention of Drug Abuse* published by the *United Nations Office on Drugs and Crime)*:

- support from policy-makers and legal framework conditions
- scientifically-based decision-making
- cooperation within and/or coordination of the different fields of activity (vertical and horizontal)
- qualification of decision-makers and practitioners
- political understanding that appropriate resources are provided and secured in the long term.

In view of the urgent challenges, also in other fields of policy, these principles are unavoidable and *cooperation* is a central paradigm.

Literature:

Foundation German Forum for Crime Prevention (ed.):

    Gelingensbedingungen für die Prävention von interpersonaler Gewalt im Kindes- und Jugendalter (2008 / 2012),

    Entwicklungsförderung und Gewaltprävention für junge Menschen -

    Impulse und Qualitätskriterienkatalog für die Auswahl und Durchführung wirksamer Programme (2013),

    forum kriminalprävention (2-2013 und 2-2014),

    www.wegweiser-praevention.de (2014)

German Youth Institute (ed.):

    Strategien der Gewaltprävention im Kindes- und Jugendalter - Eine Zwischenbilanz in sechs Handlungsfeldern (2007)

Federal Ministry of Justice (ed.):

    Hasskriminalität-Vorurteilskriminalität - Endbericht und Empfehlungen der Arbeitsgruppe (2006)

Harrie Jonkman

What do we know and what can we achieve regarding prevention work for youths?

The Report of the National Research Council / Institute of Medicine (2009): „Preventing Mental, Emotional, and Behavioral Disorders Among Young People: Progress and Possibilities" (*www.nap.edu/catalog.php?record_id=12480* **)**

Preface

The Institute of Medicine (IOM) is part of the US National Academies. It is a non-governmental institution that offers professional advice in issues regarding the health care system. Two of its numerous reports deal with the prevention of behavioral disorders: „Reducing Risks for Mental Disorders: Frontiers for Preventive Intervention Research" (1994) and "Preventing Mental, Emotional and Behavioral Disorders Among Young People: Progress and Possibilities" (2009). The latter publication in particular calls for a greater emphasis on preventing behavioral disorders and, in doing so, for concentrating primarily on measures that were proven to be effective, in order to limit the psychosocial and financial damages that behavioral disorders impose on the persons concerned and on their environment.

The German Congress on Crime Prevention shares this concern and therefore intends to further the discussion regarding evidence-based prevention in German speaking countries as well. The publication of the second report of the IOM with its thorough overview of conceptual, methodological, economic and practical issues regarding the prevention of behavioral disorders is part of this endeavor.

Since not all participants in this discussion have the opportunity to read the English original of this report, Dr. Jonkman (Verwey-Jonker-Institut in Utrecht, Netherlands) produced an English short version thereof, which is presently translated into German. This translation will be made available on the Congress'website by the end of 2014. The report brief for policymakers is reprinted here.

Dr. Jonkman presented this report and its potential for prevention in Germany on the 19th Congress in Karlsruhe to contribute to this discussion, which will be continued on the 20th German Congress on Crime Prevention in Frankfurt.

The National Academies

Report Brief FOR POLICYMAKERS • MARCH 2009

Preventing mental, emotional and behavioral disorders among young people

Progress and Possibilities

Mental, emotional, and behavioral (MEB) disorders—which include depression, conduct disorder, and substance abuse—affect large numbers of young people. Studies indicate that MEB disorders are a major health threat and are as commonplace today among young people as a fractured limb—not inevitable but not at all unusual. Almost one in five young people have one or more MEB disorders at any given time. Among adults, half of all MEB disorders were first diagnosed by age 14 and three-fourths by age 24.

Many disorders have life-long effects that include high psychosocial and economic costs, not only for the young people, but also for their families, schools, and communities. The financial costs in terms of treatment services and lost productivity are estimated at $247 billion annually. Beyond the financial costs, MEB disorders also interfere with young people's ability to accomplish developmental tasks, such as establishing healthy interpersonal relationships, succeeding in school, and making their way in the workforce.

Clear windows of opportunity are available to prevent MEB disorders and related problems before they occur. Risk factors are well established, preventive interventions are available, and the first symptoms typically precede a disorder by 2 to 4 years. And because mental health and physical health problems are interwoven, improvements in mental health will undoubtedly also improve physical health. Yet the nation's approach to MEB disorders has largely been to wait to act until a disorder is well-established and has already done considerable harm. All too often, opportunities are missed to use evidence-based approaches to prevent the occurrence of disorders, establish building blocks for healthy development in all young people, and limit the environmental exposures that increase risk—approaches likely to be far more cost-effective in addressing MEB disorders in the long run.

Interventions before a disorder manifests itself offer the best opportunity to protect young people. Such interventions can be integrated with routine health care and wellness promotion, as well as in schools, families, and communities. A range of policies and practices that target young people with specific risk factors; promote positive emotional development; and build on family, school, and community resources have proven to be effective at reducing and preventing MEB disorders. Making use of the evidence-based interventions already at hand could potentially save billions of dollars by preventing or mitigating disorders that would otherwise require expensive treatment.

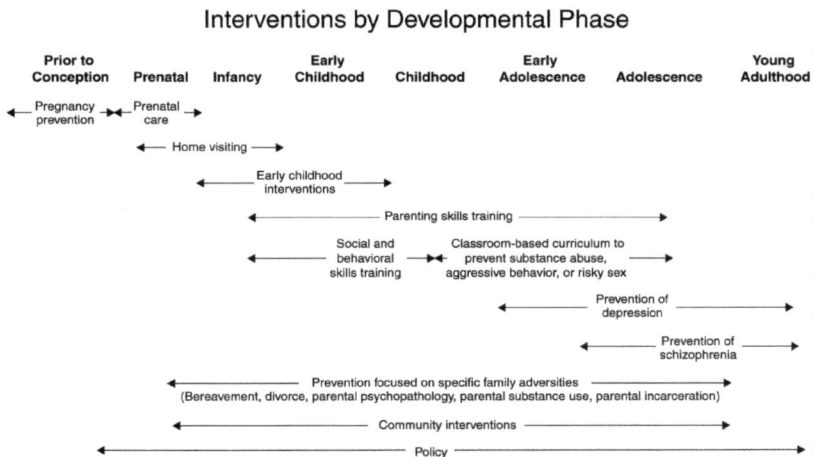

Source: Committee on Prevention of Mental Disorders and Substance Abuse Among Children, Youth, and Young Adults, 2009

Proven Approaches

A recent study by the National Research Council and the Institute of Medicine reviewed the research on the prevention of mental disorders and substance abuse among young people and recommended multiple strategies for enhancing the psychological and emotional well-being of young people. Research including meta-analyses and numerous randomized trials demonstrate the value of:

- *Strengthening families* by targeting problems such as substance use or aggressive behavior; teaching effective parenting skills; improving communication; and helping families deal with disruptions (such as divorce) or adversities (such as parental mental illness or poverty).

- *Strengthening individuals* by building resilience and skills and improving cognitive processes and behaviors.

- *Preventing specific disorders*, such as anxiety or depression, by screening individuals at risk and offering cognitive training or other preventive interventions.

- *Promoting mental health in schools* by offering support to children encountering serious stresses; modifying the school environment to promote prosocial behavior; developing students' skills at decision making, self-awareness, and conducting relationships; and targeting violence, aggressive behavior, and substance use.

- *Promoting mental health through health care and community programs* by promoting and supporting prosocial behavior, teaching coping skills, and targeting modifiable life-style factors that can affect behavior and emotional health, such as sleep, diet, activity and physical fitness, sunshine and light, and television viewing.

The key to most of these approaches is to identify risks—biological, psychological, and social factors—that may increase a child's risk of MEB disorders. Some of these risks reside in specific characteristics of the individual or family environment (such as parental mental illness or substance abuse or serious family disruptions), but they also include social stresses such as poverty, violence, lack of safe schools, and lack of access to health care. Most risk factors tend to come in clusters and are associated with more than one disorder. Currently, treatment interventions tend to isolate single problems, but there is growing evidence that well-designed prevention interventions reduce a range of problems and disorders and that these efforts are sustained over the long term. These programs often help children, families, and schools build strengths that support well-being. A focus on prevention and wellness can have multiple benefits that extend beyond a single disorder.

Policy Implications

Officials at the local, state, and federal levels all play a role in mental health promotion and the prevention of MEB disorders. Many providers and agencies are responsible for the care, protection, or support of young people: the child welfare, education, and juvenile justice systems, as well as medical and mental health care providers and community organizations. Yet resources within these agencies are scattered, not coordinated, and often do not effectively support prevention programs or policies. The result is a patchwork that does not perform as an integrated system and fails to serve the needs of many young people and their families.

National leadership is necessary to make systematic prevention efforts a high priority in the health care system as well as an integral aspect of the network of local, state, and federal programs and systems that serve young people and families. Leaders at the national, state, and local levels need to pursue specific strategies, such as:

- *A White House initiative to develop an inter-departmental strategy* that identifies specific prevention goals, directs multiple federal agency resources toward these goals, and provides guidance to state and local partners.

- *Development of state and local systems* involving partnerships among families, schools, courts, health care providers, and local programs to create coordinated approaches that support healthy development.

- *Investment in prevention and promotion,* including setting aside resources for evidence-based prevention in mental health service programs and investment in proven prevention approaches by school systems.

- *Workforce training,* including development of prevention training standards and training programs across disciplines including health, education, and social work.

- *Long-term tracking* of the prevalence and frequency of MEB disorders.

- *Implementation and evaluation of screening* with community involvement, parental support, valid tools, and interventions to address identified needs.

- *Continued research* on both the efficacy of new prevention models and real-world effectiveness of proven prevention and wellness promotion interventions;

- *Adaptation of research-based programs* to cultural, linguistic, and socioeconomic subgroups;

- *Public education,* with mass media and the internet offering the opportunity to greatly expand the reach of specific messages about risk factors and available resources, to reduce stigma, and to deliver some kinds of interventions.

Implementing a systems focus will require innovative efforts to provide societal institutions that affect young people—families, schools, health care systems, and community programs—with the tools to promote healthy development and prevent MEB disorders. Policies are also needed to help ensure families' financial security, provide safe neighborhoods and schools, improve access to health care and other services, and provide enriched early childhood environments.

Tools to equip young people who are at risk with the skills and habits they need to live healthy, happy, and productive lives are available. What is lacking are the will, social policies, and collaborative strategies to adequately support the healthy development of the nation's young people.

FOR MORE INFORMATION ...

Copies of the report, *Preventing Mental, Emotional, and Behavioral Disorders Among Young People: Progress and Possibilities,* are available for sale from the National Academies Press at (888) 624-8373 or (202) 334-3313 (in the Washington, DC metropolitan area) or via the NAP home page at www.nap.edu. Full text of the report and a free pdf copy of the Summary are also available at www.nap.edu. The study was funded by the Substance Abuse and Mental Health Services Administration, National Institute of Mental Health, National Institute on Drug Abuse, and the National Institute on Alcohol Abuse and Alcoholism.

This policy brief is one in a series of three briefs with highlights from the report.

Rita Haverkamp

Barometer of Security in Germany

Currently maintaining security remains one of the key discussion topics within public, scientific and political communities, even though our democratic and pluralistic society has achieved a generally high level of security.[1] The recurring discussion on security[2] may seem surprising when we consider the strong advantages we have regarding our welfare and economic systems. However, a high level of security may arouse greater feelings of insecurity because of the fear of losing the achieved security in the future. The future orientated dimension of security means uncertainty and therefore an unattainable state that is devoid of risks and dangers.[3]

People have their own individual ideas, to a greater or lesser extent, about what security means to them and what consequences it has on their personal life on a cognitive, emotional and behavioral level. Scientific findings on security to date, however, are limited to a selected range of aspects or selected areas. Therefore, the joint research project "Barometer of Security in Germany" (hereafter BaSiD) aimed for broader insight in the German situation of security in general as well as perceptions especially on different aspects of security. To grasp this complex and multidimensional phenomenon, the interdisciplinary partners followed diverse approaches and used a variety of research methods (representative survey, explorative study, experiment, discourse analysis etc.).

The following article will serve as an introduction to the joint research project, the theoretical background on the term security and the analysis tool, that has been designed to detect ambivalences between subjective and objective (in)security.

The Joint Research Project BaSiD

The study, funded by the German Federal Ministry of Education and Research, monitored objective and subjective securities in Germany for three years, from 2010 until 2013. While the project primarily focused on subjective security, explicitly personal perceptions, feelings and expectations on security, these findings were complemented by objective indications on four security-relevant phenomena: natural and technical disasters, terrorism, and crime. During the research process tools of data gathering were continually developed. Primary data was collected and evaluated to generate useable results regarding security provision.

---

[1]   Thanks to Kyra L. Cormier for proof-reading.

[2]   E.g., the academic discourse: Lange, Hans-Jürgen (2014): Einleitung, in: Lange, Hans-Jürgen/ Wende-kamm, Michaela/ Endreß, Christian (eds.): Dimensionen der Sicherheitskultur, Wiesbaden: Springer VS, p. 11 und Rampp, Benjamin (2014): Zum Konzept der Sicherheit, in: Ammicht Quinn, Regina (ed.): Sicherheitsethik, Wiesbaden: Springer VS, p. 51 ff.

[3]   Fritzsche, Andreas F. (1986): Wie sicher leben wir? Risikobeurteilung und Risikobewältigung in unserer Gesellschaft, Köln: Verlag TÜV Rheinland, p. 9 f.

The research network was led by the Max Planck Institute for Foreign and International Criminal Law (hereafter MPI). Partners were the Federal Criminal Police Office (hereafter BKA), Fraunhofer Institute for Systems and Innovation Research (hereafter ISI), the Institute for Sociology of the University of Freiburg (hereafter IfS), the International Centre for Ethics in the Sciences and Humanities at the University of Tübingen (hereafter IZEW), the Disaster Research Unit of the Free University of Berlin (hereafter KFS), and the Communication and Media Science of the University of Düsseldorf (hereafter KMW).

BaSiD consisted of nine modules (see Figure 1): The IZEW was responsible for module 1 which was concerned with developing the underlying concept of a mutual understanding of the term security. In module 2 the BKA and KFS created a database on objectively measurable harmful events, such as natural and technical disasters, terrorism, and crime. Module 3 incorporated a qualitative-quantitative study on individual perceptions of security, conducted by the IfS, as well as a representative public survey on security and quality of life by the MPI. In cooperation with the MPI the BKA implemented the first National Crime Victimization Survey within module 4. Module 5 was concerned with the question how security professionals as well as laymen seize familiar and unfamiliar spaces which was addressed by an experimental design by the KFS. Module 6 focused on new security technologies: The IfS attended to the deployment of biometric systems whereas the ISI examined participative procedures of technology engineering by means of three different workshops. In module 7 the KMW monitored the media coverage of natural and technical disasters, terrorism and crime. Accompanying research by the IZEW in module 8 reflected on ethical concerns regarding the interdisciplinary cooperation during the project. Finally, module 9 provided an analysis tool to classify and assess objective and subjective security.

Figure 1: Concept of the interdisciplinary joint research project

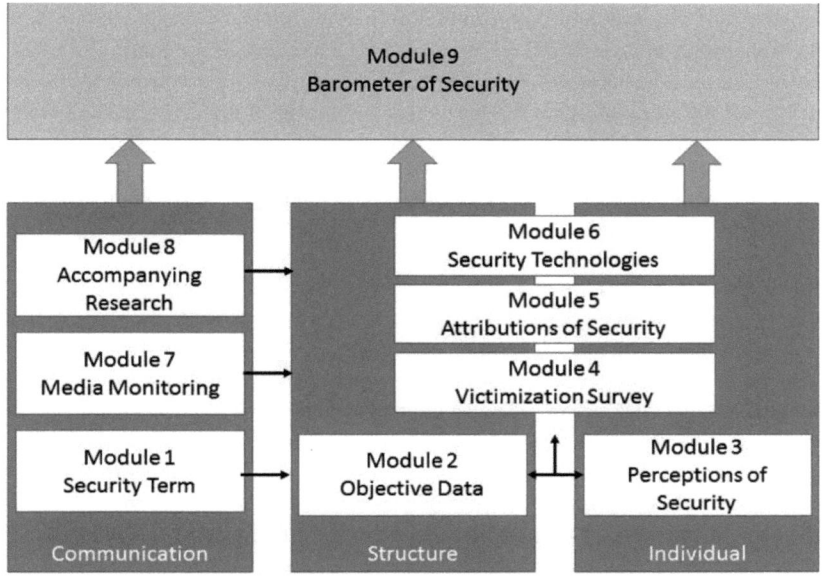

What is security?

Security represents an elementary basic need of human beings[4] which comprises their thinking, emotions, and security provisions.[5] The term refers to the absence of personal and societal risks, dangers, hazards, and threats. In spite of this negative definition, security even implies positive aspects such as quality of life and contentment, freedom from fear and worry, comfort and protection (literally: Geborgenheit[6]), as well as trust in other people and societal institutions.[7] However, trust cannot be completely associated with security because trust implies the possibility of being disappointed causing a feeling of insecurity.

Over the centuries, the concept of security has changed among individuals and societies. As a relative concept, security encompasses every part of our live and indeed

---

[4]   Cf. Maslow's hierarchy of needs, in: Maslow, Abraham Harold (1954): Motivation and personality. New York: Harper.

[5]   That means the cognitive, affective, and conative (= behavioral) constituent.

[6]   Cf. Hutta, Jan Simon (2009): Geographies of Geborgenheit: beyond feelings of safety and the fear of crime, in: Environment & Planning 27 (2), p. 252: '...the German concept of Geborgenheit [ ], which is commonly translated as 'security' but actually evokes an immediately positive sense of shelteredness, nestedness, and well-being'.

[7]   Ruhne, Renate (2003): 'Sicherheit' ist nicht die Abwesenheit von 'Unsicherheit' – Die soziale Konstruktion geschlechtsspezifischer (Un)Sicherheiten im öffentlichen Raum, in: Gestring, Norbert/ Glasauer, Herbert/ Hannemann, Christine/ Petrowsky, Werner/ Pohlan, Jörg (eds.): Jahrbuch StadtRegion 2002. Schwerpunkt: Die sichere Stadt, Opladen: Leske + Budrich, p. 61.

drives it. That's why our idea of security has also got an unlimited side that might be derived from its future orientation and the related uncertainty. [8] Therefore, not only the maintenance of security is a driving force for human activities, but also its further increase. Hence, a successful rise of objective security does not correspond necessarily with the same effect concerning subjective security if the individual still feels unsafe or even more unsafe. Furthermore, new guarantees of objective security could lead to unintended side effects accompanied by subjective insecurity. In converse, an enhancement of subjective security does not mean necessarily a growth of objective security.[9]

The already mentioned uncertain component of security means that a state without risks and dangers cannot be achieved.[10] The resultant instability attests to a societal problem situation which raises comprehensive and wide-reaching questions. The imponderability of the future and its inherent dynamic can only result in structural stability for a specific reference object and a limited time frame.[11] The related contingency of security partially explains the security paradox that can generate both more security and more insecurity.[12] As a result, security represents a complex, emotional, and normatively charged construct whose content and contours are unclear because all areas of human life are affected.[13] These considerations show that security has advanced to become a multi-faceted societal central theme in the last decades.[14]

In the BaSiD project security is understood as a social construction in accordance with numerous theoretical works[15]. Looking at the objective situation, security and insecurity are a bundle of different risks and hazards such as catastrophes and terrorism as low probability, high impact incidents, and crime as a ubiquitous phenomenon. The

---

[8]   See Ammicht Quinn, Regina (2014): Sicherheitsethik. Eine Einführung, in: Ammicht Quinn, Regina (Hrsg.): Sicherheitsethik, Wiesbaden: Springer VS, p. 19 f. and Zedner, Lucia (2009): Security, Abingdon/ United Kingdom: Routledge, pp. 144-151 who explains nine crime paradoxes.

[9]   Due to the focus on security, the relationship with freedom will not be discussed, although these concepts are connected with each other, further Andexinger, Manfred (2014): Das Spannungsfeld Freiheit versus Sicherheit – eine historisch-philosophische Reflexion, in: Lange, Hans-Jürgen/ Wendekamm, Michaela/ Endreß, Christian (Hrsg.): Dimensionen der Sicherheitskultur, Wiesbaden: Springer VS, pp. 111-124; Gusy, Christoph (2012): Vom „Neuen Sicherheitsbegriff" zur „Neuen Sicherheitsarchitektur" und Ammicht Quinn, Regina (2012): Zwischen Angstdiskursen und Akzeptanzfragen: Grundlagen einer Sicherheitsethik, both in: Würtenberger, Thomas/ Gusy, Christoph/ Lange, Hans-Jürgen: Innere Sicherheit im europäischen Vergleich. Sicherheitsdenken, Sicherheitskonzepte und Sicherheitsarchitektur im Wandel, Berlin: LIT Verlag, p. 103 ff. und p. 323 ff.

[10] Fritzsche (1986), p. 9 f.

[11] Giebel, Daniela (2012), Integrierte Sicherheitskommunikation. Zur Herausbildung von Unsicherheitsbewältigungskompetenzen durch und in Sicherheitskommunikation, Berlin: LIT Verlag, p. 59.

[12] For an early systematic approach dating from 1970, see Kaufmann, Franz Xaver (2012): Sicherheit als soziologisches und sozialpolitisches Problem. Untersuchungen zu einer Wertidee hochdifferenzierter Gesellschaften [reprint]. Berlin: LIT Verlag 2012, p. 10 ff., 157 ff.

[13] Kaufmann (2012), p. 340 f.

[14] Kaufmann (2012), p. 1, 39.

[15] Cf. e.g. Giebel (2012), p. 25 ff.

mere countability suggests objectivity that is relative from a constructivist perspective. One example is crime statistics because they cover only those offences known to the police but not those that remain unreported. According to the four considered, objective threats the project defines security in a negative sense meaning the absence of insecurity.[16] The negative definition is also based on the operationalization of security in the qualitative and quantitative approaches. Negatively connected damaging incidents might be expressed in objective risks, dangers, hazards, and threats as well as in subjective anxieties, fears, concerns, and worries. Positive aspects like trust, wellbeing, and life quality serve as explaining factors of feelings of security in the representative study of the MPI on 'Security and Quality of Life in Germany'.

The security quadrate

In order to grasp objective and subjective securities, two essential questions were consistently pursued: How secure is Germany? And how secure do people feel in Germany? These questions indicate that objective security is measurable by its statistical probability, whereas subjective security is connected with emotions. These different focal points hint at the ambivalence of objective and subjective security: as a consequence, 'being secure' and 'feeling secure' may coincide but also fall apart. Essential insights into the relationship of objective and subjective security can be derived from the Thomas theorem: 'If men define situations as real, they are real in their consequences'[17]. According to this, people's behavior is based on assessing a situation, but not on the objective circumstances.[18] In order to reflect this ambivalence, the security quadrate (see Figure 2) was developed and shows the partial inconsistency and respective discrepancy of objective and subjective security.

---

[16] Haverkamp, Rita (2014a): Grundzüge eines Sicherheitsbarometers in Deutschland – Inhaltliche und methodische Überlegungen, in: Hoch, Hans/ Zoche, Peter (eds.): Sicherheiten und Unsicherheiten, Berlin: LIT Verlag, p. 20 f.

[17] Thomas, William I./ Thomas, Dorothy S. (1928): The child in America: Behavior problems and programs, New York: Alfred A. Knopf, p. 571 f.

[18] Merton, Robert K. (1968): Social Theory and Social Structure, New York: The Free Press, p. 477, was inspired by the Thomas theorem and developed the concept of the self-fulfilling prophecy.

Figure 2: Security quadrate

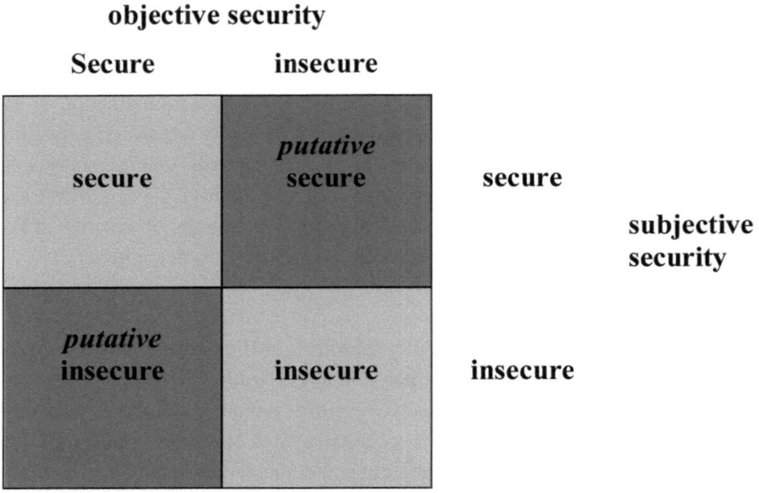

objective security

Secure	**insecure**

	putative	
secure	**secure**	**secure**
putative		
insecure	**insecure**	**insecure**

**subjective
security**

Harald Arnold (Max Planck Institute for Foreign and International Criminal Law)

The security quadrate is a four-field matrix which consists of four quadrants "secure, putative secure, putative insecure, and insecure".[19] Objective security belongs to the vertical on the left side "secure" and on the right side "insecure". In the horizontal subjective security is situated on the upper row "secure" and the lower row "insecure". The crosstab table enables to map (in)securities as follows: whereas the actual situation and their assessment correspond with each other in the quadrants "secure" and "insecure", they fall apart within the quadrants "putative secure" and "putative insecure". One famous example for such a gap between "insecure" and "putative secure" might be the heat wave in 2003. Although the heat wave caused ca. 9,355 deaths in total[20] and is regarded as the worst catastrophe of this century in Germany, the hot and stable summer seems to be remembered as a pleasant exception by a lot of people. In view of the threat potential of a heat wave, the perceived security is deceptive.

Personal and societal security

The attribution within the security quadrate needs another differentiation between personal and societal security.[21] Societal security concerns general matters with diverse facets on the macro level. One example is economy divided into, inter alia, econo-

---

[19]   Haverkamp, Rita (2014b): Das Sicherheitsquadrat – Ein Analyseinstrument zur Zuordnung von objektiven und subjektiven Sicherheiten des Verbundprojekts BaSiD, in: Kerner, Hans-Jürgen/ Marks, Erich (eds.): Internetdokumentation des Deutschen Präventionstages. Hannover 2014, www.praeventionstag. de/Dokumentation.cms/2816, p. 6.

[20]   Open-source Emergency Events Database (EM-DAT), http://www.emdat.be/.

[21]   See Haverkamp (2014a), p. 24 f.

mic and employment situation as well as consumer behavior. Due to their complexity and lack of experience, status descriptions, problem analysis, and further trends in development are largely thus beyond the individual perception and are dependent upon media reporting. The ephemeral nature of news and the accumulation of daily events make it necessary to focus and to prioritize. This practice hampers an objective reporting by overlooking, neglecting or overstating (in)securities.

In contrast, personal security characterizes one's own horizon of experience under which the person expresses personal views on various (in)securities in his or her own life. Feeling safe is based on a process in which personal estimations are developed by experiences. As a result, personal security seems to be an individual attribution and construction taking into account differences in personality and attitudes of human beings. Hence, congruencies between people and groups can be observed that mainly relate to the estimation of (in)secure places and persons by means of objective criteria (e.g., crime rates), effects of sex and age, and also the assessment of interrelations between individuals and the environment. To conclude, the separation of personal and societal securities had consequences in the quantitative-qualitative study of the IfS as well as the representative citizen survey of the MPI: each person surveyed estimated the potential of societal worries for him or her depending on their personal involvement. In the following section some findings of the MPI study will be introduced.[22]

Security in relation to personal and societal worries

Natural catastrophes, industrial accidents, and terrorist attacks are quite rare damaging incidents in Germany. Each year, these phenomena are usually recorded in the single digits. In 2013 the EM database[23] only recorded four natural catastrophes and no industrial accidents[24]. The Global Terrorism Database (GTD)[25] recorded one act of terrorism[26]. Both open-source databases have their deficiencies. The data on damaging incidents and their extent is incomplete and fragmented, causing the registered objectivity to be relative and amplified by the differentiating definitions, objectives, and collection systems. Nonetheless, reference points can be drawn from these small numbers for objective security in the three mentioned phenomena.[27] The noteworthy

---

[22] In detail Hummelsheim, Dina/ Oberwittler, Dietrich (2014): Unsicherheitsgefühle und ihr Einfluss in Deutschland. Empirische Ergebnisse einer Bevölkerungsbefragung zu Sicherheit und Lebensqualität in Deutschland 2012, in: Hoch, Hans/ Zoche, Peter (eds.): Sicherheiten und Unsicherheiten, Berlin: LIT Verlag, p. 53-74.

[23] EM-DAT is an open-source database by the Centre for Research on the Epidemiology of Disasters (CRED): www.emdat.de.

[24] http://www.emdat.be/advanced_search/index.html.

[25] The GTD is also an open-source database by the National Consortium for the Study of Terrorism and Responses to Terrorism (START) at the University of Maryland in the USA: www.start.umd.edu/gtd/.

[26] http://www.start.umd.edu/gtd/search/Results.aspx?country=75.

[27] Though crime are the most important phenomenon, crime will not be considered in detail because of its relevance for the living environment and its complexity.

low case numbers of catastrophes, industrial accidents, and terrorist attacks arrive at the cautious conclusion, that in this regard Germany is a secure country.

Considering the already introduced security quadrate an attribution in this sense is only possible on the basis of the surveyed data about subjective security sensitivities and perceptions (MPI-Survey 'Security and Quality of Life in Germany'). Therefore, Figure 3 displays societal worries of the German population. The societal worries are ranked after the personal relevance of different areas of security.[28]

Figure 3: Societal worries among the German population

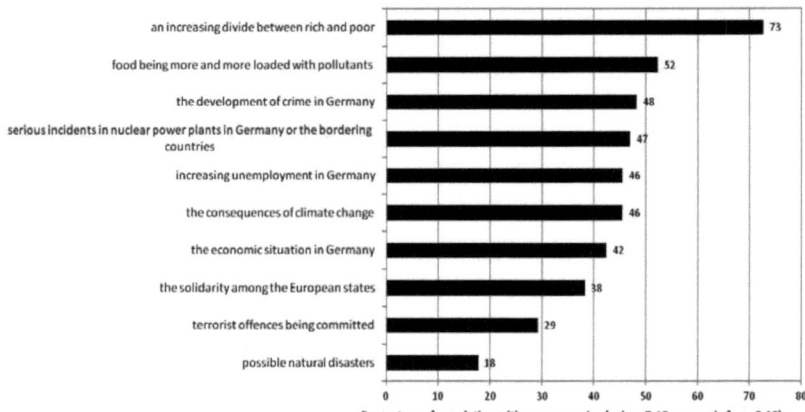

Data Source: MPI-Survey 'Security and Quality of Life in Germany' (2012), N=2.525

Regarding the mentioned phenomena, respondents have the least worries concerning natural disasters (18%) and terrorist attacks (29%) compared to the other themes in a social regard. Different from these two damaging incidents, nearly half of the respondents are worried about the development of crime in Germany.

According to the survey, crime is the third most important social sorrow concerning the questioned issues. But the total recorded offences are close to six million like the years before with a 6% decrease from the previous year. Except for 2011 police reported that the crime rate has actually diminished for every year since 2005. With regard to crime, objective and subjective security seems to fall apart for almost half of the people assessed in the security quadrate. In a societal regard, objective security exits, but also subjective insecurity among a relevant part of the population ('putative insecure'). Nevertheless, a valid and reliable answer to this divergence cannot be given at this point. First of all, the reference points of crime according to the security

---

[28]   Thanks to Dr. Dina Hummelsheim for the figures.

quadrate have to be explained, as also does the question concerning the criteria for the existence of objective security.

In contrast to Figure 3, Figure 4 shows personal worries of the Germany population again ranked after the personal relevance of different areas of security.

Figure 4: Personal worries among the German population

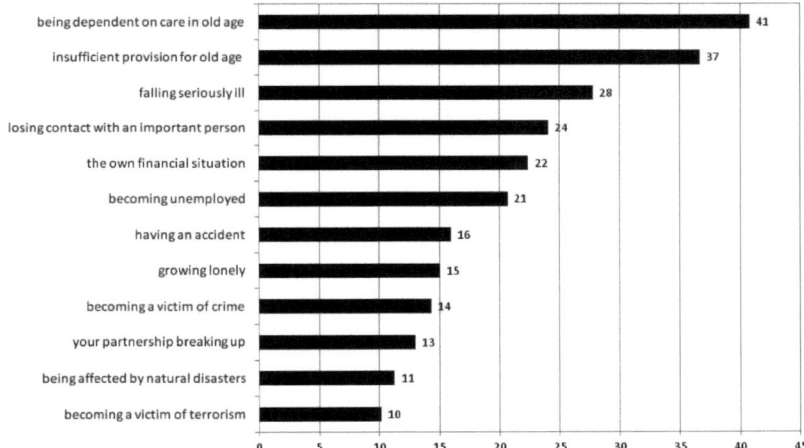

Data Source: MPI-Survey ‚Security and Quality of Life in Germany' (2012), N=2.525

Pursuant to first analysis, the respondents reported considerably less personal worries in comparison to societal worries: The majority of respondents is not worried about personal security areas. Despite worries about being dependent on care in old age (41%), the two major personal fears, insufficient provision for old age and becoming seriously ill, only bother more than one third (37%) and more than one quarter (28%). In contrast, societal worries range from 38% to 73% in eight out of ten areas of societal security. Accordingly, societal worries on terrorist attacks are on the same level as the second highest personal worry with both 28%.

On a personal level, only one-tenth of the respondents are worried about being a victim of a natural disaster or a terrorist attack. Rather fewer people (14%) are afraid about becoming a crime victim. Personal worries about becoming a crime victim are much lower than societal worries about the growth of crime in Germany (48%). In a personal regard, major worries are concerned with areas of life like care in old age, health, or the loss of a loved one.

Referring to the security quadrate, in the personal environment the data on objective security and the present database on subjective estimations of security agree with each other concerning natural disasters and terrorist attacks and thus mean 'secure' in both cases, likewise according to societal society albeit alleviated.

The statements of the respondents are, however, generally expressed societal and personal worries on diverse phenomena. Particularly, the term 'natural disasters' embraces a whole range of diverse catastrophes like the aforementioned heat wave. Also, one has to bear in mind that the attitudes are not consistent over time, but depend on the actual damaging incidents. For example, in 2013, one year after the citizen survey, another centennial flood[29], that caused the highest economic damage costs[30] during the last 25 years, took place in Germany. Shortly after this incident, respondents would probably have expressed more worries concerning natural catastrophes.

Conclusion

The so called barometer of security is a flexible and progressing instrument for analyzing objective and subjective securities. The result of the joint project is a prototype consisting of subjective and objective data from different sources and based on diverse methodological approaches (analysis of statistics, [non] representative surveys, qualitative as well as quantitative data).[31]

The introduced security quadrate is an attempt to connect theoretical and practical concepts of security. The general descriptive and typological scheme enables a basic classification of individual positions and perceptions. Starting from the two basic and opposed views on security, i.e. the subjective one and the objective one, both perceptions are systematically contrasted with each other, resulting in a simple, yet fundamental typology which allows one to expound the problems of their respective agreements and disagreements. Through this schematization, the analytical view specifies fields of insecurities that are addressed by the two quadrants 'putative secure' and 'putative insecure' (see Figure 2). An analysis in detail may reveal differences within one phenomenon concerning the feeling of security on a societal and personal level. Consequently, an elaborated assessment would consist of multiple security quadrates according to each phenomenon's ramifications and to the typology of individuals. Such an assessment even supports the identification of the (in)securities of different persons and groups on an individual and societal level.

In practice, the security quadrate could be used as an assessment tool for crime prevention to identify ambivalences in objective and subjective (in)securities among diverse types of residents. However, the limits of the security quadrate should be recognized: The scheme only allows for the classification of diverging (in)security perceptions and interests, but not for solutions to maintain and provide security in communities.

---

[29]   The first centennial flood occurred in 2002: http://www.emdat.be/result-country-profile.

[30]   http://www.emdat.be/result-country-profile.

[31]   See Haverkamp 2014a.

Klaus M. Beier

The German Dunkelfeld Project: Proactive Strategies to Prevent Child Sexual Abuse and the Use of Child Abusive Images

Background

Official statistics account for only a fraction of all child sexual abuse (CSA) and the use of child abusive images (so called 'child pornography offenses' – CPO). Those cases not reported to the authorities constitute a large part of sexual offenses against children and are in German referred to as 'Dunkelfeld' (literally 'dark field'). Consequently, preventive efforts must consider both primary prevention in the case of potential offenders as well as secondary prevention for self-referred offenders in the Dunkelfeld.

How to reach whom?

Two groups of those sexually offending against children can be distinguished:

- Those showing no sexual preference disorder, but who, for different reasons, sexually abuse children seeking a surrogate. This group comprises e.g. sexually inexperienced adolescents, mentally retarded persons, those with anti-social personality disorders and perpetrators within general traumatizing family constellations – and accounts for approximately 60% of officially known offenders;

- Those showing a sexual preference disorder, namely pedophilia (erotic preference for prepubescent minors, i.e. showing Tanner stage 1) or hebephilia (erotic preference for pubescent minors, i.e. showing Tanner stages 2 and 3). These account for approximately 40% of officially known offenders.

Sexual preference, in general, manifests itself during adolescence and remains unchanged thereafter. This is true for pedophilia and hebephilia, as well. Thus, pedophiles and hebephiles will always be at risk of offending and/or re-offending, mainly in the Dunkelfeld. Furthermore, empiric data suggests that pedophiles and hebephiles reveal high levels of co-morbidity and distress because of the problems associated with their sexual preference and that, as a result, they are more likely than other sexual offenders to seek treatment. However, community-based specialised diagnostic and therapeutic programs for these self-referred individuals remain scarce.

For that reason, at the Institute of Sexology and Sexual Medicine in Berlin, a prevention approach was developed by generating a media campaign to encourage self-identified (but officially not registered) pedophiles and hebephiles to seek professional help to avoid committing CSA and CPO.

Project Procedure

The ongoing Prevention Project Dunkelfeld (PPD) was officially launched in 2005 with an extensive media campaign which publicised the opportunity to get help. The media campaign was designed to communicate the following messages:

1. Empathy for the particular situation of the participants;
2. No discrimination because of sexual preference;
3. Confidentiality and anonymity regarding all collected data; and
4. No augmentation of feelings of guilt and shame.

The following slogan was chosen: 'You are not guilty because of your sexual desire, but you are responsible for your sexual behavior. There is help! Don't become an offender!' The campaign's poster was placed in print media and on city billboards, and a TV-spot was broadcasted on several German TV channels and in cinemas.

The translated headline of the poster was 'Do you like children in ways you shouldn't?

In 2009 the media campaign was extended to include potential and undetected child pornography offenders. The message was: 'Child pornography is sexual abuse. You are not to blame for your sexual responsiveness to child pornography, but you are responsible for your own behavior. It is your choice whether you click on it or not. Help is available! Don't become an offender. Not even online!'

Since July 2012, with the help of Google adwords, potential consumers of child abusive images are guided to the therapeutic offer of the PPD by common search keywords. Respondents to the media campaign can contact the research team anonymously (e.g. by telephone), and the staff are specifically trained to build a trustworthy and empathetic relationship during the initial contact. A personal identification number (PIN) is assigned to each respondent who:

1. self-identifies as a pedophile and/or hebephile;
2. expresses interest in the content of the project because of distress related to his sexual preference; and/or
3. expresses an interest in consulting a clinical expert.

Those respondents interested and able to attend a consultation are questioned about their criminal and sexual history as well as their sexual fantasies and behaviours. In addition, socio-demographic data (age, education, employment, family status, number of children), former experiences with health professionals, and the interviewees' handling of information regarding their sexual preference are assessed.

Outcomes

From the beginning of the project in 2005, on average, 15–20 individuals per month contacted the research office in Berlin, so that, as of March 2014, there have been 1959 applications, 845 assessments and treatment offers to 412 individuals.

The decrease from applications to treatment offers is mainly due to geographical distances – the applicants came from all over Germany. As expected, the vast majority were either pedophiles or hebephiles. Half of them had already committed child sexual abuse and three quarters admitted to child pornography offenses in the Dunkelfeld.

In a specialized one-year treatment program the participants learn to ensure impulse control by using cognitive-behavioural techniques, sexological tools (integrating the attachment dimension in terms of an increase of social functioning), as well as pharmaceutical options (mostly androgene deprivation therapy). The evaluation of the PPD was done in a non-randomized waiting list–control design with multiple assessments for 75 participants. It revealed that the primary prevention approach:

- reduces risk factors for child sexual abuse;
- prevents sexual offending against minors and reduces the number of contact offenses;
- reduces the frequency and severity of child pornography offences.

Conclusions

First results of the Berlin Prevention Project Dunkelfeld can be summarized as follows:

1. A significant number of pedophiles and hebephiles in the community are not known to the justice system and have no contact with preventive services. These pedophilic and hebephilic men are either potential offenders or real offenders. However, they remain undetected in the Dunkelfeld;

2. Many pedophiles and hebephiles who are not known to the authorities would be willing to participate in a treatment program aiming to prevent child sexual abuse and the use of child abusive images, provided they know how to access it and feel they can trust the pledge of confidentiality by experts specialized in assessment and therapy of their disorder;

3. A specially designed media campaign is able to communicate these goals;

4. The success of this preventive program is based on German legislation regarding the reporting of CSA and CPO; according to German law, it is considered a breach of confidentiality for the treating therapist to report either committed or planned CSA or CPO;

5. The current situation in other countries – even those with mandatory report laws – would allow at least a focus on potential or real users of child abusive images in the Dunkelfeld for preventive purposes. It is a fact that the use of child abu-

sive images is an indicator for a pedophilic inclination and therefore every user is an important target for prevention. The PPD has proved that it is possible to reach pedophiles and hebephiles in the community and to encourage these men to change their habit of consuming child abusive images. Furthermore it indicates the likelihood of preventing crossover to child sexual abuse – which is a promising primary prevention approach for this cause. But, of course, this will only work if trust is achieved and confidentiality guaranteed.

Prevention Network "Kein Täter werden" (Don't offend)

By now, the Prevention Project Dunkelfeld (PPD) is established in 9 further German states. These contact points constitute the Prevention Network 'Kein Täter werden' (literally 'don`t become an offender') which is coordinated at the Berlin Institute of Sexology and Sexual Medicine. Next to the one in Berlin, there are outpatient clinics of the project in Kiel (since 2009), Regensburg (2010), Leipzig (2011), Hannover (2012), Hamburg (2012), Stralsund (2013), Giessen (2013), Düsseldorf (2014) and Ulm (2014). The therapeutic services offered by these contact points are, as expected, in fact called on by affected persons. Until summer 2014, far more than 4.000 people seeking help reached out to the Prevention Network 'Kein Täter werden'. There are more contact points of the project being planned. Expanding the Prevention Network to establish nationwide primary prevention in order to avoid sexual traumatization of children and adolescents is the target. This primary prevention is recommended by the final report of the 'Runder Tisch Sexueller Kindesmissbrauch' (Round Table for Sexual Abuse), a committee installed by the German government to prevent child sexual abuse, consisting of politicians and representatives from science and relevant social groups. The experience of the Prevention Network shows that attitudes supporting abusive behavior can be reduced significantly by therapeutic means and medication support. This makes , originator-related prevention of sexual assaults work.

Relevant Literature

Amelung, T., Kuhle, L.F., Konrad, A., Pauls, A., & Beier, K.M. (2012). Androgen deprivation therapy of selfidentifying, help seeking pedophiles in the Dunkelfeld, *International Journal of Law and Psychiatry* 35, 176–184.

Beier K.M. (1998) Differential typology and prognosis for dissexual behavior – a follow-up study of previously expert-appraised child molesters. *International Journal of Legal Medicine* 111: 133–141.

Beier, K.M., Neutze, J., Mundt, I. A., Ahlers, Ch., Goecker, D., Konrad, A., & Schaefer, G.A. (2009). Encouraging self-identified pedophiles and hebephiles to seek professional help: First results of the Berlin Prevention Project Dunkelfeld (PPD). *Child Abuse & Neglect*, 33, 545–549.

Beier, K.M., Ahlers, Ch., Goecker, D., Neutze, J., Mundt, I.A., Hupp, E., & Schaefer, G.A., (2009). Can pedophiles be reached for primary prevention of child sexual abuse? First results of the Berlin Prevention Project Dunkelfeld (PPD). *Journal of Forensic Psychiatry and Forensic Psychology,* 20 (6), 851–867.

Neutze, J., Seto, M., Schaefer, G.A., & Beier, K.M. (2011). Predictors of Child Pornography Offenses and Child Sexual Abuse in a Community Sample of Pedophiles and Hebephiles. Sexual Abuse: *A Journal of Research and Treatment,* 23, 212–242.

Neutze, J., Grundmann, D., Amelung, T., Kuhle, L.F., Scherner, G., Konrad, A., Schaefer, G.A., Beier, K.M. (2012). Treatment Change in Dynamic Risk Factors (DRF) in the Prevention Project Dunkelfeld (PPD), 12th IATSO Conference 5th – 8th September 2012, Berlin, Germany.

Seto MC, Cantor JM, Blanchard R (2006) Child pornography offenses are a valid diagnostic indicator of pedophilia. J Abnorm Child Psychol 115: 610–615

Seto MC (2012). Is Pedophilia a Sexual Orientation? Archives of Sexual Behavior 38: 335–350.

Seto MC (2008) Pedophilia and sexual offending against children: Theory, assessment, and intervention. American Psychological Association, Washington, DC.

Petra Guder

Child Friendly Justice – Wishful Thinking?!

1. Introduction

In the early 20th century, the United States had a leading position regarding juvenile justice reforms which were internationally recognized and replicated. The constitution of the first Juvenile Court in Chicago was a tremendous achievement establishing a Juvenile Justice System. The architecture of the Eastern State Penitentiary in Philadelphia served as "the model for many prisons worldwide". The separation of juveniles and adults led to the "House of Refuge-Movement. The Glen Mills Schools were once the 2nd House of Refuge in the United States after New York, then based in Philadelphia. In turn, the Glen Mills Schools adapted their campus set up for a new facility out in the country in the Village Glen Mills from the "Raue Haus" in Hamburg, Germany. Back then it seemed to be much easier to learn from each others and replicate each others' models than it is today.

Today the Chicago Juvenile Court is one of the leading US-Courts in the Models for Change-Initiative launched by the US-National Council of Youth and Family Court Judges. Diversions, Deinstitutialisation, Decriminalization are the key words in all initiatives regarding effective Interventions (Blueprints, Sherman Report). They stand for a fundamental change in beliefs and practices throughout the US how to treat troubled youth successfully.

Nevertheless the United States are often associated with high incarceration rates and "Zero Tolerance"-policies. Internationally, the current reform process remains widely unnoticed. The media mainly... continues to focus on how tough on crime the United States are, whenever politicians and policy makers are blowing the whistle, that for instance the German or other Juvenile Justice System is too "soft".

There seems to be a quick readiness to replicate restrictive and retributive interventions which have already proven not to be effective – or, even worse, have negative effects, such as Boot Camps, Scared Straight Programs and Short, Sharp Shock-Arrest-Interventions supposedly on public demand – but is it really in the publics interest, that programs are implemented which do more harm than good and perhaps produce more victims in the future?

There also seems to be a commensurable reluctance to look at the respectable research, among others, by Delbert Elliott et al. regarding effective Interventions against Juvenile Violence. The programs and results are often said to be „too American", it is also argued, that they are not replicable because of cultural differences, a different system , set up of the American Juvenile Justice System and/or data protection. Despite the fact, that fundamental theories in sociology have once been developed in the United

States and are internationally acknowledged, it seems to be rather difficult to learn from recent reform strategies and to consider the implementation of intervention programs, which have already proven to be effective.

In fact, the American Juvenile Justice System does not even exist as a whole, as much as there is no such European Juvenile Justice System. Hans-Jürgen Kerner pointed it out in a recent conversation: There are "lots of black and white and different shades of grey." According to a recent study, the juvenile incarceration in the US rate has fallen 41 percent in the past 15 years, reaching the lowest level since 1975.

Today we had not only the honor, but also a great opportunity to hear and to learn firsthand from three great individuals and leaders in the field of US Juvenile Justice, what current US Juvenile Justice is all about. Hon. Judge Patricia M. Martin, Administrative Judge, Child Protection Unit, Cook County Family Court (Chicago) and past president of the National Council of Youth and Family Court Judges (NCJFCJ) and Hon. Judge David E. Stucki, current President of the NCJFCJ, had a broad historical perspective and most recent reform strategies to share. Richard Ross, Professor, Photographer and Researcher, University of California, had given us eye-opening views of incarcerated youth and youth deprived of their liberty in various institutions throughout the US. If the systems differ so much – how then can it be that some of the photographs taken in US Facilities look quite similar to those of facilities in Europe, including Germany? Is there in fact a "learning process" if it comes down to the set up of secure facilities still existing today? Is there an "Architecture of Authority" as Richard Ross described it in one of his previous, with the Guggenheim Fellowship awarded projects in 2007, documenting architectural spaces worldwide that exert power of individuals confined within them?

Research carried out by Dünkel et al. has shown, that the approaches how to tackle Juvenile Delinquency successfully, differ commensurably from country to country throughout Europe and even the system set ups differ. There are different beliefs regarding the accurate age of responsibility to be held accountable for a crime, although the vast majority of European States consider the age of 14 as appropriate. Culturally, Europe is much more diverse including many different languages, constitute many obstacles to communication. For many practitioners and even researchers is it more obvious to look at European neighbors than considering the United States as a genuine source for meaningful and effective interventions. In those countries that are in the process of establishing a Juvenile Justice System or have recently done so, there was more of a readiness to "go west". others, Scandinavian Countries and the Netherlands, which seem to have a more pragmatic approach. Contrary to that the trend and pendulum seems to swing again towards harsher tendencies to tackle juvenile crime more successfully.

2. Child Friendly Justice

Child friendly Justice Guidelines for Europe are setting a framework for European Membership Countries, how to reach Child friendly justice procedures.

The National Council of Youth and Family Court Judges of the United States has developed several procedures and standards for a child oriented, child friendly system reform.

Other countries, such as Africa have developed similar frameworks. Needless to say that the understanding and interpretation of the term "Child Friendly Justice" and the understanding of child friendly procedures and approaches differs widely. But such guidelines are only effective, if they get put in action and are not put on the upper shelf of a book case.

2.1 History of European Child Friendly Justice Guidelines
"Don't walk in front of me; I may not follow. Don't walk behind me; I may not lead. Walk beside me and be my friend" Attributed to Albert Camus

- In 2010, the Council of Europe adopted Guidelines on child friendly justice intended for use by professionals working in the criminal, civil or administrative justice systems

- Mission: Enhancement of children's access to and treatment in justice

- The Guidelines address themes such as:

- Family

- mistrust of authority and the

- need for respect, and the

- Importance for children and young people to be listened to

The issues covered include information, representation and participation rights, protection of privacy, safety, a multidisciplinary approach and training and safeguards at all stages of proceedings and deprivation of liberty.

2.2 Child Friendly Justice-Principles
- Participation
- children to be informed about their rights, appropriate ways to access justice, consulted and heard in proceedings involving or affecting
- due weight to the children's views bearing in mind their maturity and any communication difficulties they may have in order to make this participation meaningful.
- Best interests of the child

- Dignity
- Protection from discrimination

Rule of law principle should apply fully to children as it does to adults

3. Juvenile Justice and the Media

As Richard Ross already pointed out, the media does not focus so much on positive outcomes and positive news about crime decline. The Cook County experience shows, as Judge Martin told us, that the media attention was centered about negative outcomes of the juvenile court as well - it seems that good news don't sell. Misleading media reports tend to influence the public and policy makers to change procedures, mostly leading towards a call for reform to establish more harsh approaches. No wonder, that contrary to child friendly justice approaches, the media draws a different picture of the reality of juvenile justice today. Let's take a glimpse at several media headlines in Germany and the US:

Most recent Headlines regarding the US:

„Exchange Student from Hamburg shot in Missouri"

„Scandalous Death Penalty Execution"

Common associations regarding US- Juvenile Justice Policies:

„Three Strikes And You Are Out", „Zero Tolerance", „Get Tough On Crime", „Boot Camp", „Scared Straight".

Most recent headlines regarding German Juvenile Justice Policies:

"50 school truants from Hamburg facing arrest"

„Offenders are getting younger and much more brutal"

"Monsterkids"

„Extended term of imprisonment for young Offenders"

„With harsh sentencing and incarceration successful against notorious offenders – Every 2nd of all 552 intensive offenders in Berlin is incarcerated."

"Collaboration of Justice and Police successful"

(Tagesspiegel 08.02.10)

The media is a powerful tool not only informing the public but also building opinions and beliefs. But can such headlines like those mentioned above, really serve as an appropriate foundation for judging each other countries (Juvenile) Justice Policies? Can such headlines serve as an appropriate base value for a knowledgeable, research based juvenile Justice? Or are other data sources needed?

4. What works?

4.1 Expansive, international scientifically proven results

Contrary to the picture the media draws, it seems to be well worth taking a look at Juvenile Justice Periodicals, Conference Agendas and Resolutions as well as fundamental research results which were collected in the past. This International research provides a solid foundation about risk and protective factors and how to buffer negative factors. In comparison, it turns out, that there are many similarities and the subjects, fields of interests and problems seem relatively similar. Unsurprisingly, a NCJFCJ conference agenda in the US on the national and state level does in fact not read very different from one in Germany hosted by the DVJJ or perhaps elsewhere in Europe. They provide a repository for practitioners, how to design interventions effectively:

- Chicago School (early 20th Century/University of Chicago)
    - First and until appr. 1930 dominant Sociology in the US
    - Concept of Social Ecology: Processes/Relations of adjustment between human communities and their physical-geographical Environment
    - Conditions of rapid urbanization and development of subcultures and criminal environments
    - Sociology of criminal activities and environments (McKay/Park/Shaw/Thrasher), but neither picked up nor cultivated in German Criminology (accord. to KrimLex)
- Subcultural-Theory (Miller)
    - Learning Theories (a.o. Sutherland/ Cressey)
    - Group Culture Theory (Cohen 1961)
- Labelling Approach (a. o. Sack 1978)

a.o.

Longitudial Studies, some Examples:

- Laub/Sampson 2003-Delinquent Boys-Divergent Lives (Turning Points)
- Farrington 2006 Cambridge Study (Important Risk Factors youth age 8-10), Delinquent Families/risk taking/bad academics/poverty/lack of educational competency in families)
- Bannenberg/Rössner 2005: Perry-Preschool-Prevention-Project, long term effects (40+ years)/behavioral intervention for children age 3-5: not individual dispositions and developments, but the applied interventions contribute to continue or desist from deviant behaviors - Shapland 2014: Sheffield Longitudinal Study shows that offenders who had the chance to actively participated in restorative justice procedures, such as victim-offender mediation) are less likely to reoffend

- Shapland 2014: Sheffield Longitudinal Study shows that offenders, who had the chance to actively participate in restorative justice procedures (such as victim-offender-mediation) are less likely to reoffend

4.2 What do we know about norms?

This graphic, commonly known as norms pyramid, shows at what stage the most norms are learnt. The Justice System is the last resort to help develop an understanding of norms. Many other instances have a much more intensive impact before the Justice System gets even involved.

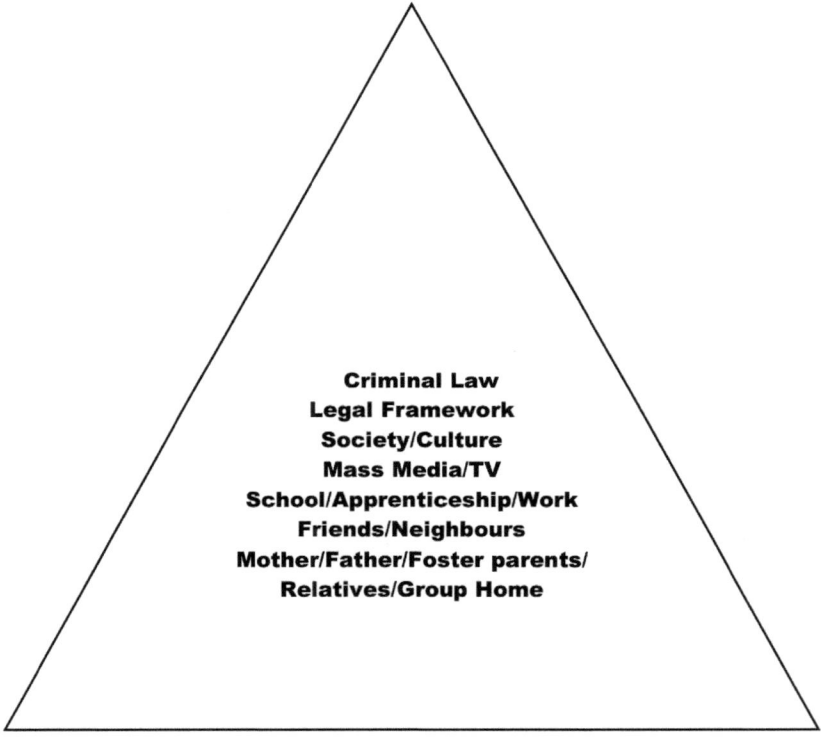

Criminal Law
Legal Framework
Society/Culture
Mass Media/TV
School/Apprenticeship/Work
Friends/Neighbours
Mother/Father/Foster parents/
Relatives/Group Home

4.3 Evaluation Studies

4.3.1 Elliott-Blueprints for Violence Prevention (1996), now Blueprints for Healthy Youth Development

The Blueprints provide an ongoing evaluation of intervention programs, which have proven to be effective. Blueprints for Violence Prevention, now Blueprints for Healthy Youth Development /Demand for a nationwide prevention initiative.

The Blueprints were initiated by:

Center for the Study and Prevention of Violence/University of Colorado/Boulder

Colorado Division of Criminal Justice

Centers for Disease Control and Prevention

Pennsylvania Commission on Crime and Delinquency

Programs 1996:	2014:
Thinking Strategies (PATHS) (Greenberg/Kusche)	• Brief Alcohol Screening and Intervention for College Students
- Big Brothers Big Sister of America (McGill)	• **Functional Family Therapy**
- Quantum Opportunities (Lattimore)	• **LifeSkillsTraining**
- **Multisystemic Therapy** (Henggeler)	• **Multidimensional Treatment Foster Care**
- **Functional Family Therapy** (Alexander)	• **Multisystemic Therapy**
- Midwestern Prevention Project (Pentz)	• New Beginnings (Intervention für Children of Divorce)
- Life Skills Training (Botvin Bestand 1998/2002:	• **Nurse-Family-Partnership**
- **Nurse-Home-Visitation (Olds)**	• Positive Action
- Incredible Years (Webster)	• Project Towards No Drug Abuse
- Bullying Prevention Program (Olweus)	• **Promoting Alternative Thinking Strategies**
- **Promoting Alternative**)	Additonal List of promising programs
- **Multisystemic Therapy Foster Care** (Chamberlain)	

Because of ongoing research some of the initial programs that could not meet the criteria anymore where removed from the list. The vast majority of programs has shown such sustainable effects that they remained on the list until today (those were italicized in table). An initiative of Hamburg University to translate the Blueprints into German to serve as an initiative for a nationwide discussion about effective programs failed because of concerns that the programs were „too American."

4.3.2 Sherman Report/Preventing crime: What works, what doesn't, what's promising.

On April 27, 1996, the 104th United States Congress enacted the Conference Report requiring the Attorney General to provide an independent, comprehensive and scientific evaluation of the „diverse group of programs funded by the Department of Justice to assist State and local law enforcement and communities in preventing crime." The University of Maryland was chosen to prepare such report. From August 1996 to January 1997 the effectiveness of intervention programs in the following areas was evaluated:

-Crime Prevention, specially youth violence

-Reduction of risk factors for youth violence, including those found within community environments, schools and families

-**Increase of protective factors against crime and delinquency**

4.3.3 What else works?

There are additional lists and databases for effective Prevention programs which have proven to work, although the criteria differ widely.

- Best Evidence Encyclopaedia (BEE)
- The U.S. Department of Education What Works Clearinghouse
- The National Registry of Evidence-Based Programs and Practices
- The Office of Juvenile Justice and Delinquency Prevention Model Programs Guide
- The Office of Justice Programs Crime Solutions
- The Coalition for Evidence-Based Policy Social Programs That Work (Top Tier)
- The Center for Disease Control Community Guide
- Judges' Ethics

4.3.4 Applied Science: US-Juvenile Justice Reform Examples

- Goal: Reduce number of children in placements/Three of the biggest court districts (Chicago/Los Angeles and New York) were able reduce placements spectacularly
- NCJFCJ Resource Guidelines
  - Improving Court Practice in Child Abuse and Neglect Cases
  - Adoption and Permanency Guidelines& Principles/Improving Court Practice in Child Abuse and Neglect Cases
  - Juvenile Delinquency Guidelines & Principles/Improving Court Practice in Juvenile Delinquency Cases
  - Graduated Sanctions Guidelines
  - Guidelines for Disproportionate Minority Contact
  - Graduated Sanctions Guidelines
  - Judges Ethics

Further initiatives:

- Office for Juvenile Delinquency and Delinquency Prevention (since 1974) (OJJDP)
- Director since 2013: Robert Listenbee, until then one of the leading reformers in the State of Pennsylvania
- Coordinating Council on Juvenile Justice and Delinquency Prevention
- Federal Advisory Committee on Juvenile Justice
- Models for Change

Foundations

- Mc Arthur Foundation
- Annie Casey Foundation (Models for Change Initiative, provides funding for states, who meet criteria for change initiatives)/Funding of „Juvenile in Justice".

Examples:

- Pennsylvania/statewide implementation of Blueprints
- Funding of Juvenile in Justice-Documentary to support change

Implementation of new procedures and diagnostic Instruments:

- Risk and Strengths / Needs-Assessments
- Competency based ./. Deficit oriented
- Diversion
- Decriminalization (of status offenders, a. o. school truants to eliminate arrests)
- Deinstitutionalisation in favor of community based intervention programs
- Improvement of the participation of parents and children in judicial procedures

4.4 Last but not least

4.4.1 Death Penalty abolished for Juveniles

The Supreme Court abolished capital punishment for juvenile offenders on March 2, 2005, ruling 5 to 4 that it is unconstitutional to sentence anyone to death for a crime he or she committed while younger than 18.

In concluding that the death penalty for minors is cruel and unusual punishment, the court cited a „national consensus" against the practice, along with medical and social-science evidence that teenagers are too immature to be held accountable for their crimes to the same extent as adults.

Breakdown of the 72 people on death rows who were juveniles when they committed their crimes:

- Texas: 29
- Alabama: 14
- Mississippi: 5
- Ariz., La., N.C.: 4 each
- Fla., S.C.: 3 each
- Ga., Pa.: 2 each
- Nev., Va.: 1

Source: The Associated Press

4.4.2 Supreme Court abolishes Life without parole for Juveniles

In 2012, the Supreme Court ruled that the death penalty for all crimes and life without parole for crimes other than homicide is unconstitutional (Miller Decision). The rulings have forced states to think very differently about how to hold juveniles, but to date (2014) only 13 out of 28 states have complied with the supreme court ruling to abolish mandatory life without parole for juveniles in their states.

4.5 Reform Problems

- States are politically highly independent
- Sanctions and intervention options differ widely, individually applied interventions are dependent the juveniles place of residence
- State policies are dependent on how the political relevant positions are filled (compare: Recent research conducted by Susanne Karstedt, UK)
- High skepticism among practitioners against evaluation and research findings
- reluctance against scientifically proven interventions ("we know by ourselves, what works trough experience")
- Data protection concerns regarding multidisciplinary collaboration
- Cultural concerns against implementation of effective, scientifically proven intervention programs
- Slow reform process- it is difficult to change what is
- even though actually a international scientifically proven level of knowledge exists: "The wheel does not really be reinvented."

5. Conclusion

The problems listed above could easily describe any other scenario in any other country and/or for example on the European Continent. Thinking about how difficult it turned for Dünkel et al to provide a European comparison of Juvenile Justice systems, illustrates that the scenario, the stakeholders and activists for reform are facing in the US could be taken anywhere on the planet.

Some arguments do not sound new for everyone, who wants to facilitate and/or initiate change: We never did that before," "we never did it like that," "we are good enough," "our system is better than others,", alleged data protection or cultural concerns cripple or at least hinder initiatives for change. Hidden agendas hamper open and productive discussions, considerations and priority of individual and/or organizational benefits lead often to half-hearted compromises. Informed knowledge is much needed to overcome these obstacles in order to help troubled children more effectively. Those are the ones, which are supposed to be the center of every discussion, decision, attempt to integrate them into society successfully and help their parents to increase their parenting skills. The United States has not found all the answers, and the EU has not found all the answers either. One of the conclusions of this workshop becomes very clear: The problems children, families and courts face are similar in the US and EU - why then not learn from each other?

Why is it, that a school truant in Hamburg has a high chance to get locked up in an secure juvenile arrest facility for not paying his/her fine and being criminalized for his/her behavior while at the same time a school truant in Hamburgs twin city Chicago is no longer considered a status offender and not being locked up in a arrest facility anymore for the very same behavior in order to decriminalize such behavior?

David Stucki informed us about the US-Initiative to raise the age for the application of juvenile law to 18 and is referring to scientifically proven data suggesting that. Why then, contrary to that, are European States debating to lower the age of responsibility and on the other end, to strictly limit the application of juvenile law to 18?

Why does one country in Europe establish a specific arrest law for juvenile offenders while in another (the US) research has proven, that such short term arrests do harm more than they do good and increase instead of decrease the risk of reoffending? Would such research not be also applicable for those youth at risk in Europe receiving short term arrest sentences and as a consequence have to lead to the elimination of such similar policies?

Is it really a cultural difference, which leads to completely contrary decisions at the very same time?

People like Richard Ross are much needed to point their finger into the right direction, into the direction of the children as the center of every action.

It speaks for the US Reform Process that the work of Richard Ross was funded by the Annie E. Casey Foundation to help promoting change. It is, by the way, a very good example how media support could turn bad news into a constructive debate for change for the better. This is a good lesson to learn from the US besides all efforts which have been taken or are under way to reform the juvenile justice system based on valid research data and make justice more child friendly, even though if this term does not specifically exist in the US. Although US juvenile courts have been in operation for over 115 years finding and evaluating best practice programs is an emerging practice in the states today. While the attempt of Child Rights Activists in the US to ratify the Childs Rights Convention is still widely hindered by some State concerns and a conservative attitude towards children rights versus parents rights. The concern the ratification could restrict/affect the single states independence, many of our colleagues, if working in the field or conducting research are in fact working towards a child friendly reform of the Juvenile Justice System. This is at least promising.

The European Child friendly Justice Guidelines promote further child-friendly actions and encourage member states of the EU to:

- promote research into all aspects of child-friendly justice, including child-sensitive interviewing techniques and dissemination of information and training on such techniques;
- exchange practice and promote co-operation in the field of child-friendly justice internationally

It is well worth not to limit this exchange of practice and the co-operation to European Member States and to open this window more widely to gain a broader perspective.

It is true that the US have still not ratified the UN Convention of the Rights of the Child – but to conclude it can be truly said, that the US have in fact made tremendous efforts toward Child friendly Justice without using this specific term. Listening to the words of Patricia Martin, Richard Ross and David Stucki it becomes quite obvious, that the US and the EU have a great deal to share about similar situations of children and families in need of court intervention, especially in the areas of positive outcomes. The reform process in the United States is certainly a good learning experience to look at and to come to a continuous exchange of ideas in the future. From this day forward ongoing exchange provides the best opportunity to improve the lives of our youth and will make their court experience a real child friendly one by collaborating towards a child friendly justice around services, programs, studies, trainings, sharing data and evaluative methods between the US and the EU. This workshop has been a good first step, but only a first step. The result of this workshop could not be summarized any better than with the words Judge Patricia Martin said at the end answering questions from the audience: „We have much to share and learn from each other. We are losing generations of youth and therefore we need to work together to resolve and improve our methods of reform in a more expedite manner." Wishful and wise thinking, constant exchange of ideas, application of research data to policy making and daily practical work will help us to improve our systems in a child friendlier manner and will ensure to make child friendly justice every day a little better than it was yesterday.

David Stucki

The Role of the National Council of Juvenile and Family Court Judges (NCJFCJ) in the Current Reform Process

1. Introduction

The juvenile justice system in the United States has a long history of struggling to balance its social welfare foundations with social control demands. In 2014, we now see our system edging away from the punitive orientation of the last several decades. One example of this important change can be seen in recent U.S. Supreme Court decisions – such as eliminating life without parole as a disposition for juveniles. This move back toward rehabilitation and restoration as guiding principles is likely a result of scientific advances in areas such as understanding brain development, healing after trauma, and improving substance abuse treatment. For many, continuing to craft a developmentally appropriate juvenile justice system that appreciates "adolescence as a mitigating factor" remains a priority goal for system reform.

2. Current Reform Efforts

There are several components of current reform efforts that illustrate this move toward a developmentally appropriate juvenile justice system:

1. For example, research has established that mixing low-risk youth (e.g., runaways) with high-risk youth (e.g., armed robbers) results in worse outcomes for the low-risk youth compared to no intervention.

2. In the context of detention and similar institutions, this dynamic has been called "deviancy training" – and points to the need for robust diversion systems and strong structured decision-making protocols.

2.1 The Juvenile Justice and Delinquency Prevention Act (JJDPA)

2.1.1 Alternatives to Detention

Our understanding of this phenomenon is perhaps most strongly demonstrated through the Juvenile Justice and Delinquency Prevention Act (JJDPA) that includes criteria about not using detention in cases of status offenses (e.g., truancy). Coupled with widespread support for elimination of the Valid Court Order exception in the pending re-authorization of the JJDPA – which is fully supported by the NCJFCJ – we are now seeing jurisdictions working to develop alternatives to detention that keep lower risk kids engaged in their community versus locked up in unhealthy environments.

2.1.2 Keep Kids in School and out of Court

Diversion programs are only one part of efforts to ***ensure the least restrictive options are used across the juvenile justice system.*** There is a large push, in general, to "keep kids in school and out of court" by dismantling what some have termed the "school to prison pipeline". This approach seeks to return discretion and authority back to schools to deal with student behavior via "teachable moments" and other methods without the confines of zero tolerance policies. The flow of cases to court for low-level offenses occurring at school is cutoff – preventing children from becoming ensnared in the justice system and being put at risk for additional system penetration.

2.1.3 Decriminalization

Another prong by which reform efforts are seeking to reduce the number of children that come before the court and placed at risk for unnecessary involvement in the juvenile justice system is re-defining what, exactly, constitutes an offense. For example, underage victims of commercial sexual exploitation are increasingly being dealt with as dependent versus delinquent youth. In treating these children as victims versus offender (i.e., prostitute), they can avoid harmful stigmatization and receive supportive services, treatment, etc. that often are not available through the juvenile justice system. Indeed, eliminating trafficking of children for sexual purposes is a priority issue in the USA. The NCJFCJ, along with partners such as Human Rights for Girls, are working to develop tools to support judges and courts to effectively identify and appropriately intervene with these victims.

2.1.4 Incarceration as Last Resort

Another example of current reform efforts is how we treat those relatively few youth that must be incarcerated due to serious and violent offenses. Although some in the United States have called for the complete elimination of secure confinement with youthful offenders, this is not likely a realistic goal, or perhaps not even a wise goal. Rather, it is more realistic we work to ensure that:

- incarceration is only used with the most serious youth offenders (by some estimates, only about 20% of delinquent youth will continue on to a life of criminal activity – of which only a small percentage would be considered serious/violent offenders requiring incapacitation); and

- conditions of confinement are humane and rehabilitative.

3. Current Trends in Juvenile Justice

3.1 Understanding of Trauma

Perhaps one of the most promising current trends in juvenile justice is incorporating our understanding of the impact of trauma on human development into practice and policy. Courts are working to do this by first conceptualizing then operationalizing what it means to be trauma-informed. For many, being trauma-informed means acknowledging that, by definition, the majority of people that come before the court will be injured in some way. Embracing this assumption then means implementing universal precautions in practice to help promote perceptions of safety, agency, and connectedness – the three domains to promote healing of those injured. Efforts such as these to become increasingly trauma-informed are not just centered within the court – but throughout the juvenile justice system and include treatment providers, probation, and detention.

Although this work is still in early stages, we are leveraging prior work by the ***National Child Traumatic Stress Network*** on trauma-informed systems, and are already seeing improvements in outcomes. For example, a juvenile detention center in the United States that mandated trauma training for all staff and changed how it approached children when they are "acting out" reduced restraints by over 90% in a one year period with an associated decrease in both child and staff injury. On the horizon for reform efforts in juvenile justice are a number of emerging trends; topics and issues that will likely be on the center stage of work over the next 3-10 years.

3.2 Sanctuaries

One of these trends builds upon the trauma-informed work just mentioned and involves creating "sanctuaries" for youth involved in the juvenile justice system. Based on the sanctuary model developed by Dr. Sandy Bloom and colleagues, this approach seeks to develop environments and practices – across systems of care – to be havens that encourage a sense of safety, control, and connectedness. In turn, these are the conditions that promote healing in those injured (e.g., those experience traumatic stress reactions). Given individuals with traumatic histories are often in a state of hyper-arousal that involves constantly scanning for threats – developing environments in detention, courts, etc. that limit unnecessary and counterproductive arousal is critical.

3.3 Changes in Treatment of Juvenile Sex Offenders

In the next few years, we will see substantial changes in how juvenile sexual offenders are treated.

Juvenile sexual offenders are often considered the most difficult group of offenders with whom we work, and mandatory registration requirements highlight the degree to which society view them as a threat to community safety. Historically, treatment of these youth has focused on incapacitation to ensure community safety, then working with the offender to manage deviant arousal and put in place a safety and supervision plan.

Research over the last decade, however, suggests this approach to treatment of juvenile sexual offenders is misguided. Rather, current research suggests that the majority of juvenile sexual offenders will not recidivate – and in fact have some of the lowest recidivism rates for any offense type. Further, research suggests that atypical or deviant sexual interests is relatively rare in this group, and that many offenses are more likely related to poor boundary issues, age, education, etc.

To that end, current thinking about the treatment of juvenile sexual offenders is that the majority can be handled in the community and are best served through modalities such as Multi-Systemic Therapy (MST) and education regarding healthy sexuality.

3.4 Further Professionalization of the Juvenile Justice Field

Further Professionalization of the juvenile justice field is another emerging trend. Much like similar efforts in the field of social work, it is likely we will see juvenile justice careers framed by standards of education and training. It is probable we will be seeing degree programs specializing in working with youth in the justice system. We will likely see increased numbers of certification and licensure opportunities. In working toward professionalizing this field, we are indeed honoring the value we place on our youth and those working with all youth to ensure safe and productive citizens.

3.5 Restorative Practices

In the coming years, it is anticipated we will see a return to the use of restorative practices in the juvenile justice field. This will likely involve us turning to other systems and cultures – such as tribal courts – for practices like peacemaking and healing circles that can be used in juvenile courts and the juvenile justice system.

4. The Impact of Research in the Juvenile Justice Field

4.1 Specific Studies and Research

In the next decade, researchers will strive to identify evidence-based practice with groups not often studied (i.e., non-white / non-male). Research must be expanded to include specific studies on females, cultural differences, rural versus urban, LGBTQ, etc. as developmental and intervention needs are not always universal. That is to say that what works for a 16 year old white male very well might not work for anyone who is not a 16 year old white male.

4.2 Disproportionate Minority Contact/Implicit Bias

In the thinking about the near future, one of the most vexing problems in the juvenile justice system will receive a substantial increase in attention: disproportionate minority contact (DMC). Despite decades of work to reduce DMC in the juvenile justice system, very little progress has been made and/or maintained. Recent conversations initiated by the Office of Juvenile Justice and Delinquency Prevention indicate reducing DMC will be a priority in the coming years, and an effort that will likely be led by public / private partnerships in working with states. As part of this work, researchers and practitioners alike will need to develop strategies to not just reduce institutional bias, but reduce bias in individual decision-making. The most difficult aspect of reducing individual bias is testing and implementing interventions to reduce implicit bias. Implicit bias operates outside of our awareness and has been linked to biased behavior in many different populations (e.g., police officers, physicians, etc.). Although implicit bias is linked to normative information processing in humans, its effects on decision-making cannot be underestimated, and successful attempts to reduce DMC will almost certainly need to include consideration of "being human" in working with others not like ourselves.

4.3 Establishing 18 Years as Age of Jurisdiction

Lastly, we will likely see resurgence in establishing the age of jurisdiction as 18 years across all states. In some states, the age of jurisdiction can be quite low for some offenses (e.g., 14 years). This again is inconsistent with our founding principles of our Juvenile Justice System. Consistent with research findings regarding the adolescent brain as a "work in progress" and not fully formed until approximately 23 years of age, the NCJFCJ has taken the position that all states should recognize the age of jurisdiction as 18 years. Indeed, this shift alone might be the largest indicator of progress toward building a truly developmentally appropriate juvenile justice system.

4.4 Epigenetics

In terms of the more distant future of juvenile justice, it is difficult to anticipate what major development will occur outside of those outlined here we hope will come to fruition. That said there is one area of science that holds much promise for working with children and families. This is the science of epigenetics. "Epi" means to act upon, and refers to the process by which chemical markers control gene expression without modifying the actual gene.

To illustrate this, I will use a library as an example. In thinking about epigenetics, it is helpful to think of your genes as a vast library of books-some of which are easily read and others that are not (e.g., they are stuck behind other books, are on a very high shelf, etc.). One factor that can facilitate access to all of the books in your library is a librarian (i.e., chemical markers). If the librarian is stressed, he or she might not be as adept in locating books. On the other hand, if everything is running smoothly, he or she can make accessing books much more efficient and productive.

Research suggests the same dynamic applies in terms of chemical markers responding to toxicity or stress in the environment. When there is stress on an organism, markers might suppress or express genes as a result. What is interesting with epigenetics is that the organism under stress may or may not show symptomology related to gene expression (e.g., anxiety).

However, the expression can be passed on to future generations, and under the right circumstances, that offspring would experience the symptomology of the trauma experienced by the parent or grandparent or great grandparent, etc. This, in part, could help explain historical trauma and why "just get over it just isn't enough".

Researchers today are working to understand how we might be able to manipulate various chemical markers to shut off or turn on genes that prior environmental stress impacted negatively in some way. Obviously much work remains to be done to achieve this goal – but the potential this science holds for improving well-being and interrupting intra and inter-generational suffering is impressive.

5. Conclusion

As a Judge, I have a unique vantage point in the broader system. From my perspective as a decision maker, I have only one guiding principle:

Is what I am doing making a positive difference for this child and this family standing in front of me?

I have always found this approach to be helpful. Even as we look at the many issues discussed here on a Macro level, I encourage you to also look at the Micro level:

Is what I am doing making a positive difference for this child and his family?

This is an exciting time to be a professional in the Juvenile and Family Justice System in the United States. I am sure it is also true for all of my colleagues worldwide who are dedicated to make the Juvenile Court System and the outcomes for our Children every day a little better and "child friendlier" than it was yesterday.

Much remains to be done in the United States. Achieving these goals will require a substantial change in laws, screening instruments, research funding, etc. – as well as a fundamental shift in how our society perceives the value of youth and the effectiveness of punishment and deterrence.

Patricia M. Martin

From First Court Model to Model Court: The history of the Cook County Juvenile Court

1. Preface

For most of its history the public has largely ignored the court. For better or for worse, little attention was paid to the Cook County Juvenile Court. During the early years of the court various leaders tried to uphold the lofty ambitions of the juvenile court founders. Intrinsically tied with the history and idea of the court to help children rather than punishing them is "Suitcase Mary" Barthelme. Barthelme, the first Cook County Public Guardian and later a juvenile court judge, earned her nickname because of her practice of giving suitcases neatly packed with dresses toiletries and other necessities to the girls who appeared in court. Throughout the time beliefs changed, what to do with troubled and neglected children and influences of politics and media conflicted with solid knowledge, how to treat these children successfully and allow them to have a future and to become a productive citizen until today.

Historically media attention has driven the public's interest and awareness of the court. Whether it was conditions at the Juvenile Detention Center or child's death and the crack cocaine epidemic in the 1990's, public attention and media attention have a tendency to coincide. Sometimes this has brought needed resources. Other times it has brought wrong-headed solutions that took years to correct. I will talk about the media a little later. During the 15 year tenure as presiding judge, we have tried to be very open to the media so that they may receive a balanced view of the work that we do.

2. Historic Periods of the Juvenile Court

The History of Cook County Juvenile Court consists of three specific periods which represent major shifts for the court:

First period: Founding of the court

Second period: 1960's when juvenile justice and child protection cases diverged

Third period: The last twenty years when the court underwent major reform

2.1 First Period

The Cook County Juvenile Court was the first court of its kind in the United States. The state of Illinois created the court in 1899. To have a full understanding of the court, however, it helps to know a little bit about the Chicago of the late eighteen hundreds.

In 1871, Chicago suffered the Great Chicago Fire. The fire destroyed more than 18,000 buildings and left one third of the city's population homeless. Over the next 30 years, Chicago would rebuild. In 1893, to showcase its progress, Chicago hosted the World's Fair or as it is known in Chicago the Columbian Exposition. The people of Chicago hoped that the fair's 27.5 million visitors would see a new, growing, prosperous Chicago. Indeed, Chicago was all of these. It was new. The world's first steel framed skyscraper, the Home Insurance Building, was built in 1884. The city was growing. Between 1870 and 1900 Chicago's population increased more 500% to nearly 1.7 million people. The population growth reflected not only a migration to Chicago from other parts of the country but an influx of a great many newly settled immigrants from Europe. And the city was prosperous.

This population growth and booming economy were a boon but also presented challenges. For example, there was labor unrest such as the Haymarket Bombing and Riot on May 4, 1883 in which 7 policemen and 4 workers died with as many as 60 police and 70 civilians wounded. There were the Union Stockyards which gave Chicago the title of "Hog Butcher to the World," the conditions of which were memorialized in Upton Sinclair's 1906 novel, "The Jungle." At the same time, the Progressive Movement was taking hold in the United States with some of its leading proponents located in Chicago. It was in this environment that the Chicago Juvenile Court began.

The issue of children becoming criminals had been discussed for some time. Children were arrested for many minor offenses such as truancy, petty theft, and stealing rides on street cars. Once arrested the children were held in police jail and tried in police courts. The offenses frequently resulted in fines but if the families could not pay the fines, the children were sent to the same city jails as adults. In 1884, future Illinois governor John Altgeld speaking of this system referred to it as:

[A] "great mill which, in one way or another, supplies its own grist, a maelstrom which draws from the outside, and then keeps its victims moving in a circle until swallowed in the vortex."

At the time of the founding of the Juvenile Court, placards read, **"Who is the Criminal – the State or the Child?"**

Not surprisingly, because of Chicago's rapid growth many residents lived in tenements. The founders of the juvenile court thought that it was these poor social conditions that brought children into the criminal justice system. They believed that the state first neglected those children and then punished them. The thought was that the court could reduce crime by providing services to children to ameliorate their conditions. Thus from its inception the court linked delinquency and abuse and neglect.

Unfortunately, this very early linking of abuse and neglect to future criminal behavior still haunts the court. In saying this, I do not dispute that child maltreatment is a risk factor for delinquency. I do believe, however, that by tying the two together too closely that we reinforced prejudices towards abused and neglected children and their families. Today, our research has shown that these children are treated more harshly in such areas as scholastic discipline. I submit that this a residual effect of regarding maltreated children as budding criminals.

Returning to the early years of the court, despite the enormous step forward that the juvenile court represented in many ways it was built on a criminal justice model. For example, children and their families were monitored by probation officers and children who did not remain with their parents lived in an institutional setting. Of course there were quite a number of early problems with the juvenile court that focused on societal issues rather than the best interests of children. For example, there were those who sought to shut down the court. There were accusations that the court was akin to child slavery, tearing children from poor families to ship them to other states and nations.

Problems were not confined to the court's opponents. There were conflicts between those who supported and wanted to help the court. Catholic and Protestant affiliated charities argued about how social services would be provided. The worry among both Catholics and Protestants being that the juvenile court would somehow proselytize the children who came before it. Remnants of this dispute remain today in our statutes. The Illinois Juvenile Court Act states that parents retain the right to determine their children's religious affiliations unless parental rights are terminated. Federal law expressly bars race as factor in choosing foster placements but child welfare agencies may take religion into account when choosing a foster home for a child.

The procedures employed by the court reflected a belief that the child was innately good. The child was denied the rights afforded to adult criminal defendants. As the United States Supreme Court (relying on a 1909 Harvard Law Review article) summarized:

"[The child was] to feel that he is the object of the state's care and solicitude, not that he was under arrest or on trial. The rules of criminal procedure were therefore altogether inapplicable. The apparent rigidities, technicalities, and harshness which they observed in both substantive and procedural criminal law were therefore to be discarded. The idea of crime and punishment was to be abandoned. The child was to be „treated" and „rehabilitated," and the procedures, from apprehension through institutionalization, were to be „clinical," rather than punitive."

The reformers who founded juvenile court envisioned a court focused on improving the conditions of children. By the 1930s the pendulum had swung again towards punishing children. In the 1940s and 1950s society expressed its concern regarding the "escalating rate" of juvenile delinquency. These developments set the stage for the next major shift.

2.2 Second Period

The 1960s were a time of turmoil in the United States. Examples of that turmoil were readily evident in Chicago. There were riots during the democratic convention. Haymarket square returned to the news with the bombing of the police memorial erected in the square to commemorate the police officers killed in the 1886 bombing. The civil rights struggle that began in the 1950s continued. Primarily as a result of that struggle, federal courts were rapidly expanding guaranties of equal protection, due process, and individual rights. Meanwhile the juvenile court continued in an informal atmosphere. The court continued to sit, in theory, in a non-adversarial capacity. While some spoke of the benign paternalism of the court, others disagreed.

-In re Gault Ruling

In 1967, the Supreme Court resolved this dispute in its landmark ruling, In re Gault. In Arizona, on a June morning in 1964, 15 year old Gerald Gault and a friend made an obscene phone call to one of Gerald's neighbors. Thus began Gerald's journey to the Supreme Court. Within a week, Gerald was found delinquent and committed to the Arizona State Industrial School for the period of his minority unless discharged sooner. An adult convicted of the same crime could have been sentenced to a fine of between 5 and 50 dollars or imprisonment for up to two months. Gerald faced a potential confinement of six years. The Supreme Court ruled that Arizona had violated Gerald's constitutional rights. Specifically, the Supreme Court found that juveniles accused in delinquency proceedings had the right to notice of the charges, the right to counsel, the right to confront and cross-examine witnesses, and the right against self-incrimination. The Gault case marked a turning point in how delinquency hearings would occur. It also marked a divergence between juvenile justice cases and child protection cases. Henceforth, juvenile justice cases took on more of an atmosphere of a criminal case. Child Protection cases retained their civil nature.

When I reread the Gault case, I was struck not so much by the failings that the Supreme Court pointed out but by certain admonitions that that court quoted in its opinion:

There was a quote from one judge warning that a juvenile court must not "degenerate into a star chamber proceeding with the judge imposing his own particular brand of culture and morals on indigent people. . . ." Another from a law review article warned that „The judge as amateur psychologist, experimenting upon the unfortunate children who must appear before him, is neither an attractive nor a convincing figure." What struck me about those quotes was the call that they made to judges to be humble and not to overreach in our use of our authority. I find that admonition particularly compelling when juxtaposed to the injustices committed and referenced in the Gault case.

2.3 Third Period

I am going to spend the majority of my remaining remarks on child protection matters. Before I do that, however, I would like to discuss one more development in juvenile justice, BARJ or balanced and restorative justice.

2.3.1 BARJ Principles

Balanced and restorative justice has three purposes:

- the community
- hold the offender accountable
- equip the offender with competencies to enable the offender to live a productive and responsible life.

The State of Illinois codified these three BARJ principles in 1998 during a complete rewrite of the delinquency article of the Juvenile Court Act.

Protecting the community:

All of us have the right to live in a safe community. The first prong of balanced and restorative justice recognizes the rights of victims. This prong goes beyond commitment of those minors who present a danger to the community. It recognizes the need to promote, develop, and implement community based programs aimed at preventing delinquency.

Accountability:

Accountability means that minors understand that their actions have consequences. Accountability is broader than punishment. Accountability means that the offender understands the effects of his actions on the victim and the community.

Competency development:

This means teaching skills with which the offender can build a productive life. Competency development takes a holistic approach through programs such as multi systemic therapy, MST. MST is an intensive intervention geared towards working with the entire family as a unit.

2.3.2 Cook County Intervention programs based on BARJ Principles

In Cook County there are a variety of programs intended to implement these principles. There are diversionary programs such as peer juries. There is offender victim mediation and victim offender conferencing to assist the victim in securing meaningful restitution. There are programs such as victim impact panels and community panels for youth. These programs help offenders understand how their actions have affected their victims and the community at large.

Probation plans often require minors to provide community service. This way minors can work to benefit and rebuild their communities while the minors learn positive skills. Our probation department also offers interventions aimed at specific types of crime. Probation has a program called Retail Theft School. I have to admit that I am not fond of this program's name. It sounds like a program that teaches retail theft. In actuality it is a partnership between probation, the state's attorney office, and private loss prevention officers to teach those arrested for retail theft the effects of their behavior, including the effects upon themselves.

As you can see from this brief list of programs, BARJ is an attempt to balance societal interests, victims' rights, and offenders' rights. The BARJ principles are inter-related. They build upon each other. Accountability includes not only punishment but an understanding of the harm caused. Protecting communities isn't just about law enforcement; it's about people becoming invested in their communities. Building competency includes gaining new skills and therapeutic interventions. With that I am now going to move away from delinquency to child protection.

2.3.3 Child Protection Courts

In the United States child protection courts deal adjudicate cases of child abuse and neglect. This is the area in which I have spent the majority of my judicial career. For the last 15 years, I have been the Presiding Judge of the Cook County Child Protection Division. I work with 14 other judges to whom are entrusted the care of 6,100 children. We work closely with the Illinois Department of Family Services and various attorney offices to improve the lives of these children and their families. Our goal is the best interest of the child. First, we try to determine if a child may remain safely with his or her family. If the child must be removed, we attempt to work with the family towards a safe and speedy reunification. If reunification cannot be achieved or is impracticable, we explore other permanent options for the child such as adoption or guardianship with a private individual. This is essentially the framework within every child protection court in the United States operates. Allow me to share with you our road to this destination.

Child protection systems have always had to confront the problems of children growing up in foster care. It is now widely recognized that removal of a child from the child's parents, even when necessary to save the child's life can be traumatic for the child. Even more widely accepted is the fact that childhood traumas may have lasting consequences.

In child protection, that initial trauma may be compounded by multiple placements in foster care, further abuse or neglect, unresolved needs, and countless other factors. In the 1970s, policy makers began to recognize the problem of foster care drift. A situation in which a child entered the child welfare system only to move from foster home to foster home and then "age out" without the skills or support system to be a productive adult. Often times foster care drift was the result of repeated, failed efforts to reunite parents and children no matter how extraordinary those efforts were. Intertwined with repeated failed attempts at reunification was the difficulty in terminating parental rights and freeing the child for adoption.

2.3.3.1 The Role of the Adoption Assistance and Child Welfare Act of 1980

These problems eventually resulted in our Congress enacting the Adoption Assistance and Child Welfare Act of 1980. The Act set up a framework under which our courts still operate. I alluded to that framework earlier in describing our court. Focusing on Illinois, after the Adoption Assistance Act was enacted Illinois drafted a state plan corresponding to the Act's provisions. In practice, however, the plan was not followed. This resulted in a number of lawsuits demanding that our Department of Children and Family Services, DCFS, improve its practices in serving its wards.

- "Super-Predators"-Concern

At the same time there was again a growing concern about juvenile crime and new drug, crack cocaine, becoming prevalent in the inner city. Intrauterine exposure to crack was predicted to have enormous consequences. It was suggested that these babies would lack the ability to form attachments and not develop empathy. Combined with the fear of juvenile crime, this would eventually give rise to a new boogeyman, "super-predators"-juveniles, utterly lacking consciences, committing heinous crimes. Of course the truth fell far short of the Hollywood movie plot that was presented.

-The Role of the Media

Enter a third element, the media. There were a number of sensational media reports of maltreated children. This spawned outrage that DCFS had not acted in time to prevent the maltreatment. Thus, the Illinois DCFS was squeezed between outrage that it was not removing children and outrage that it was not caring properly for the children that it did remove.

2.3.3.2 The Wallace Case and its impact on the Family Court

All of this set the stage for what happened in April 1993. A mentally ill mother, Amanda Wallace, killed her three year old son, Joey. The details of the murder were shocking. For the public, however, one detail was too much to bear. Two months before his murder, a juvenile court judge had reunified Joey with Amanda. The editorial pages erupted. The court was a disgrace and DCFS was inept. More media attention, in November of that year case of children starvation emerged during the weekend of the United States's national day of Thanksgiving. Then in the winter of 1994, 19 children were found living in squalor in an apartment on Keystone Avenue in Chicago.

The bubbling cauldron of child welfare finally boiled over. Worried over the criticism of inaction combined with routine screenings for drug exposure in maternity wards resulted in more new cases than ever entering court. In 1994, over 10,000 children were brought to the court's attention. If you will recall, earlier I mentioned that our total current caseload is roughly 6,100 children. Illinois would go on to have the highest removal rate of children in the country.

At the same time, as a result of the Wallace case, few children returned home for fear of what would happen "if something went wrong." The court's caseload ballooned to over 50,000 children. At one point 17.2 of every 1000 children in Illinois were in foster care. The situation led to a widespread call for reform.

3. From Reform to Reform: Current Reform Strategies

In retrospect, I wonder how similar this scenario must have been to the original reforms that led to the creation of the court in the 1890s. Blue ribbon commissions convened, private foundations and universities offered their resources and services, and governmental bodies lavished attention. A new courthouse was built. New leaders were brought in to the child protection system. More judges were assigned and quasi-judicial personnel were hired.

The child protection system adopted a strategy to attack at both the front end of the system and the backend of the system. On the front end, new tools for assessing risk were developed. New legislation, redefining what constitutes neglect, was passed. DCFS provided more and better services to parents to enable them to care safely for their children.

The mid-nineties and the decision of Illinois to simultaneously address problems at both the front and back ends of the child welfare continuum. At the same time as we were undergoing these reforms, Congress was addressing the failure of the Adoption Assistance Act to achieve its goals nationally. The federal government created an incentive system to increase the number of adoptions. Illinois found itself in the vanguard of this new adoption movement. In 1997 and 1998, Illinois accounted for 14% and 18% respectively of all adoptions reported to the federal government from all 50 states.

In addition to adoptions, Illinois developed other tools to help children find permanency. For example, Illinois obtained a federal waiver to subsidize guardianship. This enabled families to receive a subsidy if they agreed to become the private guardians of foster children. This program proved to be an effective tool to enable extended family to care permanently for children without disrupting existing family structures,

On the backend, a push to locate safe and permanent placements for children was launched. Permanency became a mantra. The Cook County Juvenile Court became a participant in the National Council of Juvenile and Family Court Judges' model court project.

4. NCJFCJ Nationwide Strategies for Reform

4.1 NCJFCJ Model Court Program

Let's talk a little about the NCJFCJ model court program. When we hear model court, we tend to envision an ideal court. I wish we were ideal courts but that is not what the NCJFCJ meant to imply when creating the model court program. The program is one through which various jurisdictions agree to become "laboratories" or models of change. The courts agree to collaborate with their various stakeholders and attempt to improve outcomes for children and families. In return, the NCJFCJ provides technical support and training opportunities.

When Cook County joined the model court program, we made two commitments to the NCJ FCJ. The first was to work collaboratively with our stakeholders. In my opinion, one of the chief benefits of becoming a model court was that it caused us to create and institutionalize a mechanism for cooperation between the court, DCFS, our attorney offices, and other stakeholders. This group, the Table of Five, although we exceeded five members long ago, still meets monthly to discuss and resolve problems. The group has proven invaluable. We have been able to solve numerous systemic problems through these meetings. We have been able to discuss and rectify problems with diversionary programs. We have been able to help our partners manage changes in law that would otherwise overwhelm them. Most importantly, we have developed a culture of trust and respect.

We better understand the challenges that each of us face. Moreover, when things have gone wrong, we have moved beyond assigning blame. Our collaboration is solution driven. We recognize our obligations to the children and families we serve and recognize that we need solutions to fulfill those obligations.

4.2 NCJFCJ Change Model Program

Our second commitment to the NCJFCJ was to become a change model. We agreed that we would work creatively to improve outcomes for children and families. To do this we continually assessed our deficiencies and our needs. Once we identified those needs, we experimented with a variety of programs to address them. The model court program, in turn, provided us with a nationwide network of other laboratories to which we could look for ideas and programs. Over the years, we have hosted and attended site visits during which one model court observes a program of another model court. These visits create a forum through which a model court can learn from another court's experiences. This way we can avoid pitfalls and snares that the other court has had to navigate.

In addition, the model court program has given Cook County access to some of the top experts in child welfare. The National Council has repeatedly brought valuable trainings to Cook County. As our model court matured, we were able to bring our experiences to new model courts. Though these exchanges, Cook County has introduced programs that are imitated nationwide. These exchanges, have also allowed us to copy programs from elsewhere.

5. Conclusion

I had been a judge in juvenile court for a brief time in 1996 and 1997 when our reform was still in its infancy. I returned to the court as presiding judge in 2000. At the time of my return, the juvenile court's caseload had declined to under 30,000 children.

My goals in becoming presiding judge were too build on the successes of my predecessors, empower those who came before the court, and to improve the lives of children in foster care. On this last goal, I am a firm believer that if we are going to remove children from their families only if our alternative is an improvement.

I am still working on these goals. In terms of building on previous successes, the court has done well. Over the last six years the court has averaged 1150 new cases. I would like to note that we now have one of the lowest removal rates in the country along with no adverse effects on re-abuse or child deaths. As I have mentioned twice our total caseload is approximately 6,100 children well below our peak of 50,000 children and the number when I began, 30,000 children.

With respect to my other goals, I introduced a program to give children who are likely to leave the court as adults a greater role in participating in plan for their future. Likewise, I have introduced programs to empower families to help craft solutions to their problems. Our mediation program employs trained mediators to facilitate discussions between parents, caseworkers, foster parents, and others involved in a child's life. Mediation, we hope empowers participants and provides a ready alternative to actions imposed on them by the court.

I regret that I have had time to share with you only a small portion of the court's history and but a sample of the truly impressive effort of the last 115 years. Nevertheless, I hope that you have enjoyed this journey from court model to model court. If all of us work together, on the local, regional, national or even international level we will be most influential to better children's lives. They are and will ever be our future.

Richard Ross

Juvenile in Justice

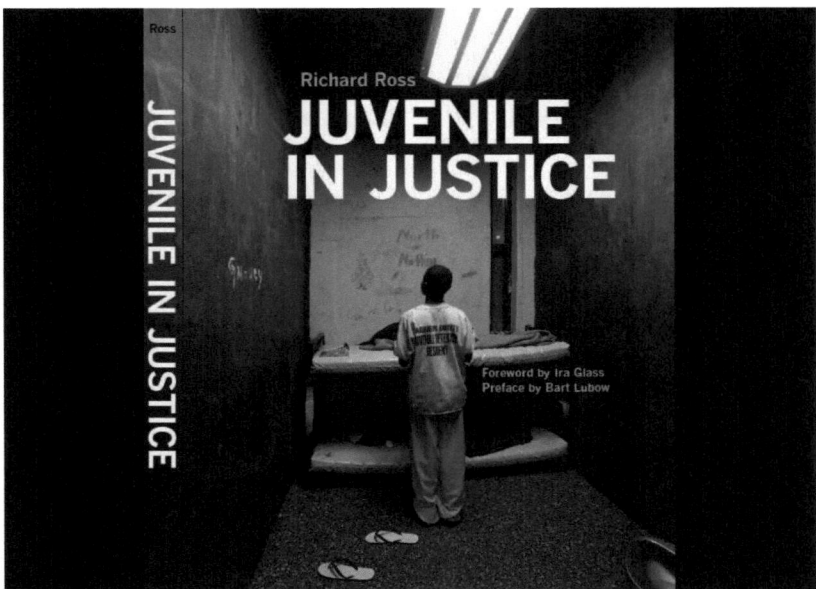

"There is no keener revelation of a society's soul than the way in which it treats its children". Nelson Mandela

1. Introduction to Juvenile in Justice

Disclaimer: I am not a judge, attorney,P.O. etc. I am an artist. I am a human being.

For the past 5 years, I interviewed and photographed more than 1,000 detainees, some as young as 8 years old, in more than 350 detention facilities in 30 different states throughout the US. At the outset of this project I wanted to give a voice to those with the least amount of authority in any U.S. confinement system. This has been a difficult journey of learning about a world that is populated by administrators-a complex hierarchy of judges, staff, guards, families, and finally the juveniles. All the people in this chain, in one manner or another, had to agree to let me sit in a cell and allow me to listen to the story of the child. It has been a very long process. There are well meaning people in this system who are doing their best to change the lives of the juveniles in their care-both, inside and outside the institution. Some institutions and people were distrustful and wary, some self-critical, some proud and defensive. Regardless, gaining access was an ongoing negotiation until the last minute, when I was outside of the cell, talking to the juvenile and asking him or her for permission to enter his or her cell and world.

During the making of this project I knew that disseminating the images I was producing would burn bridges in front of me. Since the work became public, I have been giving license to the images, free of charge, to all facilities and advocates in the field.

2. Project Goals

- Give visual tools to advocates
- Change current practice
- Frame the issues for next generation

The goal is to have an impact. I want a visual image to have an impact.

THEN THIS BECOMES A POWERFUL TOOL.

3. Art is a weapon

"The study of art that does not result in making the strong less willing to oppress the weak means little." (Booker T. Washington)

Art is a weapon to change the future.

„This is beautiful photography, beautiful in the way it conveys the stark, simple truth of children in prison. Yet to see it as photography is to miss the point. This is sociology, and psychology and criminology and public policy, but it is also about man`s capacity to do evil to his fellow man, or in this case, the children of men." (John Fleming, Editor, Juvenile Justice Information Exchange.

4. The power of Words

Trauma/PTSD	Poverty	Adult Sentencing
Rape	Gun accessibility	Foster Care
States Rights	Broken Families	Trends
LGBT	Brain Development	Immigration
Clothing	Solitary Confinement	Language
Sanitation	Mandatory Sentencing	CPS
Respect	Jurisdictional	Safety
Visitation	Hierarchies	Nutrition
Sexual Exploitation	Gang Enhancement	Social Contract
Status Violation	Gangs	Health
POA-ing	Education	Sleep
Media	Substance Abuse	Tribal Cultures
	Sex Education	

Even though I came from architecture…I found all these issues. And I was overwhelmed. All of these are legit research topics

THE LANGUAGE IS THE KEY:

A person can be a prisoner—means liberty is taken away. But they may not be a convict, because they haven't been found guilty of a crime. They are still a detainee.

This is the word they use in Guantanamo.

Terminology: prisoner, convict, detainee, offender, client…..how does this affect one's self perception???

These are kids. Look at the scale. Who are these people? How do you treat a terrorist – how do you treat a kid?

The power of words:

„**Youth**" has a 7:1 positive response

„**Kid**" has a 12:1 positive response

„**Child**" has a 15:1 positive response

5. Examples
-Orleans Parish Prison

Sheriff Guzman rents out space to other parishes overcrowding his facilities. They have also closed juvenile facilities….which means they go to the same places adults are held

The future will look back on this period of mass incarceration in our history with the same disdain we presently view the shameful past of slavery in America. Your grand-children may ask why you were oblivious to this and didn't protest.

A kid, 12 year old, sent here for getting in a fight at school, then kicking a cop car and refusing to wear his seat belt. *Now sentenced to two weeks to do his homework in a cell.*

-Washow County Nevada

Detention supervisor sent this image to all principals in her district. This is not a place for kids. He is waiting for his Mommy, who is an undocumented day worker and can't get off until 6 to get him.

-Caldwell, Idaho

The girl is a meth user, kicked out of school for truancy. This is not a drug rehabilitation center, or somewhere she can catch up on units. Prostitute? L.A. Central 2013: Prostitute vs. Sex Trafficking?!

The internal life schema reads: Parents don't parent. Caregivers don't care. Protectors don't protect. Nurturers don't nurture. Trusted adults can't be trusted. Thus, the only person I can depend on is myself. I have to be on guard. I have to protect and care for myself. I have to do whatever it takes to survive.

-Ronald Franklin-Miami Dade

Kid received 4.5 years –lives in the balance.

-Colorado - Young Offenders Program

Orientation Training Phase:

MILITARISM DOES NOT CURE TRAUMA and PTSD

Hanging sentences….what sense does that make?

INSTITUTIONS ARE HOARDERS OF BAD PRACTICE.

-Maryvale, California

"What percentages of girls have been sexually abused when they come here?" "What percentage?" "Everyone. All 88 girls in our custody."

ALL the girls here have been molested and have had incomplete childhoods. 90 girls, former orphanage. Level 12 California state security.

-Postville, Iowa

Mother with ankle bracelet, waiting with baby to testify against inhumane working conditions. Some of the kids from Postville encountered in Washington and San Diego....awaiting repatriation.

Another example:

"Eyes on" for last 19 months, 24/7.

How does that help someone who is at risk of hurting themselves?

How much does it cost to keep someone idly watching a youth 24/7?

How could those funds be used to help them? For community resources?

Let's address what facilities that detain kids are and what they mean:

These facilities are Dangerous, Ineffective, Unnecessary, Wasteful, Obsolete, Inadequate. These are the wrong facilities for the 88% and inhumane facilities for the remaining 12 %--regardless. They are ineffective.

Some institutions are under federal orders to close or change.

California is example of court order to lower pop—Jerry Brown Gov. says they're too dangerous.

6. Newly built facilities

Hawaii/

New facility built at $ 160 Million Dollar for 55 kids.

As Kevin Costner, "If you build it, they will come"---or rather, they will be sentenced.

Another facility, build for $135 million dollars, opened in 2007; the kid is the only one in this entire wing because he is 18.

Who benefits?

7. Statistical Data:

1996:	Today:
10,000+ kids in CYA	**Today less than 800**
2,000+ afro-american kids in California charged with murder	**Today about 200**

This is the safest most law abiding generation in the current era of data collection.

Why don't we read or hear about this from media or politicians?

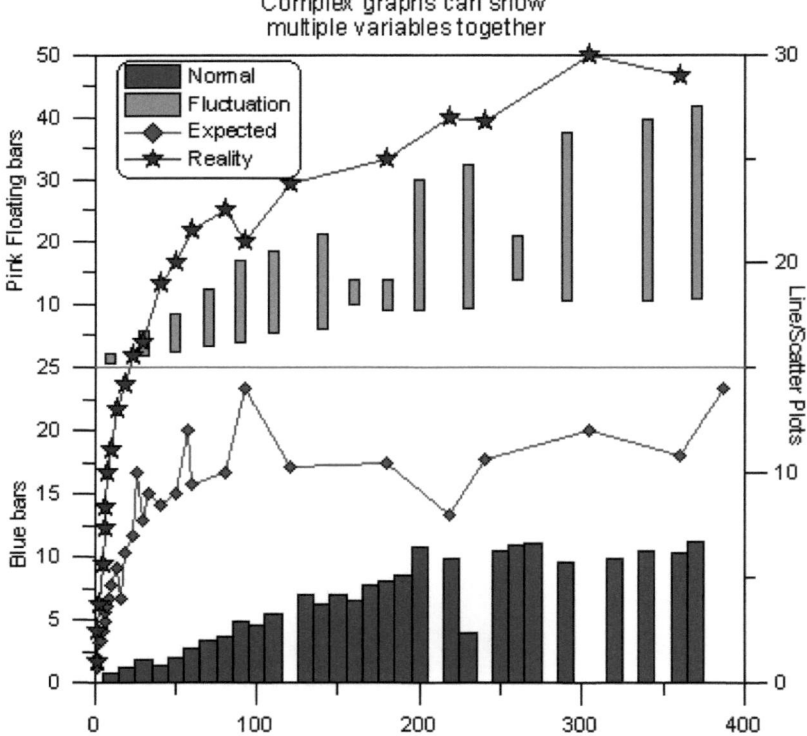

Incarceration rates in all O.E.C.D. countries, 2013*

*Number of persons imprisoned
per 100,000 population*

United States	710
Chile	266
Estonia	238
Israel	223
Poland	217
Mexico	210
New Zealand	192
Slovakia	187
Hungary	186
Turkey	179
Czech Rep.	154
Britain	147
Spain	147
Portugal	136
Australia	130
Luxembourg	122
Canada	118
Greece	111
Belgium	108
Italy	106
South Korea	99
Austria	98
France	98
Ireland	88
Netherlands	82
Switzerland	82
Germany	79
Denmark	73
Norway	72
Sweden	67
Slovenia	66
Finland	58
Japan	51
Iceland	47

Contrary to all statistics and facts,

a professor of politics and public affairs on the political science faculty at Princeton University, John DiIulio, created and popularized the super- predator concept. He coined the term superpredator (1995b) to call public attention to what he characterized as a "new breed" of offenders, "kids that have absolutely no respect for human life and no sense of the future. . . . These are stone-cold predators!" (p. 23). Elsewhere, DiIulio and co-authors have described these young people as "fatherless, Godless, and jobless" and as "radically impulsive, brutally remorseless youngsters, including ever more teenage boys, who murder, assault, rob, burglarize, deal deadly drugs, join gun-toting gangs, and create serious [linked] disorders" (Bennett, DiIulio, & Walters, 1996, p. 27).

America's reliance on juvenile incarceration is unique among the developed nations of the world. I costs an average of $88,000 a year to hold a juvenile in detention. We have over 2 million people incarcerated in the United States.

The War on Poverty Became the War on Drugs 1987-2007 Every given day are appr. 700000 young people incarcerated or institutionalized. Research suggests that young people, who spent longer time in such facilities, do not have a lower recidivism rate than those with shorter sentences.

The average costs for a 9-12 months are $ 66-88.000 Dollar. The State of California spends annually $ 224.712 to house one kid in the new "green" facility in Oakland. The city of Oakland spends annually $ 4925 per child in public schools.

This is data and the way it is visualized. And Annie E Casey is great for data. But I grew up in a world of singular images:

Children as young as 7 years old can be prosecuted and tried in adult court in 22 states and the District of Columbia.

This Girl was given Meth by her mother when she was 7. Girl is doing 35 years for homicide, mother is free.

Graham vs. Florida, Miller vs Alabama Life without parole.....impact to change the world........**Changed**...But no MANADATORY life without parole...but can be looked at case by case....and kids can get 90 years....etc.

8. Parens Patriae

"Parent of the nation,"

In law, refers to the power of the state to intervene against an abusive or negligent parent, legal guardian, or informal caretaker, and to act as the parent of any child or individual who is in need of protection.

If a parent put a child in a closet such as this for poor behavior would the child be removed from the family? Or would the parent be arrested?

WHEN STATE IS PARENT- how do they have authority to do what you wouldn't let a parent do? If a parent locked their child behind a door like this…would you not take action? 88 % are locked up for non-violent crimes…POA-ing

THIS IS NOT AN INDIVIDUAL OCCURRENCE---IT IS SYSTEMIC. What is the role of parens patriae? Institutions are the hoarders of bad practices.

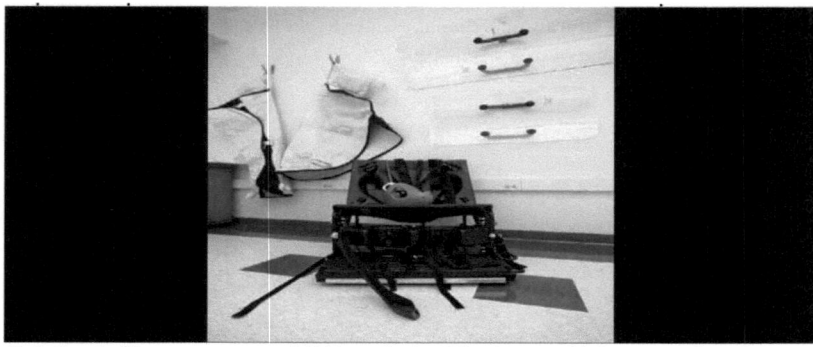

Oak Creek. If a parent put a child in a device like this would the parent be taken into custody and punished?

Who do you become when your world keeps you in shackles?

7. Minorities

BUT AS A TRANSSEXUAL?? – being held in isolation for protection? "It is pretty difficult being gay and Christian in a land of homophobes. Actually, it's pretty impossible here." 14 year old beaten up by her girl friend two weeks earlier. A.B., age 14, Tulsa, Oklahoma

Native American issues?

South Dakota 8% of the state is Native American 40% of detention and confinement is Native American. There are 26 detention centers on reservations. Jurisdiction is complex. And tribal justice frequently is at odds with "American" justice as "Justice by strangers" which is anti ethical to Native American thinking.

Racial issues?

Latino youth are 4x more likely to receive an adult sentence for the SAME crime as white children. Afro-American Kids are treated harsher than white kids, even if their charges and (offending) history are identical.

8. Outlook

There are effective solutions and interventions. If a kid does not represent a present and clear danger to the public, it is unnecessary and expensive, to remove troubled youth from their communities. The average results are not any better, but often much worse, than community based interventions and supervision. Typically, programs which include counseling and treatment reduce recidivism. Programs focusing on control and pressure are showing negative or no effect

HE IS LOOKING AT YOU. THERE IS A RESPONSE WE WANT TO GET.

Karlsruhe Declaration of the 19th German Congress on Crime Prevention

May 12 and 13 in Karlsruhe

In the last quarter century, crime prevention has been established and developed in many ways in Germany. A new field of action and policy has developed at the level of communities, states, and the federation with programs and measures that are directly or indirectly aimed at preventing and reducing crime and/or at least mitigating its consequences and improving the feeling of safety among the public.

As a social responsibility which must be implemented in a networked and interdisciplinary manner across departments and institutions, crime prevention requires the active cooperation of many social forces and disciplines in three central areas of activity: the practice, policy, and science of prevention.

For this reason, the 19th German Congress of Crime Prevention is focusing on the tasks in these areas of activity in and for crime prevention with the demand „Prevention requires practice, policy, and science" and has commissioned a scientific expert opinion which especially addresses these questions: whether and to what extent these three areas of activity have fulfilled their tasks; what challenges had to be and still have to be overcome; what conclusions can be drawn from this and what requirements can be made in order to further develop, establish, and systematize crime prevention through the three areas of activity.

Based on the opinion of Dr. Wiebke Steffen „Crime prevention requires the practice, policy, and science of prevention", the German Congress on Crime Prevention authored this **„Karlsruhe Declaration"** together with its organizing partners: Bundesministerium für Familie, Senioren, Frauen und Jugend (BMFSFJ) [Federal Ministry of Family Affairs, Senior Citizens, Women, and Youth], DBH Fachverband für Soziale Arbeit, Strafrecht und Kriminalpolitik [Professional Association for Social Work, Criminal Law, and Criminal Policy], State of Baden-Württemberg, Polizeiliche Kriminalprävention der Länder und des Bundes (ProPK) [Police Crime Prevention of the states and the Federation], the City of Karlsruhe, Stiftung Deutsches Forum für Kriminalprävention (DFK) [Foundation German Forum for Crime Prevention], WEISSER RING e.V..

Crime prevention: challenges of the new field of action and policy

In the last quarter century, crime prevention has been established and developed in many ways. As a consequence of this development, the familiar original prevention protagonists (police and justice system) are now supported by additional protagonists such as schools, children and youth help organizations, and civil society organizations. Cooperation commissions have been instituted at all levels – local, regional, national, international – in order to live up to the understanding of crime prevention as a social responsibility which requires cooperation between protagonists and institutions.

Compared to criminal repression, crime prevention takes precedence in terms of content and time: also in terms of protecting the population from crime (victim protection) and improving the feeling of safety, it makes more sense to prevent crimes before they happen than to prosecute them afterwards. No matter how successful criminal prosecution is, it cannot repair damage already done or even reverse events.

While the guiding principle of the precedence of prevention over repression is not controversial as a crime policy principle, it has not yet led to a comparative success in creating the necessary (legal) framework conditions at all levels and ensuring that the necessary personnel and financial resources are provided, not to mention laws, measures, institutions, and organizational measures being specifically oriented towards prevention. Particularly at the federal level, progress has not gone beyond very general considerations and openly proclaimed convictions.

Especially in view of a generally favorable development of crime, the **German Congress on Crime Prevention** encourages all levels and actors in crime prevention not to let up in the crime-prevention efforts but rather to redouble them if possible.

At the **local/communal level,** the *concept of communal crime prevention* has had a positive effect on the development of crime prevention. Working together to fight crime and fear of crime across departments and in institutionalized form and preventing crime in those areas that it arises and is enabled is an approach which has proved itself. This form of dealing with the complexity has become indispensable. However, we also have to acknowledge deficits, structural deficiencies, and steps in the wrong direction. Even though it has been around for a long time, the practice of communal crime prevention still has a lot of room for improvement.

The **German Congress on Crime Prevention** still considers the concept of communal crime prevention as „just plain common sense" and asks **politicians** to institute corresponding commissions everywhere. Studies should be conducted on the development of communal crime prevention in the direction of an institutionalized communal security policy, for instance by setting up staff positions for crime prevention in the respective communities, districts, and regions.

Due to the tight budget restrictions in many communities, their financial basis shows clear room for improvement so they can meet their crime preventive obligations to the necessary extent and so that the other actors at the communal level can continue their outstanding and indispensable work in crime prevention and possibly even further expand it.

Cooperation commissions have also been formed at the **state level** in accordance with the understanding of crime prevention as a social, inter-departmental, and interdisciplinary responsibility: there are state prevention councils or similar commissions in almost all states, however, with very different organizational, personnel, and financial equipment. They are just as indispensable as consulting organs of the respective state governments with the goal of reducing the incidence of crime and improving the feeling of safety as they are in supporting the communal level by providing know-how and expertise, by instituting commission and project databases, by offering qualifications and training, and by providing an opportunity to share experiences.

The *German Congress on Crime Prevention* demands that *State Prevention Councils* should be formed not only in all states but also that they should be suitably equipped in terms of organization, personnel, and funding. The integration of councils into the government and not a specialized ministry should also be studied, as should the creation of a „*staff position for crime prevention*" at the state level. These measures may identify and support the desirable development of crime prevention to a systematic prevention strategy/prevention policy at the state level.

In contrast to many communities and most states, there has not been an increased focus in policy on crime prevention and its sustained development, as demanded by science and practice, at the **federal level**.

On the contrary: crime policy at the federal level not only sticks with its criminal-law reaction patterns, but has even enhanced them.

The *German Congress on Crime Prevention* urges a long overdue course correction of criminal policy towards crime prevention and away from merely repressive means according to the slogan „more of the same". This course correction towards crime prevention as an alternative, non-punitive answer to the challenge of preventing crime and improving the feeling of safety expressly stands against the currently dominant trend in criminal policy of creating a control-oriented preventive criminal law which promotes the preventive state into which Germany has been changing for a few years (see also the Munich declaration of the 17th German Congress of Crime Prevention).

In order to support and clarify this course correction, the *German Congress on Crime Prevention* considers the creation of a „*National Center for Crime Prevention*" with at least sufficient resources in terms of organization, personnel, and funding to be urgently necessary; this could possibly be implemented by expanding the Stiftung Deutsches Forum für Kriminalprävention (DFK) into such a center and integrating the expertise of significant institutions and research institutes. We should mention, for instance, federation/state-financed institutions such as the Kriminologische Zentralstelle (KrimZ) [Criminological Center] and the Polizeiliche Kriminalprävention der Länder und des Bundes (ProPK). This center should not be connected to a ministry but to the Federal Chancellery.

It should be verified at **all levels** how the proposal of the renowned Canadian criminologist *Irvin Waller* can be realized to invest 5% of the current expenses for the reaction to crime – police, justice system, and penal institutions – into effective crime prevention.

Crime prevention must be based on evidence: challenges for practice, policy, and science

Crime prevention must be based on evidence, i.e. on the basis of theoretical and empirical scientific insights. This not only applies to prevention in practice but also to prevention policy. This knowledge has also been developed and provided for practice and policy by criminology as the relevant interdisciplinary reference science and the other relevant disciplines such as psychology, sociology, education, economy.

While a scientific-empirical foundation of projects and programs for crime prevention has continuously gained in significance for **prevention practice** in the past two decades, **criminal policy** appears to be deaf to empirical insights. This is at least true for federal criminal policy whose trends and procedures have not integrated the results of scientific-criminological research in any recognizable form. The two *Periodical Security Reports* commissioned and submitted by the respective Federal Governments have essentially no impact on criminal policy in Germany. We can certainly not speak of a knowledge-based criminal policy at the federal level.

The *German Congress on Crime Prevention* welcomes the increasing scientific foundation of practical prevention work, in particular increasingly frequent and common scientific supervision and verification of planning, implementation, and effect of prevention measures and programs (Implementation and Evaluation). It encourages science and practice to continue on this path of cooperation, also in terms of the qualification and training of personnel and the development of information systems and databases.

The *German Congress on Crime Prevention* expressly points out that a rational criminal policy must be based on a solid empirical foundation. This knowledge was developed a long time ago and has been available for some time. The urgently necessary increased focus on crime prevention and its sustained expansion, in particular at the federal level, should not fail because criminal policy continues to turn a blind eye to the theoretical and empirical knowledge which supports and even demands this course correction.

The *German Congress on Crime Prevention* believes that the creation of – really – *Periodical Security Reports* based on legal regulations or a decision of the German Parliament is urgently necessary. These reports should be compiled by an interdisciplinary scientific commission on a regular basis, for instance once in every legislative period.

Many scientific disciplines are and have been involved in developing the **knowledge** about what works and what doesn't, what makes sense in terms of crime prevention and what doesn't; but a key player has always been criminology whose continued existence in German universities is at risk.

Since this could have effects on crime prevention, the *German Congress on Crime Prevention* encourages universities to intensify the instruction in particular in sociological and juristic faculties and to bundle, coordinate, and promote the diverse criminological activities by creating interdisciplinary criminological centers. The association between criminology and criminal law, which is potentially too close, should possibly be sacrificed and criminology established as an independent social science. A well-positioned criminology department is a necessary (if not sufficient) prerequisite for the implementation of the requirement for interdisciplinary prevention science – in correspondence with inter-departmental preventio practice and prevention policy.

The *German Congress on Crime Prevention* welcomes the Foundation Chair „Crime prevention and risk management" that was established in 2012 at the University Tübingen. In order to give crime prevention the necessary weight in the research spectrum of criminology and other disciplines, this Chair must be financed past 2017 and made permanent.

For more information about the requirements for crime prevention, its possible benefits, and the benefits it has already created, the 19th German Congress on Crime Prevention refers to the conferences of the 12th, 13th, 14th, 15th, 16th, 17th, and 18th German Congresses on Crime Prevention and the demands and appeals of the respective declarations.

Karlsruhe, May 13, 2014

Program of the 8th Annual International Forum

Monday, 12. May 2014

11:00 - 12:30 – Convention Center: "Schwarzwaldhalle"
Opening Plenum of the German Congress on Crime Prevention
(German with interpretation into English)
- **Welcome by the Executive Director of the German Congress on Crime Prevention**
  Erich Marks, German Congress on Crime Prevention
- **Address of Welcome**
  Manuela Schwesig. Federal Minister of Family Affairs, Senior Citizens, Women and Youth
- **Address of Welcome**
  Dr. Frank Mentrup, Lord Mayor of the City of Karlsruhe
- **Address of Welcome**
  Reinhold Gall, Minister of the Interior of the State of Baden-Württemberg
- **Address of Welcome**
  Professor Dr. Hans-Jürgen Kerner, Congress President and President of the German Foundation
  for Crime Prevention and Assistance of Criminal Offenders
- **Address of Welcome**
  Dr. Wiebke Steffen, Author of the Report for the Congress
- **Keynote Speech**
  Professor Dr. Manuel Eisner, University of Cambridge

14:00 - 15:00 – Convention Center: Room 1.31
Current Developments in Implementation Research
Prof. Dr. Dean L. Fixsen, University of North Carolina, USA

15:30 - 16:30 – Convention Center: Room 1.31
Prevention connects! – The Twinning-light Project 'Strengthening Capacities
of the Ministry of Interior for Crime Prevention' (Croatia - Baden-Württemberg)
Frank Buchheit, State Office of Criminal Investigation Baden Württemberg, Germany
Ruža Karlović, Police Academy, Croatia

17:00 - 18:00 – Convention Center: Room 1.31
Unraveling school violence
Dr. Seong-Hoon, Park, Korean Institute of Criminology (KIC), South Korea
Dr. Seung-Hyun Lee, Korean Institute of Criminology (KIC), South Korea

Chairs: Dr. Marc Coester (German Congress on Crime Prevention)
                 Dr. Burkhard Hasenpusch (Crime Prevention Council Lower Saxony)

Alternative:
14:00 - 18:00 – Convention Center: Room 2.06
US Juvenile Justice. From the first juvenile court of the United States in Chicago 1899 and the
Chicago School to the Model Courts for Change

18:00 - 20:00 – Convention Center: Gartenhalle
Evening Reception of the German Congress on Crime Prevention

Tuesday, 13. May 2014

Day of debates
"Europe and prevention: the needs of local decision makers and practitioners"
Organized by the European Forum for Urban Security in partnership with the German Forum for Urban Security

09:00-11:30 – Convention Center: "Hans-Thoma-Saal"
Translation available in English, German and French

The EU landscape 2014 – 2020. Institutional renewal, policy renewal
Overview of EU policies relating to prevention

The European scope of local crime prevention
Panel discussion on European inter-city and cross-border cooperation in crime prevention

11:30 - 12:30 - Catering Area Convention Center - Opportunity for Lunch

12:30 - 15:00 – Convention Center: "Hans-Thoma-Saal"
Translation available in English, German and French

Expectations of new EU policies and programmes in the field of justice & home affairs?
Panel discussion to analyse the EU Stockholm programme in the light of the Efus Manifesto and to identify the needs of local authorities

An open letter by crime prevention stakeholders to the renewed European institutions
Concluding session formulating the position and needs of local-decision makers and practitioners

Alternative:
14:00 - 15:00 – Convention Center: "Schwarzwaldhalle"
Strategic importance of cyber security
Melissa Hathaway, Harvard, Belfer Center for Science and International Affairs, President Hathaway Global Strategies LLC, Cambridge, USA

15:00 - 16:00 - Convention Center "Schwarzwaldhalle"
Closing Plenum of the German Congress on Crime Prevention
(German with interpretation into English)
- **The "Karlsruhe Declaration" from the German Congress on Crime Prevention**
  Dr. Wiebke Steffen, Author of the Report for the Congress
- **Closing Remarks**
  Prof. Dr. Hans-Jürgen Kerner, Congress President
- **Big Data – Chances and risks for prevention**
  Prof. Dr. Viktor Mayer-Schönberger, Universty of Oxford
- **Outlook and closing address**
  Erich Marks, Executive Director of the German Congress on Crime Prevention

Authors

Prof. Dr. Dr. Klaus Beier
Charite Universitätsmedizin, Germany

Frank Buchheit
State Office of Criminal Investigation in Baden-Württemberg, Germany

Prof. Dr. Marc Coester
Berlin School of Economics and Law, Germany

Petra Guder
Glenn Mills Academy, Germany

Prof. Dr. Rita Haverkamp
Endowed Professorship of Crime Prevention and Risk Management, Germany

Dr. Claudia Heinzelmann
German Congress on Crime Prevention

Dr. Harrie Jonkman
Verwey-Jonker Institute, Netherlands

Wolfgang Kahl
German Forum for Crime Prevention (DFK), Germany

Daniela Köntopp
Student of the degree course „Master of Advanced Anglophone Studies"

Erich Marks
German Congress on Crime Prevention, Hannover, Germany

Patricia Martin
Circuit Court of Cook County, United States of America

Richard Ross
University of California, United States of America

Dr. Wiebke Steffen
German Congress on Crime Prevention, Germany

David Stucki
Stark County Ohio Family Court, United States of America

Jörg Ziercke
Bundeskriminalamt, Germany